Distributional Impacts of Climate Change and Disasters

NEW HORIZONS IN ENVIRONMENTAL ECONOMICS

Series Editors: Wallace E. Oates, *Professor of Economics, University of Maryland, College Park and University Fellow, Resources for the Future, USA and* Henk Folmer, *Professor of Research Methodology, Groningen University and Professor of General Economics, Wageningen University, The Netherlands*

This important series is designed to make a significant contribution to the development of the principles and practices of environmental economics. It includes both theoretical and empirical work. International in scope, it addresses issues of current and future concern in both East and West and in developed and developing countries.

The main purpose of the series is to create a forum for the publication of high quality work and to show how economic analysis can make a contribution to understanding and resolving the environmental problems confronting the world in the twenty-first century.

Recent titles in the series include:

Distributional Impacts of Climate Change and Disasters

Concepts and Cases

Edited by

Matthias Ruth

University of Maryland, USA and University of Bremen, Germany

and

María E. Ibarrarán

Universidad Iberoamericana Puebla, Mexico

NEW HORIZONS IN ENVIRONMENTAL ECONOMICS

Edward Elgar

Cheltenham, UK • Northampton, MA, USA

Published by
Edward Elgar Publishing Limited
The Lypiatts
15 Lansdown Road
Cheltenham
Glos GL50 2JA
UK

Edward Elgar Publishing, Inc.
William Pratt House
9 Dewey Court
Northampton
Massachusetts 01060
USA

A catalogue record for this book
is available from the British Library

Library of Congress Control Number: 2009930851

Mixed Sources
Product group from well-managed
forests and other controlled sources
www.fsc.org Cert no. SA-COC-1565
© 1996 Forest Stewardship Council
FSC

ISBN 978 1 84844 037 1

Printed and bound by MPG Books Group, UK

Contents

Contributors

Roy Boyd received his bachelor's in economics from the University of New Mexico in 1976 and a master's (1979) and PhD (1981) in economics from Duke University. His main field of specialization is in environmental and natural resource economics, and he has written extensively on forestry, climate change, energy, resource taxation and computable general equilibrium. Dr Boyd has worked at the University of Wisconsin in Milwaukee (1981–84), the Federal Trade Commission (1984–86), the Department of Agriculture (1986–88) and Ohio University (1988 to the present). He is currently a professor of economics at Ohio University, and his interests include forest policies in tropical regions and climate change modeling. A book on climate change in Mexico, *Hacia el Futuro: Energy, Economics and the Environment in 21st Century Mexico*, was co-authored with María Eugenia Ibarrarán and published in 2006.

Antoinette Brenkert is a research scientist at the Joint Global Change Research Institute. She has extensive experience in modeling and data analysis for natural systems and for integrated assessment. She developed, with others, structured methods for analyzing country, sector and local vulnerabilities to climate change and methods to develop integrated socio-economic and environmental scenarios of the future. Brenkert is the principal developer of the Vulnerability/Resilience Indicator Model, including a full sensitivity analysis, using a Monte Carlo approach.

Dana Coelho is a Presidential Management Fellow with the US Forest Service. Her professional interests are in strategic conservation planning and ecosystem services, communications and building partnerships. She holds a master's in sustainable development and conservation biology and a master's of public policy from the University of Maryland. While at the University of Maryland, Coelho worked as a research associate with the Center for Integrative Environmental Research, fulfilling various research, writing, editing and web design responsibilities. She also coordinated a weekly seminar in ecological economics and served as president of Graduate Women in Public Policy, a student organization.

Angie Dazé is a climate change coordinator for CARE International, where her work focuses on community-based adaptation in west and southern Africa. Previously, she worked as a program manager for CARE Canada where her work focused on environment and climate change issues, particularly in Asia. Before joining CARE Canada in Ottawa, she worked for the organization on a community-based project in Bangladesh, which helped people to adapt to the adverse impacts of climate change including flooding, increasing salinity, drought and waterlogging. Dazé has also worked as a climate change specialist for the policy branch of the Canadian International Development Agency (CIDA). Her field experience also includes projects in the water and environmental health sector in Nepal and Guyana.

Heiko Garrelts is a researcher on environmental governance and risk management and is currently a member of the Center for Sustainability Studies (artec), University of Bremen. He has diplomas in political sciences and landscape planning. His research deals with decision-making processes in different policy fields, above all nature protection and climate change policy. He is especially interested in the interplay of different levels of policy-making, the role of non-governmental organizations and issues of the science–policy interface.

Timothy Gulden is a research scholar at the Center for International and Security Studies at Maryland (CISSM) and an adjunct professor at the University of Maryland School of Public Policy. He has been a guest scholar at the Brookings Institution's Center on Social Complexity and attended the Santa Fe Institute's Complex Systems Summer School. He works on a wide range of issues where the understanding of complex dynamics is critical to the formulation of effective policy. His recent projects include the development of a system for the oversight of hazardous biological research, an analysis of the spatial and temporal dynamics of civil violence in both Guatemala and Iraq, and an exploration of the security implications of policy responses to climate change.

María E. Ibarrarán, a professor at Universidad Iberoamericana Puebla in the Department of Economics and Business, is a member of the Center for Studies on Poverty and Exclusion. She obtained a PhD in geography and a master's in energy and environmental studies from Boston University. She also holds a bachelor's in economics from Instituto Tecnológico Autónomo de México. Her research interests are energy and environmental economics, particularly related to the social and economic impacts of climate change and air pollution. In 2006 she published a book (with co-author Roy Boyd), *Hacia el Futuro: Energy, Economics* *and the Environment in 21st Century Mexico* (Springer). She has worked on air quality in Mexico City and on mitigation policies to address climate change with Nobel Laureate Mario Molina.

Laurence Kalkstein is a professor of geography and regional studies at the University of Miami, and president of the International Society of Biometeorology, the largest biometeorological organization in the world. He received his undergraduate degree from Rutgers University and his master's and PhD from Louisiana State University. He is the principal investigator on a number of contracts dealing with the assessment, development and implementation of heat–health watch-warning systems for major cities around the world. These systems are funded by both private and government organizations such as the National Oceanic and Atmospheric Administration (NOAA)/National Weather Service and the Environmental Protection Agency (EPA), both in the US, the United Nations World Meteorological Organization, various electrical utilities, local health departments and agencies in other countries. At present, more than 20 such systems are in operation in the United States, nine are running in Italy, three in Canada, one in China and one in Korea. Throughout his career, Dr Kalkstein has published more than 120 peer-reviewed manuscripts and book chapters in leading climatological, geographical and medical journals and has been editor for two major climatological journals: *Climate Research* and the *International Journal of Biometeorology*.

Paul H. Kirshen is Research Leader with Battelle Memorial Institute. Previous to this he was director of the Tufts University Water: Systems, Science, and Society Graduate Education Program and professor in the Civil and Environmental Engineering Department. He has many years of experience serving as principal investigator of complex, interdisciplinary, participatory research related to water resources and coastal zone management and climate variability and change. He has also developed decision support tools using weather and climate information for reservoir management and agriculture in New England and elsewhere. He has worked in West Africa throughout his career, most recently on incorporating seasonal climate forecasts into agriculture and water resources management. He has taught courses in water resources engineering and integrated water resources management. He received his ScB from Brown University and his master's and PhD from Massachusetts Institute of Technology.

Christina Koppe is a scientist working with the Deutscher Wetterdienst DWD (German Meteorological Service) in the Department of Human Biometeorology. In her PhD thesis she developed a method that allows a health-relevant assessment of the thermal environment, taking into account short-term adaptation of the population to the local meteorological conditions of the past weeks. This method is the basis for the German Heat Health Warning System and a medium-range heat information system for Europe, which was developed in the framework of the EU-funded EuroHEAT project. Her research interests are, among other things, the impacts of heatwaves on human health in current and future climates and the possibilities to predict and prevent these impacts on the short- to long-range timescales. Dr Koppe takes part in different national and international activities that look at such impacts and ways to prevent them.

Hellmuth Lange has been teaching at the University of Bremen, Germany since 1973. He has been director of the Center for Sustainability Studies (artec) at the University of Bremen and speaker of the German environmental sociologists' Environment and Society section of the German Sociological Association. He is co-director of the interdisciplinary graduate school Global Change in the Marine Realm (GLOMAR) and member of the board of the Research Network Environment and Society of the European Sociological Association. Trained as a sociologist and political scientist, his general research areas are sociology of work and industrial relations, science and technology studies, and environmental sociology. His most recent work focuses on assets for improving environmental behavior in the realm of both OECD countries and the new middle classes of developing countries and, on the other hand, climate change as a challenge to regional governance, including risk management.

Elizabeth Malone is a senior research scientist at the Joint Global Change Research Institute. Her interests focus on policy-relevant sociological research in global change issues, developing studies that integrate disparate worldviews, data sources and scientific approaches. Recently, she has been working on developing structured methods for analyzing country, sector and local vulnerabilities to climate change. Associated with that work she has been exploring approaches to scenarios of the future that integrate socio-economic and environmental information. She edited, with Steve Rayner, *Human Choice and Climate Change*, a four-volume assessment of social science research relevant to global climate change; they jointly authored the summary volume and an invited paper for *Nature* on the conclusions.

Mario Molina obtained his undergraduate degree in Chemical Engineering at Universidad Nacional Autónoma de México (1965), and then studied in Germany (1967), before obtaining his PhD in physics and chemistry from Berkeley (1972). Dr Molina was professor at the Massachusetts Institute of Technology from 1989 to 2004, professor and researcher at Universidad Nacional Autónoma de México between 1967 and 1968; at University of California at Irvine from 1975 to 1979; and at CALTECH from 1982 to 1989. In 1995, Mario Molina shared with F. Sherwood Rowland and Paul Crutzen the Nobel Prize in Chemistry for their work in atmospheric chemistry and the effect of chlorofluorocarbons (CFCs) on the depletion of the ozone layer. This was the first time that a Nobel Prize was awarded to research on man-made effects on the environment. The discoveries led to an international environmental treaty, the Montreal Protocol, which bans the production of industrial chemicals that reduce the ozone layer. Dr Molina was named one of the top 20 Hispanics in Technology, 1998. Today, Dr Molina is one of the world's most knowledgeable experts on air pollution and the effects of chemicals on the environment and is very active in studying other environmental problems such as climate change.

Simone Orlandini is an associate professor of the Department of Agronomy and Land Management of the University of Florence (DISAT-UNIFI). He graduated in agricultural sciences, University of Florence, with a thesis concerning field crops, and received a PhD in agrometeorology (University of Sassari) with a thesis concerning the application of agrometeorological models for the control of grapevine diseases. Dr Orlandini currently teaches in computer science, biometeorology and bioclimatology at the University of Florence and serves as director of the Interdepartmental Centre for Bioclimatology of the University of Florence. He is *accademico ordinario* of the Accademia dei Georgofili di Firenze, editor of the *Journal of Agrometeorology* and member of the editorial board of the Italian *Journal of Agronomy*. Dr Orlandini is the author of more than 200 scientific, technical and didactic papers.

Winfried Osthorst is a researcher working on environmental politics in multilevel arrangements, particularly in European contexts. At present he is associated scientist at the interdisciplinary graduate school, Global Change in the Marine Realm (GLOMAR), and a member of the Center for Sustainability Studies (artec), both at the University of Bremen. He has diplomas in sociology and public administration, and a PhD in social sciences. His work focuses on the analysis of political processes with consequences for environmental quality. Fields of work cover waste management, land use change in coastal areas, spatial planning, urban development and port development.

Anthony G. Patt earned a legal degree from Duke University and a PhD in public policy from Harvard University. He is currently research scholar at the International Institute for Applied Systems Analysis (IIASA), near Vienna, Austria, in their program on risk and vulnerability. His primary research focus is on how to improve the use of scientific information for decision-making, particularly with respect to climate change. He often conducts controlled experiments, both in the laboratory and in the field, to identify patterns of information use. Dr Patt has conducted extensive research on the use of climate forecasts as a tool for sustainable development in Africa. A five-year study, completed in 2005, that he led in Zimbabwe was the first to identify the economic value that farmers received from seasonal forecasts, using a field-based research methodology, and one of the only studies to quantify the benefits of participatory communication practices for scientific information. More recently, he led an assessment of the use of forecasts across multiple economic sectors over the entire African continent, identifying the institutional factors associated with successful forecast communication and use. Dr Patt's other work includes studying expectation formation by investors in European electricity markets, as a way of understanding the effects of policies meant to promote renewable energy, and studying the use of climate science in European overseas development assistant policy. He was a contributing author to the Intergovernmental Panel on Climate Change's Fourth Assessment Report.

Jesse C. Ribot is an associate professor at the Department of Geography at the University of Illinois, Urbana-Champaign and previously served as a senior associate in the Institutions and Governance Program (IGP) of the World Resources Institute, where he directed the Decentralization and Environment Initiative of IGP's Environmental Accountability in Africa Program. Dr Ribot was a fellow at the Max Planck Institute for Social Anthropology, a Woodrow Wilson scholar, a research associate at the Harvard Center for Population and Development Studies, a fellow at the Yale Program in Agrarian Studies, and a lecturer in urban studies and planning at Massachusetts Institute of Technology. He has conducted research on issues of environmental justice, environment and decentralization, social vulnerability in the face of environmental change, access to natural resources and the effects of resource markets on local livelihoods.

Matthias Ruth is Roy F. Weston Chair in Natural Economics, director of the Center for Integrative Environmental Research at the Division of Research, director of the Environmental Policy Program at the School of Public Policy, and co-director of the Engineering and Public Policy Program at the University of Maryland. His research focuses on dynamic modeling of natural resource use, industrial and infrastructure systems analysis, and environmental economics and policy. His theoretical work heavily draws on concepts from engineering, economics and ecology, while his applied research utilizes methods of non-linear dynamic modeling as well as adaptive and anticipatory management. Applications of his work cover the full spectrum from local to regional, national and global environmental challenges, as well as the investment and policy opportunities these challenges present. Dr Ruth has published 12 books and over 100 papers and book chapters in the scientific literature. He collaborates extensively with scientists and policy-makers in the USA, Canada, Europe, Oceania, Asia and Africa.

Farid Selmi is a PhD student at the Center for Sustainability Studies (artec) and a member at the International Graduate School for Marine Sciences – Global Change in the Marine Realm (GLOMAR), both at the University of Bremen. His current research interests focus on processes that reconcile the social and ecological prerequisites for sustainable community development, thus determining the enabling conditions for societies in transition in questions of participation and adaptation. Since 2005, his research has been focused on Indonesia, his case study area. He holds a master's degree in aquatic tropical ecology (ISATEC) from the University of Bremen.

Scott Sheridan is an associate professor of climatology in the Department of Geography at Kent State. He has a bachelor's and a master's in meteorology from Rutgers and Texas A&M, respectively, followed by a PhD in climatology from the University of Delaware in 2000. Dr Sheridan's research interests include several areas of applied climatology, mostly involving the effects of climate on humans. He has had considerable experience in analyzing heat vulnerability; he has worked on the development of heat watch–warning systems for more than two dozen cities worldwide, and has explored public behavior during heat warnings, the potential for changed frequency of heatwaves in the future, as well as the interactions of heat and air pollution on human health. He has collaborated with the World Meteorological Organization headquartered in Geneva and a number of other national agencies throughout Europe and North America. As a result of his work in this field, he was recently promoted to editor-in-chief of the *International Journal of Biometeorology*.

Karen Smoyer-Tomic is a senior research analyst for HealthCore, as well as research fellow and adjunct associate professor at the University of Delaware and adjunct associate professor in Public Health Sciences at the University of Alberta, Canada. Dr Tomic's expertise is in the physical, built and social environmental determinants of health, with a focus on the role of social, housing and infrastructural factors affecting the pathway between climate and air pollution exposures and human health. More recent work involves disparities in spatial accessibility to health resources and the role of urban sprawl on environment and population health. Dr Smoyer-Tomic is author of more than 40 peer-reviewed research articles, reports, book chapters and conference proceedings; has been an invited keynote speaker at 24 venues; and has presented at more than 40 professional meetings internationally. Her research on environmental health has been highlighted in television, newspaper and radio interviews, and she has served on international health advisory boards, grant review panels and journal review committees. Previously she was a tenured associate professor in earth and atmospheric sciences at the University of Alberta. She received her bachelor's degree in biology and geography and a master's in geography from the University of Delaware, and her PhD in geography from the University of Minnesota, specializing in the geography of health and health care, biostatistics and public policy. She advocates for improving environmental health and reducing disparities among vulnerable populations and has served as health committee chair for the Pencader Hundred Community Center for low-income populations, and currently is a board member of the Delaware Cancer Consortium Environmental Committee.

Pablo Suarez is a researcher on climate and disasters, focusing on the use of information for reducing vulnerability. He is associate director of programs for the Red Cross/Red Crescent Climate Centre, climate change advisor for Oxfam America's Private Sector Team, and consultant for the United Nations Development Programme (UNDP). Pablo has consulted for the World Bank Development Economics Research Group, the United Nations Environment Programme (UNEP), the Global Environment Facility (GEF), the International Institute for Sustainable Development (IISD), the American Association for the Advancement of Science (AAAS), the Potsdam Institute for Climate Impact Research (PIK) and other international organizations, working in more than 40 countries. He is a visiting fellow at the Boston University Frederick S. Pardee Center for the Study of the Longer-Range Future, and a guest scholar at the International Institute for Applied Systems Analysis (IIASA). Pablo has a degree in water and civil engineering, a master's in community planning and development, and a PhD in geography. His current work addresses community-level adaptation to climate change, institutional integration across disciplines and geographic scales, and the use of video and other innovative communication tools for awareness, advocacy, and capacity building.

Foreword

One aspect of climate change that has been studied with less detail so far is that related to its economic and social impacts. This is due, perhaps, to the intrinsic complexity that characterizes long-term social and economic predictions, because they involve unprecedented environmental situations; or maybe to the wide variety of material, organizational and cultural reactions from human society to climate change. The truth is that some communities will suffer severe shocks from the new climate conditions on Earth, such as isolated and underdeveloped island countries, whereas others will face global warming better informed and with more economic resources, and thus with greater possibilities to deal with extreme weather events.

We should worry more about people who have never enjoyed technological advances, and now see their way of life, their culture and even their very existence threatened by the climate change. For instance, people from sub-Saharan Africa have been fighting for years, in bloody political and military internal conflicts, for land that is increasingly less productive and dry, providing a testimony of what might happen in other parts of the world if the average temperature rises more than about 2–3° C. In all continents, migration of people is increasingly common because billions of them have seen their natural and economic resources nearly exhausted. What should prevail is not the law of the strongest, but instead a commitment from the international community to support their efforts to deal with adverse environmental conditions.

The impacts of climate change in terms of geography and time scale have diverse and difficult-to-understand consequences for the nations and societies of the entire world. In this book we find a very useful exploration of macroeconomic approximations connected to these consequences, as well as innovative ideas to measure vulnerability through numerical indicators and country resilience to climate risks. For sure, the new tools developed in this book will be extremely helpful for building an accurate economic diagnosis and to achieve a greater consensus among the nations of this planet, all of which face the long-term consequences of climate change.

Mario Molina

Acknowledgments

This book explores the impacts of climate change on a wide variety of sectors and places, their vulnerabilities, and mitigative and adaptive capacities. It showcases the work on countries at different development levels by researchers who focus on distributional impacts of climate change within different areas of society. We wish to thank the authors for their contributions, which make this book a unique compilation of the state of the art. Special recognition needs to be given also to Tara Gorvine at Edward Elgar's Massachusetts office, for her guidance along the way. Last but not least, our personal appreciation and thanks go to our families and friends for their love and patience throughout the years.

PART I

Background

1. Introduction: distributional effects of climate change – social and economic implications

Matthias Ruth and María E. Ibarrarán

Climate change has global impacts relative to both its causes and its effects. These impacts, however, are not distributed evenly but can create dissimilar effects across different latitudes, altitudes and even groups of people, within the same location. For example, some parts of the globe may be impacted by a large number of hurricanes, while others suffer from frequent episodes of drought. Other parts may be more prone to vector disease due to temperature rise or to land loss from sea level rise. Simultaneously, different groups of people may be affected, to differing degrees, because the distribution of these effects combine with yet another important distinction – the coping capacity of different countries, and of the individuals within those countries. Access to information is a key issue in preventing, and adapting to, current and expected impacts from climate change. There is wide variation in the real availability of such information to different groups. Other key issues concern the ways in which stakeholders act on that information.

Climate change tends to increase the frequency and the intensity of weather-related natural disasters. Depending on the location of populated areas, this puts many people at risk with respect to access to water, coastal flooding, disease and hunger. This can leave them with a more degraded environment. Economic, social and environmental impacts, in turn, further increase vulnerability to natural disasters and tend to set back development, destroy livelihoods (especially of the poor), and increase disparity both nationally and worldwide. Acknowledging and understanding these differences can lead to better adaptation processes for all.

In this book we address the many aspects of the distributional issues resulting from climate change from a wide range of perspectives. In general, we discuss some issues at the international level, making reference to worldwide differences at a country level. We also explore the different vulnerabilities that exist among countries and, finally, some at the country level. This enables us better to capture the nature of the distributional impacts of climate change by tackling the precise differential vulnerability of people and places. People are affected differently by many factors: their income level, the age and gender structure of their population, access to information and environmental assets, and social and human capital. They also respond differently in the ways that they mitigate the effect of climate change and adapt to it because of their economic capacity, institutional development and strength of social cohesion.

This book is divided into two parts. Part I sets the stage by focusing on the relationship between climate change and natural disasters and by broadly exploring the economic and social impacts they cause. Following this Introduction, in Chapter 2 Elizabeth Malone and Antoinette Brenkert describe a vulnerability–resilience indicator model that uses 18 proxy indicators, grouped into eight elements, to assess on a quantitative basis the comparative potential vulnerability and resilience of countries to climate change. The model integrates socio-economic and environmental information such as land use, crop production, water availability, per capita gross domestic product (GDP), inequality and health status. Comparative results for 160 countries are presented and analyzed.

In Chapter 3, María Ibarrarán and Matthias Ruth make the connection between climate change and macroeconomic performance. Their assessment is based on information from climate impact assessments and data from natural disasters. The latter are pertinent to the extent that climate change will increase the severity and frequency of severe weather events, putting more people at risk by influencing access to water, coastal flooding, disease and hunger, and leaving them with a more degraded environment. This in turn leads to increased vulnerability. The study by Ibarrarán and Ruth points at the different vulnerabilities to natural disasters that exist in developed and developing countries. Even within countries, impacts vary significantly across population and economic sectors. When losses from natural disasters are large, their cumulative effects can have notable macroeconomic impacts which feed back to, and further pronounce, existing income inequalities. Impacts tend to be most pronounced for women, the very young, the elderly, and ethnic or racial minorities.

Part II of this book discusses particular impacts of climate change, focusing on their differential effects on specific populations and ecosystems. For example, in Chapter 4 Laurence Kalkstein, Christina Koppe, Simone Orlandini, Scott Sheridan and Karen Smoyer-Tomic explore the discrepant effects of climate on health, for certain demographics and income levels, differentiated by gender and socio-economic status. Their analysis focuses on the impacts of extreme heat, and the effect of climate change on asthmatics, drawing on a large and growing base of literature dealing with these two issues in the US and elsewhere.

Chapter 5, by Anthony Patt, Angie Dazé and Pablo Suarez, analyzes the differential impacts of climate change on women – a group which frequently lacks empowerment and participation in decision-making. It points to the fact that women are demonstrably better at decision-making of the type that climate adaptation requires. This includes embracing change, trusting and incorporating scientific knowledge, learning how to make decisions under conditions of uncertainty, and thinking long term. This suggests opportunities for win–win outcomes through greater empowerment and inclusion of women in decision-making at all scales. Patt, Dazé and Suarez argue that greater inclusion may reverse the inequitable distribution of impacts. Furthermore, greater inclusion could improve adaptive decision-making in general, reducing the negative impacts of climate change on the entire community. Case studies from Bangladesh and Tajikistan illustrate the challenges and opportunities that exist when addressing the gender dimension of adaptation initiatives.

In Chapter 6, Roy Boyd and María Ibarrarán address the differential impacts of greenhouse gas mitigation efforts in Mexico – a country with great inequality among incomes, vast energy resources and increasing environmental problems. Historically, the distribution of income in Mexico has been highly skewed with relatively large areas of extreme poverty. Currently, energy and environmental policies are being discussed in order to mitigate climate change. Boyd and Ibarrarán point out that these policies have a significant impact on equity and income distribution. Further, they argue that such equity issues cannot be ignored since any viable policy should be thought of as 'fair', and policy-makers cannot easily bypass the needs and wishes of a large portion of their constituency. Using a dynamic computable general equilibrium model Boyd and Ibarrarán simulate the impact of these policies on economic growth, carbon emissions, the capital stock and the economic welfare of a number of income groups. Proportionally, the highest usage of energy occurs in the lowest-income groups. Consequently, increased investment and exploration in the natural gas sector have had distributionally progressive effects. For the same reason, investments in energy-saving technologies have also had the largest positive impacts on low-income groups. The same cannot be said for efforts relative to the deregulation of electricity prices and carbon taxes. Existing subsidies to electricity use were designed to benefit agricultural production and consumption by low-income groups. Boyd and Ibarrarán show that, as a result, the removal of those subsidies largely benefit the wealthy. Similarly, carbon taxes have a more severe impact on lower-, as opposed to higher-, income groups.

The distributional implications of climate change cannot only be seen in developing countries and poor, rural regions but are also in urban areas of industrialized nations. Matthias Ruth, Paul Kirshen and Dana Coelho explore these implications in Chapter 7. They discuss expected impacts in urban areas of the industrialized world, drawing from recent literature and case studies. Thereafter, Ruth and his colleagues explore the causes behind differential urban vulnerabilities based upon analyses of urbanization, urban infrastructure and metabolism, and environmental quality. Their analysis presents options to manage better the inevitable differences that exist in urban areas in order to reduce vulnerabilities.

Between the identification of options and their implementation often lies the field of information dissemination – dissemination regarding climate change, impacts, vulnerabilities and adaptation options. This dissemination occurs (or should occur) amongst both higher-level decision-makers as well as individuals in the affected population. Although information about antici-pated climate conditions can support adaptation, its mere availability is not a sufficient condition to ensure vulnerability reduction among those whose current situation deserves the highest priority. Without adequate consid-eration to equity issues, widespread generation of climatic forecasts discon-nected from the real obstacles to their communication and use could result in a socially differentiated distribution of benefits. Accordingly, in Chapter 8, Pablo Suarez, Jesse Ribot and Anthony Patt discuss the following three models of the role of predictions in decision-making for reducing vulner-ability: perfect information (which assumes optimal dissemination and use of forecasts), vulnerability to hazard (which focuses on improving responses to events that cause harm), and vulnerability to outcome (which proposes to reverse processes that make people vulnerable in the first place). The authors argue that if the development of climate forecasts remains embedded in (and directed by) the perfect information paradigm, those with the most pronounced needs are not likely to reap the benefits of improved climate pre-dictability. Participatory initiatives can integrate these approaches – helping to improve predictions and their communication channels, coping with pre-dicted events and triggering community-based processes aimed at reversing marginalization and vulnerability.

Unabated, increased vulnerability and marginalization will likely result in increased social tensions and conflict. Like the direct impacts of climate change, many of the conflict-related risks associated with climate change are likely to impact the poor most severely. This unfortunate fact is acknowledged by those who study resource scarcity as a driver of conflict. Still, there remain other important, less direct connections between climate change and human conflict. These connections bring another level of dis-cussion into the distributional analysis. In Chapter 9, Timothy Gulden argues that civil conflicts in the less developed parts of the world can also pose real threats to wealthy nations; and that technological responses, if not handled with adequate care, have the potential to threaten even the wealthiest citizens of the most powerful countries.

Drawing on their experiences in both developed and developing countries, in Chapter 10 Hellmuth Lange, Heiko Garrelts, Winfried Osthorst and Farid Selmi address the question of how adaptation becomes an issue of political decision-making and leads to conceptual changes in the realm of the political-administrative system. The focus of their analysis lies in policy and institutional design, the choice of policy instruments and the timing of interventions.

To highlight the core mechanisms influencing conceptual adaptation to risks in terms of policy change, the authors compare three empirical cases: the only gradual adaptation of coastal protection towards climate change in Germany, the introduction of new flood management regulations in Germany after a riparian flood in 2002, and a new disaster risk management regime in Indonesia as reaction to a series of severe disasters during recent years. Lange and his colleagues show that these processes of adaptation differ in terms of scope and pace. However, in contrast to widespread conceptualizations of adaptation, they do not prove to be pure problem-oriented, straightforward processes. Rather, threats and impacts represent just one factor that explains the amplitude in terms of pace and scope. Further relevant factors are innovative risk-related management concepts. In the cases studied, such alternatives already existed within public or professional discourse before the extreme events occurred. Thus they were also available immediately afterwards.

Lange, Garrelts, Osthorst and Selmi argue that the decisive factors which influence risk management and adaptation actions are: actors, conflicts of interest and institutional settings. The mediums of these factors are competing discourses. Beyond their effect on social groups, discourses legitimize or delegitimize institutionally underpinned concepts and habits. Thus, discourses have an explicit distributional quality since they assign roles and resources to actors and institutions.

This book begins to fill a gap in the existing literature by covering the differentiated impacts of climate change. It raises important equity issues that become relevant at global, regional, national and subnational levels in terms of what the expected effects of climate change are in a wide variety of topics, and how adaptation actions may help reduce vulnerabilities. We conclude in Chapter 11 by summarizing and synthesizing insights encapsulated in the chapters here, and by discussing possible solutions to cope with the distributional effects from climate change and their social and economic implications.

2. Vulnerability, sensitivity and coping/adapting capacity worldwide

Elizabeth Malone and Antoinette Brenkert

INTRODUCTION

Tension exists between the need to conduct global analyses of climate change and the likely highly differentiated small-scale impacts of climate change. Because of the global nature of the issue – neither greenhouse gas concentrations nor global climate are regional or local phenomena – studies of greenhouse gas emissions and their impacts on the climate are essential to define the scope of the issue, especially to address issues of potential mitigation. However, since climatic impacts on natural and socio-economic systems are likely to be felt and responded to at regional and local levels, the heterogeneous conditions of individual societies necessitate more localized studies. Furthermore, the impacts of climate change will be different within any particular society, since rights and resources are unevenly distributed.

Responses to the question of the appropriate research level – global, regional/country or local – have generally used one of two prevailing approaches. One approach is to conduct highly aggregated, quantitative studies of emissions and concentration levels. A second approach is to conduct disaggregated, often purely qualitative, case studies of single countries or localities. These different approaches have opened two gaps: an inability to compare countries and regions with regard to their resilience to climate change impacts, and a lack of studies that account for societal inequalities that will themselves be affected unequally by climate change. These gaps prevent decision-makers from carefully weighing options that have short- and long-term implications.

Analyzing the relationships between exposure and sensitivity to climate change and climate variability, in addition to the potential of adaptive capacity building and coping, is a crucial aspect in decision-making processes regarding where to invest, who should make the investment (government, firms, non-profits, private citizens, and so on), and when.

To begin to fill the research gaps, we developed a quantitative tool, the Vulnerability–Resilience Indicator Model (VRIM). This model integrates socio-economic and environmental information to provide a quantitative comparative basis upon which to assess an area's vulnerability and resilience to climate change and variability.

THE VULNERABILITY–RESILIENCE INDICATOR MODEL (VRIM)

The VRIM was designed to meet two specific challenges identified in the recent impact assessments of the Intergovernmental Panel on Climate Change (IPCC) (Watson et al. 1996; 1998; McCarthy et al. 2001). The first challenge is to improve approaches for comparing climate change impacts across diverse elements and populations. The second is to model socio-economic transformations as well as climate changes in assessing the future significance of climate change. This is important because many climate change impact studies assume static social and economic structures in estimating the sensitivity of hydrological or terrestrial systems to projected climate regimes. Assumptions based on static structures, however, are highly unrealistic since substantial socio-economic changes are likely to unfold at the same time that climate changes are occurring.

The VRIM is a multilevel model that aggregates a number of proxy values into elements. These elements, in turn, are aggregated into sensitivity and adaptive capacity values and then finally into a vulnerability–resilience index. The first two levels of the structure are shown in Figure 2.1. The third level comprises 2–3 proxy variables under each element. All 18 proxy variables used in this study are listed by element in Table 2.1 (see also Brenkert and Malone 2005) along with a description of what the proxy stands for and how it functions in the model. Notably, when

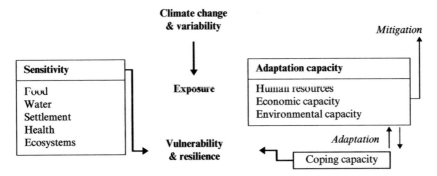

Figure 2.1   *The structure of the Vulnerability–Resilience Indicator Model (VRIM)*

*Table 2.1   Summary of what the proxies stand for and the functional
relationships*

Aggregate Elements	Element	Indicators/ data	Proxy for	Functional relationship
Sensitivity	Settlement/ infrastructure sensitivity	Population at flood risk from sea level rise	Potential extent of disruptions from sea level rise	Sensitivity ↑ as population at risk ↑
		Population no access clean water/ sanitation	Access of population to basic services to buffer against climate variability and change	Sensitivity ↑ as population with no access ↑
	Food security	Cereal production/ crop land area	Degree of modernization in the agriculture sector; access of farmers to inputs to buffer against climate variability and change	Sensitivity ↓ as production ↑
		Protein consumption/ capita	Access of a population to agricultural markets and other mechanisms (e.g., consumption shift) for compensating for shortfalls in production	Sensitivity ↓ as consumption ↑
	Ecosystem sensitivity	% agricultural land	Degree of human intrusion into the natural landscape	Sensitivity ↑ as % agricultural land (% land managed) ↑

Table 2.1   (continued)

Aggregate Elements	Element	Indicators/ data	Proxy for	Functional relationship
		Fertilizer use/ cropland area	Nitrogen/ phosphorus loading of ecosystems and stresses from pollution	Sensitivity is ↓ if use < 60 kg/ ha or > 100 kg/ha; ↑ when use = > 60 and < 100 kg/ha
	Human health sensitivity	Completed fertility	Composite of conditions that affect human health including nutrition, exposure to disease risks, and access to health services	Sensitivity ↓ as fertility ↓
		Life expectancy		Sensitivity ↓ as life expectancy ↑
	Water resource sensitivity	Renewable supply and inflow and water withdrawal	Ratio of water supply from renewable resources and withdrawals to meet current or projected needs	Sensitivity ↑ as % water used ↑
		% irrigated land	Water demand	Sensitivity ↑ as % irrigated land ↑
Coping & adaptive capacity	Economic capacity	GDP(market)/ capita	Distribution of access to markets, technology, and other resources useful for adaptation	Coping/adaptive capacity ↑ as GDP per capita ↑
		An income equity measure	Realization of the potential contribution of all people	Coping/ adaptive capacity ↑ as poverty or inequity ↓

Table 2.1   (continued)

Aggregate Elements	Element	Indicators/ data	Proxy for	Functional relationship
	Human and civic resources	Dependency ratio	Social and economic resources available for adaptation after meeting other present needs	Coping/ adaptive capacity ↓ as dependency ↑
		Literacy	Human capital and adaptability of labor force	Coping/ adaptive capacity ↑ as literacy ↑
	Environmental capacity	Population density	Population pressure and stresses on ecosystems	Coping/ adaptive capacity ↓ as population density ↑
		SO_2/ state area	Air quality and other stresses on ecosystems	Coping/ adaptive capacity ↓ as SO_2 ↑
		% land unmanaged	Landscape fragmentation and ease of ecosystem migration	Coping/ adaptive capacity ↑ as % unmanaged land ↑

sensitivity of the proxy is high (↑) resilience will be low (↓) in the base year. When capacity to respond is high (↑) resilience will be high (↑). The objective is to develop a flexible tool where proxies can be added and/or substituted, depending on the focus of the question that is to be explored. The current elements represent aspects of the socio-economic and environmental structure that show sensitivity and/or capacity to respond to changes in the elements of the structure. Changes include those attributable to expected development and/or climate change and climate variability, either gradual or abrupt (tsunamis, hurricanes, and so on).

Exposure, defined as the nature and extent of changes in an area's climate variables such as temperature, precipitation and extreme weather events, is not explicitly incorporated except for exposure to potential sea level rise. The impact of future exposure will depend on the extent to which socio-economic and environmental capital will have changed, by forward-looking adaptation and/or by setbacks from the negative impacts of hazards and climate change. Thus, building a model through which local exposure can be tested is a prerequisite for testing the impact of exposure.

The labels 'sensitivity' and 'adaptive capacity' point to the accepted framing of certain vulnerability–resilience aspects as likely having negative impacts from climate change, or likely to provide positive means to cope and adapt in the face of climate change. Although the aggregate elements are also given these labels, in fact aspects in one category may be present in others. For example, environmental capacity could be greatly reduced through misuse or neglect of the environment, increased pollution and loss of biodiversity. Similarly, aspects of the sensitivity elements – including human health, ecosystem sensitivity, food security and settlement sensitivity – might be more resilient in the future. The proxy variables listed in Table 2.1 were chosen to represent more than their strict denotative meaning. For instance, under food security, the proxy variable 'protein consumption per capita' means not only the intake of protein, but also the quality of the diet in general terms and the availability of food. Similarly, 'completed fertility' implies general female health, and the quality and availability of prenatal care. Thus, the actual numbers generated by the model become less meaningful as numbers over time and, instead, stand for a more general description of human and environmental well-being.

However, because of the aggregate nature of this study, neither the proxy variables nor the elements cover the range of potentially important attributes. For example, within 'settlement/infrastructure sensitivity' the extent and condition (for example, age, energy efficiency) of buildings and infrastructure are not accounted for. Thus, a study that focused on mitigation would need to include at least one additional proxy variable to represent this information. Similarly, in 'food security' more profitable energy crops such as sugar cane for ethanol may crowd out food crops. Again, a study that focused on questions of energy and sustainability would need to represent this issue by means of proxy variables.

A brief discussion of each element, and the associated proxy variables, will demonstrate the comprehensiveness of the set. This discussion will then be followed by one on issues relating to the representativeness, colinearity and completeness of the set.

Settlement/Infrastructure Sensitivity

This element includes effects on economic activities in the industrial, energy and transportation sectors, as well as on human settlements.

Climate variability and change have direct impacts through flooding, droughts, changes in average temperatures (for example, leading to thawing of permafrost), temperature extremes and extreme weather events (for example, hurricanes). In addition, climate variability and change can affect markets for goods and services in these sectors, as well as natural resource inputs important to production. Settlements in coastal margins are affected through both sea level rise and storm surges. In addition, both these areas and inland settlements can be affected by weather-related events that act directly on infrastructure (for example, leading to land-slides) and indirectly through effects on other elements (for example, water supply, agricultural activity and migration patterns). Although patterns of effect are different for urban and rural settlements, both are sensitive to climate variability and change.

Three proxies are used in this element. The projected number of people affected by potential rise in sea level is based on the estimated number of people affected by sea surges. The populations in a country without access to safe water and sanitation represent a lack of basic infrastructure and services.

Food Security

This element represents the potential for changes in the availability of food in a particular geographic area. It encompasses both production of principal foodstuffs (for example, crops, livestock, fish) as well as socio-economic issues such as type of production system, access to production inputs that can offset changes in climatic conditions, and access to markets for the purchase of food. Climate variability and change can affect food sensitivity through a variety of mechanisms, particularly related to food production. Variability in temperature and precipitation affects crop production directly; and indirectly, for example, through erosion of soils, and pest and disease outbreaks. In addition, floods, droughts and periods of extreme temperatures affect livestock and fisheries production. Climate change is also projected to have impacts on agricultural production through changes in atmospheric concentrations of CO_2. This affects productivity and water use efficiency, particularly in C3 plants. Impacts on agricultural production may also be felt through changes in availability of water resources for irrigation.

Two proxies represent food sensitivity: cereal production and protein consumption. Cereal production per unit area captures the degree of modernization in the agriculture sector and the access of farmers to production inputs that can be used to buffer against the effects of climate variability and change. Protein consumption per capita is a proxy for the degree of modernization in the processing and distribution of agricultural goods for consumers.

Ecosystem Sensitivity

Ecosystems and the functions they provide to individuals and society are sensitive to variability and change in climate. These functions may include: providing food, fiber, medicines and energy; processing carbon and other nutrients; purifying and regulating water resources; and providing recreation and intrinsic value. Both the composition and distribution of ecosystems have changed in response to shifts in climate, and future shifts are projected in response to the rate and magnitude of climate change. Similar to impacts in agriculture, changes in atmospheric composition affect the competitive balance among different types of plants, as well as changes in soils and in the incidence of diseases and pests. Ecosystems are also influenced by other environmental stresses, including pollution (both run-off in water courses and deposition from the atmosphere), increasing extraction of resources, and incursion and fragmentation. These factors also affect the sensitivity of ecosystems to climate variability and change.

Two proxies represent the sensitivity of ecosystems: the percentage of agricultural land, and fertilizer use. The percentage of agricultural land is a proxy for the degree of human activity in and management of the natural landscape, which would increase the sensitivity of ecosystems to climate variability and change. Fertilizer use per unit area is a proxy for ecosystem stresses resulting from pollution as it is indicative of nitrogen and phosphorus loading of ecosystems.

Human Health Sensitivity

The health of human populations is affected by climate variability and change. This affect can occur through direct mechanisms (for example, heatwaves in conjunction with episodes of poor air quality, especially in urban areas) as well as indirect pathways (for example, changes in prevalence of vector-borne and non-vector-borne infectious diseases). Populations with different levels of technical, social, and economic resources differ in their sensitivity to climate-induced health impacts.

Two proxies represent sensitivity of health to climate variability and change: completed fertility and life expectancy. These variables represent a variety of conditions that affect human health, including nutrition, exposure to disease risks, and access to health services.

Water Resource Sensitivity

Climate variability has a large impact on the general hydrology of a landscape and on the availability of water at local and national scales. Climate change is expected to have an ever greater impact, through changes in precipitation and temperature, leading to more severe storms, floods and droughts. Moreover, as the socio-economic aspects of a society are affected through changes in water availability, government policies are expected to respond.

Two proxy variables represent the sensitivity to water availability. Renewable supply and inflow and water withdrawal indicate the sustainability of current water practices and project practices in the future. The percentage of irrigated land captures the amount of water demanded for an ever changing population and its sustenance.

Economic Capacity

Wealth generally provides access to markets, technology and other resources that can be used to adapt to climate variability and change. Hence, the first proxy in this element is gross domestic product (GDP) per capita. The second proxy, a measure of inequality, represents the degree to which wealth or income is unevenly distributed. Where the distribution of wealth or income is very unequal, adaptive capacity will also be unequally distributed.

Human and Civic Resources

Human and civic resources represent another critical component of coping and adaptive capacity. This component includes literacy, level of education, access to retraining programs, and other factors that determine how flexible individuals are in adapting to new employment opportunities or shifts in living patterns as a result of climate variability.

Two proxies represent human resources. The dependency ratio measures the proportion of economically active and inactive individuals in a population. A higher rate of dependency indicates that economically active individuals have many others to support, and that resources for adapting to changes in climate will be more limited. The literacy rate measures the skills necessary for individuals to adapt to change.

Environmental Capacity

As discussed above, natural systems are sensitive to climate stimuli and must adapt to climate variability and change. Adaptation may involve a variety of eco-physiological changes such as changes in species mix, migration, or even the loss of species or ecosystems. The survival of current ecosystems will depend not only on the degree of climate variability or rate and magnitude of climate change, but also on the current baseline conditions of the systems themselves.

Three proxies represent the resilience or coping and adaptive capacity of ecosystems. Population density indicates the amount of pressure people are placing on their ecosystems. Sulfur dioxide emissions show the level of industrialization of an area, another way to assess stress on the natural systems. Percentage of unmanaged land indicates a kind of 'safety valve' and land that buffers or dilutes human impacts on the environment (although it may also describe land that is barren and unproductive).

Limitations of the Set of Proxies

Critics may argue that the proxies are not representative enough; that the set is incomplete; and that the proxies within the set are overlapping. These are issues for any indicator set. Most discussions of sets address the first concern but not the latter two. Notable examples include the Environmental Sustainability Index documentation (YCELP and CIESIN 2002), the Wellbeing Index (Prescott-Allen 2001) and the indicator set used by O'Brien et al. (2004) for India.

First, the representative character of any proxy generally can be questioned. A land use proxy may not explicitly account for either soil characteristics or historic civil strife in an area. Current land use is the result of several factors. No proxy can perfectly represent an abstract category. The adequacy of a proxy should be based on its ability to summarize a number of important properties and to be quantified. A practical consideration is the availability of good-quality data for meaningful comparisons.

Second, the set of proxies used in the VRIM does not include relevant and important characteristics such as governmental capacity, cultural worldviews and beliefs, and institutional opportunities and limitations. Although proxies for these characteristics have been developed and applied in other quantitative studies, they are generally open to bias and often do not include enough good-quality data. For example, the Environmental Sustainability Index (YCELP and CIESIN 2002) includes variables such as 'IUCN member organizations per million population', 'Civil and political liberties', and 'Democratic institutions'. The data for civil and political liberties is taken from Freedom House and incorporates the results of a selective survey, in which the 'most valued' sources are 'the many human rights activists, journalists, editors, and political figures around the world who keep us informed of the human rights situation in their countries' ('About the survey', Freedom House 2008). The Wellbeing Index (Prescott-Allen 2001) includes a category called 'Freedom and governance'; three of its four variables are taken from Freedom House data. The fourth is from Transparency

International's Corruption Perceptions Index. There is an obvious bias toward Western-style freedom and democracy in both of these indexes. Accordingly, we do not include these factors in our quantitative analysis.

Third, many of the proxies in the VRIM set overlap and are not independent. For instance, protein intake makes obvious contributions to human health, as does fertilizer use on cereal production, and so forth. It is not possible to have proxies that are completely independent. Dependencies must be acknowledged as part of the analysis of results. Independent components are not a requirement of an effective vulnerability index, however. Each indicator proxy is chosen for a different reason and represents a different aspect of vulnerability. For example, if a population (as reflected in per capita data) is important in multiple indicators, it is because the effects of that population are significant for multiple areas. The indicator set will accurately reflect the effect of the population on the overall vulnerability index.

For example, GDP per capita is somewhat correlated with life expectancy. GDP per capita is included in the vulnerability–resilience index as a proxy for access to markets, technology and other useful adaptation resources. Life expectancy is a proxy for human health. Since these are different aspects of vulnerability, it is important to get a measure of both without imposing explicit weights. This rubric holds unless there is a theoretical basis for doing otherwise (for example, scenario assumptions or particular situations). Their correlation and consequent larger effect on the index is acceptable since they are more important than other variables that only affect a single aspect of vulnerability.

A wide international comparison of a range of variables inevitably leads to problems regarding data availability. As a result, we sought to construct the index so we could include as many countries as possible. The final list, however, does not cover the entire world.

Finding the balance between coverage and comprehensiveness entails three options: using fewer variables with a wider geographic coverage, reducing the sample of countries for the full index, including only those for which there is sufficient information, and devising statistical methods to preserve both the entire sample of countries and the entire set of variables. We chose the second option even though it could introduce a bias towards highly industrialized countries. International statistical publications (for example by the World Bank and the FAO) yielded lists of up to 201 countries. We reduced this list to 160 countries given the scarcity of data for some countries such as most small island nations. We also deleted Iceland, due to its specific land use; the Democratic Republic of the Congo, due to its extremely high water availability; and Singapore, due to its extremely high population density.

Scaling and Hierarchy

In this global study we implemented the 'range method' of proxy indexing (see Brenkert and Malone 2005). Analogous to the method used in calculating the Human Development Index (HDI) (UNDP 2005), our range method standardizes scales and prevents variables from being unintentionally weighed. Each proxy variable is scored on the same scale by calculating its score within the range of values of the specific proxy participating in the analysis. As a result, the potential bias of large ranges, and the impact of outliers, are limited. We determined the location of the indicators according to the assumptions of 'high' ($\uparrow$) and 'low' ($\downarrow$) as described in Table 2.1.

Table 2.2 describes the aggregation of values hierarchically based on geometric means. Sensitivities are calculated as positive numbers, indicating their level of resilience, instead of negative ones indicating their sensitivity. Thus, the index emphasizes resilience rather than vulnerability. The

Table 2.2 Proxies are indexed according to the range method

	Range method
Steps in the hierarchy	• geometric mean of proxies → element indices • geometric means of indices → sensitivity or coping/adaptive capacity • geometric mean of all indices → resilience index
Sensitivity index	kept as positive value
Indexing	based on the range of values
Determination of the scaled proxy value: alternatives depend on its value's ranking as 'good' or 'bad' within the range of proxies representing the range of geographic entities to be compared	$\text{Shift} + \dfrac{100 * (P - \text{Pmin})}{(\text{Pmax} - \text{Pmin})}$ $\text{Shift} + \dfrac{100 * (\text{Pmax} - P)}{(\text{Pmax} - \text{Pmin})}$

Notes:
P is the country or state's proxy or indicator value.
Pmin and Pmax are the minimum and maximum proxy values representing the range of geographic entities to be compared.
'Shift' is a value that must be used to avoid scores very close to 0. Results were found to be not very sensitive to any shift value larger than one.

Source: Brenkert and Malone (2005).

elements labeled as sensitive become less sensitive when expected socio-economic development takes place. Projections of the indicators reflect increases in resilience under normal socio-economic development when land-use issues and pollution are taken seriously. The resilience indicator is the geometric mean of the eight element indicators.

USING THE INDICATORS AND TAILORING THE APPROACH TO VARIOUS APPLICATIONS

The VRIM's set of quantitative indicators allows for comparisons of regions, countries, states or provinces, or of smaller localities, in terms of their vulnerability and resilience to a current and changing climate (Brenkert and Malone 2005). Previously, we tested the methodology for Indian states.[1] The result was a ranking of the states for their vulnerability and resilience to potential climate change and climate variability. The ranking was evaluated for socio-economic and environmental conditions in 1990. We (Malone and Brenkert) then analyzed prospective changes in the vulnerability and resilience of the Indian states to potential climate change and variability in line with scenario projections by the integrated assessment model MiniCAM (Edmonds et al. 1997) and its postprocessor Sustain (Pitcher 1997).

A current project on Mexico focuses on the impacts of potential drought on the future vulnerability and resilience of the various Mexican states (Brenkert et al. 2006). For that study we added precipitation to the water availability element and substituted 'percent of irrigated land' for 'percent managed land' in the ecosystem sensitivity element.

For the study reported here, we updated our previous limited global database (Moss et al. 2001) to year 2000 for 160 countries. We also added a percentage of irrigated land calculation to the water sensitivity element, calculated resilience indices from the proxies, and ranked the resilience indices showing the sensitivity and adaptive capacity aspects of resilience. Finally, we provided insight in the consequences of the method used for projections through an uncertainty analysis.

METHODS FOR PROJECTIONS

Scenarios of the future should be plausible and consistent. They should explore alternative overall pathways and diverse trends within these pathways. Historic data might provide a basis for projecting future trends in income as simple continuations of current trends. However, growth in

Table 2.3   *SRES factors for each region in 2020 and 2050 (there might be bumps or dips in 2035)*

Regions		Population		GDP (MER)		Crop production		Unmanaged land		SO$_2$ emissions	
		A1v2	A2A1	A1v2	A2A1	A1v2	A2A1	A1v2	A2A1	A1v2	A2A1
USA	2020	1.20	1.19	1.78	1.67	1.48	1.49	0.92	0.95	0.50	0.66
	2050	1.21	1.20	2.30	1.91	2.02	1.97	0.83	1.05	0.28	0.38
Canada	2020	1.12	1.14	1.63	1.52	1.96	1.57	0.95	0.98	0.81	0.93
	2050	1.03	1.11	1.94	1.71	2.53	2.05	0.95	1.00	0.52	0.67
OECD Europe	2020	1.01	1.05	1.63	1.53	1.57	1.55	0.92	0.95	0.26	0.51
	2050	0.92	1.02	1.93	1.77	2.36	2.20	0.80	0.99	0.19	0.30
Japan	2020	1.02	1.05	1.64	1.35	1.94	1.71	0.95	0.95	0.79	1.05
	2050	0.89	1.00	1.81	1.56	2.61	1.90	0.95	1.02	0.60	0.85
Australia &	2020	1.29	1.38	2.03	1.96	1.76	1.90	0.88	0.93	0.69	0.94
New Zealand	2050	1.30	1.62	2.80	2.86	2.17	2.71	0.74	0.91	0.48	0.65
Eastern Europe	2020	1.10	1.11	2.06	1.12	1.87	1.86	0.91	0.94	0.99	0.78
& Former Soviet Union	2050	1.01	1.11	5.47	1.46	2.85	2.44	0.80	0.99	0.90	0.68
China	2020	1.31	1.34	10.13	5.02	1.69	1.76	0.89	0.95	2.43	1.81
	2050	1.38	1.56	39.49	11.99	2.17	2.56	0.80	0.93	1.29	2.14
Middle East	2020	2.23	2.42	4.27	3.39	1.45	1.49	0.91	0.97	1.06	1.06
	2050	3.73	4.89	21.23	11.54	1.77	2.21	0.89	0.94	0.76	1.84
Africa	2020	1.51	1.59	3.27	2.34	0.99	1.00	0.91	0.96	1.56	1.42
	2050	2.08	2.41	23.76	4.87	1.33	1.41	0.82	0.97	3.25	1.81
Latin America	2020	1.61	1.73	4.04	2.66	1.49	1.56	0.92	0.94	1.39	1.56
	2050	2.08	2.47	14.70	6.79	2.22	2.01	0.74	1.01	0.97	2.15
Southeast Asia	2020	1.43	1.52	6.71	3.44	1.86	1.82	0.91	0.94	2.49	2.00
	2050	1.68	1.98	30.24	8.51	3.01	2.54	0.82	1.00	2.77	2.75

income starts from different baseline values in different countries and will undoubtedly increase at different rates in different places. Although trends may not persist into the twenty-first century, the general relationships among various socio-economic factors may continue.

To develop our resilience–vulnerability scenarios, we began with the descriptions of the IPCC's *Special Report on Emissions Scenarios* (Nakicenovic and Swart 2000) (those scenarios that do not include emissions reduction policies) in the form of outputs from the MiniCAM integrated assessment model (Edmonds et al. 1997) regarding GDP per capita, changes in population, land use, agricultural production and sulfur emissions. The characterizations of the two scenarios used (fast and high growth, and the delayed growth scenarios) are shown in Table 2.3.

In the 'rapid growth' scenario (A1v2) economic development is robust and population growth moderate. Population peaks around the year 2065.

Over time, current distinctions between poor and rich countries decrease. For most people, health and social conditions greatly improve. With increases in income, dietary patterns shift towards increased consumption of meat and dairy products. Land use also shifts to sprawling urbanization and intensification of agriculture. In this scenario, global annual CO_2 emissions are 17.5 Gt C in 2095 and the average temperature increases 2.47°C.

In the 'delayed development' scenario (A2 to A1) economic development in Africa and parts of Asia and Latin America is less vigorous because of continuing institutional setbacks. People, ideas and capital are less mobile so that technology diffuses slowly with the result that international disparities relative to productivity, and hence income per capita, are maintained or increased. Fertility rates decline only slowly; the global population is close to 12 billion by 2100. Some attention is given to potential local and regional environmental damage. Total global carbon emissions amount to 21.4 Gt C/yr in 2095. Vulnerability would be expected to be particularly high in those areas where economic development is delayed and environmental problems are not addressed.

We then hypothesized that relationships between pairs of proxy values could provide unique country-level pathways for the 160 countries in the VRIM database. We therefore determined the statistical relationships between GDP per capita and various indexed proxy variables, and used the base year statistical relationships between GDP per capita and various indexed proxy variables in the VRIM projections (see Figure 2.2 for examples where the x axis is GDP per capita and the y axis the indexed proxy, and Table 2.4 for all proxy projections). These correlations are strong among GDP per capita and birth rate, life expectancy, access to safe drinking water, access to safe sanitation, access to agricultural markets and other mechanisms, and the literacy rate. Correlations are weak among GDP per capita and the Gini index and dependency ratio.

Results: Ranking in the Base Year of 2000 for a Global Comparison

The 160 countries were sorted according to the resilience indicator values (middle bars), as shown in Figures 2.3a–d. These figures also include resilience in sensitivity (top bars), and adaptive capacity (bottom bars). Relative rankings mostly line up with expectations.

In the first quartile, Norway ranks highest with high adaptive capacity. This high ranking is attributable to high economic capacity as a result of a high income and a high-scoring equity index. Most of the Organisation for Economic Co-operation and Development (OECD) countries are located in the top quarter of countries (including the top ten spots), as are three

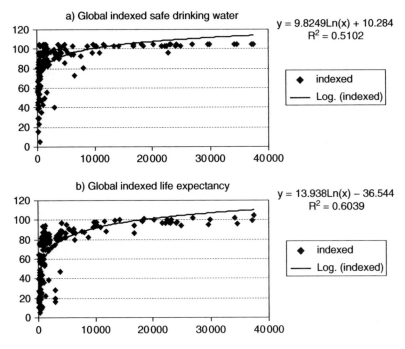

Figure 2.2   Correlations between GDP per capita and indexed proxy values

oil-rich Middle East countries. Papua New Guinea ranks high through its high resilience in the sensitive elements, which in turn is due to its high-scoring ecosystem resilience and water availability.

Countries in the second quartile score higher in their resilience in the sensitivity element than in their adaptive capacity except for oil-rich Oman and Libya. This is a geographically diverse set, with Africa, the Pacific Islands, Latin America, Eastern Europe and Asia represented. Scores are about 15 percent lower on average than scores in the top quartile.

The third quartile is headed by China, with South Korea immediately following. On average, overall scores are roughly 28 percent lower than the scores of the first quartile. Some former Eastern European countries – like Romania, Kazakhstan, Azerbaijan and Georgia – have higher coping and adaptive capacity than sensitivity, because they score high in human resources. African countries – like the Republic of the Congo, Kenya and Tanzania – and Costa Rica have higher coping and adaptive capacities than sensitivity, because of their high environmental capacity. India, located in this quartile, scores 107th out of 160 countries. This is similar to, but slightly improved over the finding in our earlier study (Brenkert

Table 2.4   SRES scenarios and statistical relationships used for the 11 regions defined for the MiniCAM integrated assessment model, showing the method for projections of each proxy

	Element	Proxy	Consequences of change	Projected with:
Sensitivity	Settlement/ infrastructure sensitivity	Potential extent of disruptions from sea level rise	Resilience over time ↓ as population at risk increases over time and sea level rises	Population change from the SRES scenarios; sea level rise from MiniCAM output
		Access of population to basic services to buffer against climate variability and change	Resilience over time ↑ as GDP per capita increases over time	Indexed safe drinking water access = 9.8249Ln(x) + 10.284 $R^2 = 0.5102$ Indexed safe sanitation access = 14.794Ln(x) − 39.598 $R^2 = 0.6051$
	Food security	Degree of moderni- zation in the agriculture sector; access of farmers to inputs to buffer against climate variability and change	Resilience over time ↑ as production technology increases over time↑	Crop yield changes from MiniCAM output
		Access of a population to agricultural markets and other mechanisms (e.g., consump- tion shift) for compensating for shortfalls in production	Resilience over time ↑ as protein consumption increases and the undernourishment index decreases	Indexed nutritional index = 9.9259Ln(x) + 9.5935 $R^2 = 0.4848$

Table 2.4   (continued)

Element	Proxy	Consequences of change	Projected with:
Ecosystem sensitivity	Degree of human intrusion into the natural landscape	Resilience over time ↓ as % agricultural land increases	Land use change from MiniCAM output
	Nitrogen/ phosphorus loading of ecosystems and stresses from pollution	Resilience over time ↑ when fertilizer use increases up to 60 kg/ha but ↓ over time with levels > 100 kg/ha	Fertilizer use changes based on land use changes from MiniCAM output
Human health sensitivity	Composite of conditions that affect human health including nutrition, exposure to disease risks, and access to health services	Resilience over time ↑ as fertility decreases to a sustainable level	Indexed birth rate $= 11.219\mathrm{Ln}(x) - 9.711$ $R^2 = 0.4699$ (Note: Actual birthrate $= -0.7696\mathrm{Ln}(x) + 9.0092$ $R^2 = 0.4699$)
		Resilience over time ↑ as (healthy) life expectancy goes up	Indexed life expectancy $= 13.938\mathrm{Ln}(x) - 36.544$ $R^2 = 0.6039$
Water resource sensitivity	Ratio of water supply from renewable resources and withdrawals to meet current or projected needs	Resilience over time ↓ as % available fresh water demand increases	Water demand changes based on agricultural production from MiniCAM output
	Water demand	Resilience over time ↓ as % land irrigated increases	Percentage irrigated land changes based on land use changes from MiniCAM output

Table 2.4 (continued)

	Element	Proxy	Consequences of change	Projected with:
Coping & adaptive capacity	Economic capacity	Distribution of access to markets, technology, and other resources useful for adaptation	Resilience over time ↑ as GDP per capita increases	GDP and population changes from SRES scenarios
		Realization of the potential contribution of all people	Resilience over time ↑ as poverty or inequity decreases	Indexed Gini index = $-2.0386\mathrm{Ln}(x)$ $+ 66.266$ $R^2 = 0.0328$
	Human and civic resources	Social and economic resources available for adaptation after meeting other present needs	Resilience over time ↓ as the % of people dependent on the working population increases	Indexed dependency ratio $= 4.7917\mathrm{Ln}(x)$ $+ 20.776$ $R^2 = 0.1415$
		Human capital and adaptability of labor force	Resilience over time ↑ as literacy increases	Indexed literacy rate = $9.8574\mathrm{Ln}(x)$ $+ 6.7554$ $R^2 = 0.3777$
	Environmental capacity	Population pressure and stresses on ecosystems	Resilience over time ↓ as population density increases	Population changes from SRES scenarios
		Air quality and other stresses on ecosystems	Resilience over time ↓ as SO_2 increases and vice versa	Sulfur emissions based on agricultural production from MiniCAM output
		Landscape fragmentation and ease of ecosystem migration	Resilience over time ↑ as % unmanaged land increases	Land use changes based on agricultural production from MiniCAM output

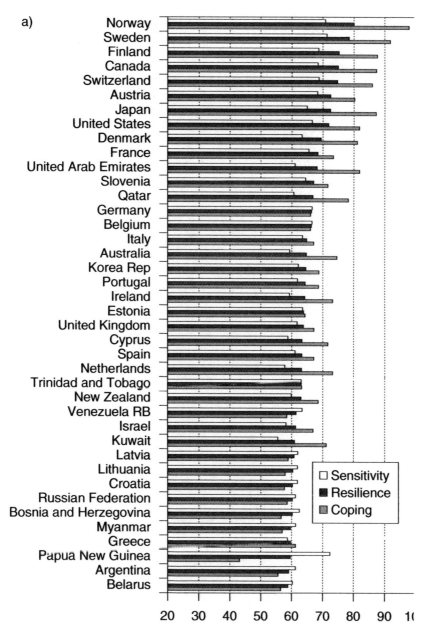

Figure 2.3   Ranking of countries according to their resilience indicator values; their sensitivity and adaptation capacity values are also shown

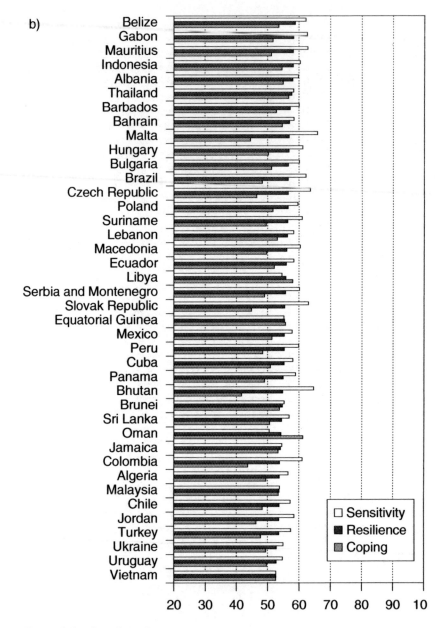

Figure 2.3   (continued)

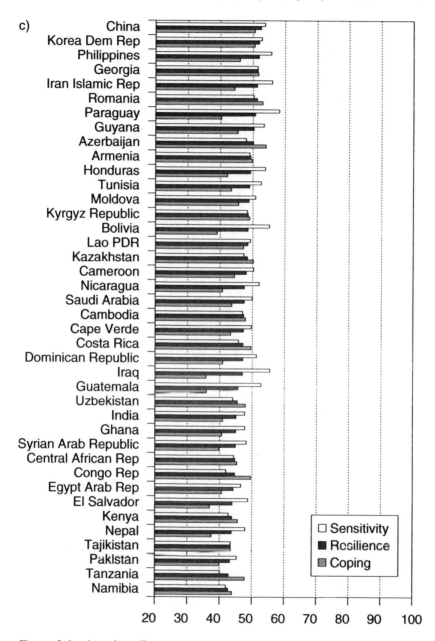

Figure 2.3   (continued)

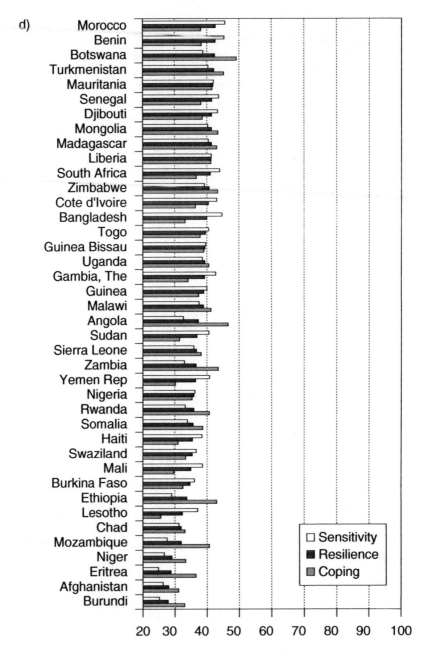

Figure 2.3   (continued)

and Malone 2005, Table 8). Using 1990 data, India ranked 74th out of 103 countries.

The fourth quartile contains mainly African countries, with Turkmenistan, Bangladesh, Haiti, Afghanistan and Yemen as the exceptions. Yemen shows up here because of its high inequity and low food security and water availability. Some African countries – such as Botswana, Angola, Zambia, Ethiopia, Mozambique, Niger, Eritrea and Burundi – have higher adaptive capacity than resilience in the sensitivity elements. Scores for fourth-quartile countries range from 50 to 65 percent lower than the highest score in the first quartile.

These rankings mostly produce expected values and, therefore, are not very illuminating in themselves. However, they may serve as a basis for choosing countries from each quartile to examine in detail.

A sample of 15 countries spans the range of indicator values and represents each of the MiniCAM regions. A closer look at these countries provides insight into the sources of the rankings. For instance, is a certain adaptive capacity ranking low because the human resources proxy is very low or for some other reason? Figure 2.4 illustrates this.

Highlights of the individual sources of index values include the following: Norway's GDP per capita in combination with the equity index provides the highest resilience ranking among these countries. Spain has high scores in economic capacity, settlement security, food security and human health compared to the other countries, partially offset by the lowest scores in ecosystem resilience and environmental response capacity to climate. China scores highest in food security (due to cereal production) and human health, and has among the highest scores in human resources. Yemen scores lowest in people in the workforce and is low in economic capacity due to inequity. This country also scores low in water availability and cereal production, and has a high birthrate. Chad scores lowest in settlement security due to lack of access to clean water and sanitation. Senegal also scores low in settlement security, but for a different reason: many people living in sea-surge-prone areas.

RESULTS: VRIM PROJECTIONS

Projections of resilience follow the methodology outlined earlier in this chapter. If the same change rates were used to project the baseline values, countries would travel parallel pathways into the future. A change in ranking can only result from responses that are unique to countries and/or from alternative scenarios. Figure 2.5 shows projections for the 15-country sample, for the high-growth and delayed-growth scenarios of the future into 2065. The

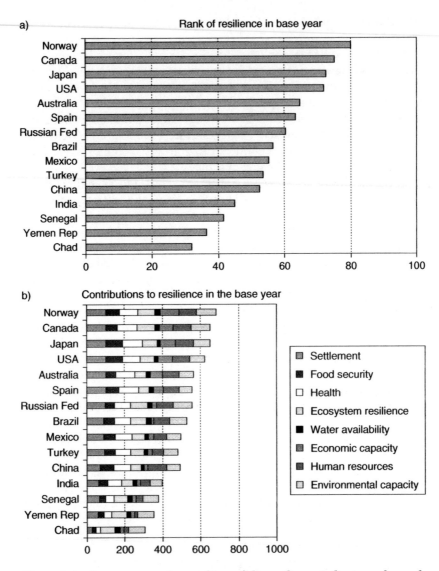

Figure 2.4   Base year results: ranking of the resilience indicator value and the element indicator values for example countries

relative rankings of the four lowest-ranked countries do not change in either scenario. Although the pathways differ (Figure 2.5), the relative rankings do not change in either scenario (Figure 2.6). In the high-growth scenario, countries tend to converge more than in the delayed-growth scenario.

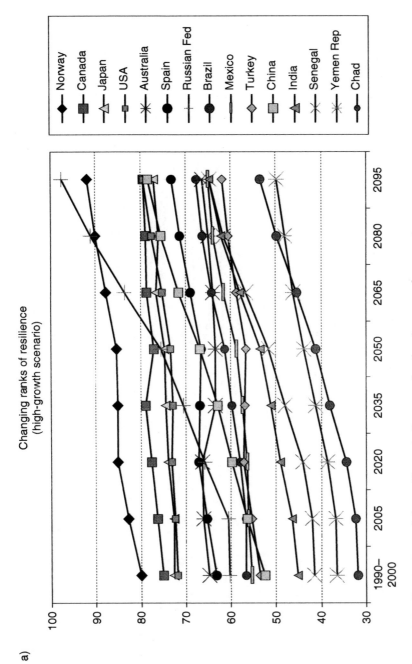

Changing ranks of resilience
(high-growth scenario)

a)

Figure 2.5   Projections of the resilience indicator value for the example countries

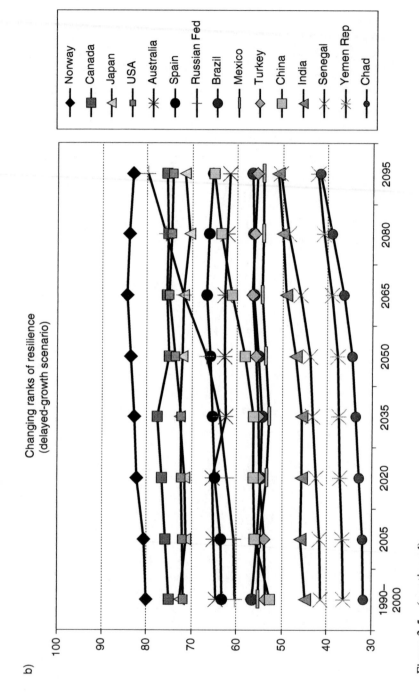

Changing ranks of resilience
(delayed-growth scenario)

Figure 2.5 (continued)

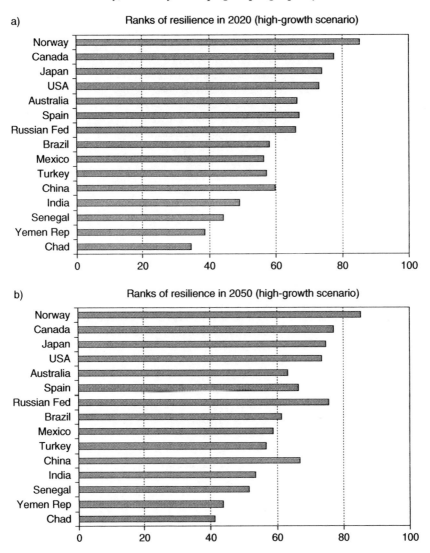

Figure 2.6   *Changes in ranking by 2020 and 2050 for the example*
            countries

The high-growth scenario shows a greater increase in resilience for the developing countries than for the developed countries consistent with the scenario description of A1v2. In the high-growth scenario, China has the largest increase in resilience compared to all other countries. It changes ranks from fifth from the bottom among the 15 countries around the turn

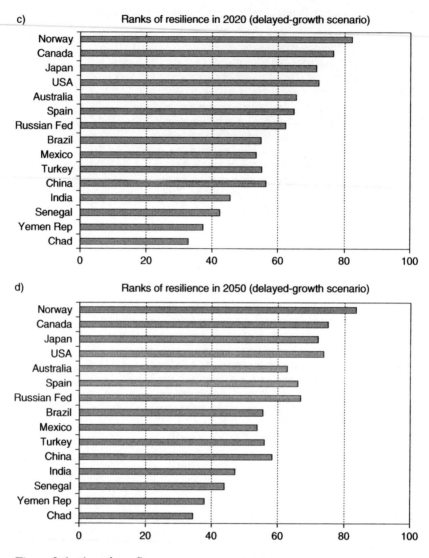

Figure 2.6   (continued)

of the century to 'developed country' resilience by 2050. This ranking is
equivalent to Spain and even outranks Australia. In the delayed-growth
scenario China's resilience increases only a fraction faster than other
developing countries, ranking eighth by 2050. Russia also shows potential
increase in resilience, especially in the high-growth scenario, by maintaining ecosystem resilience.

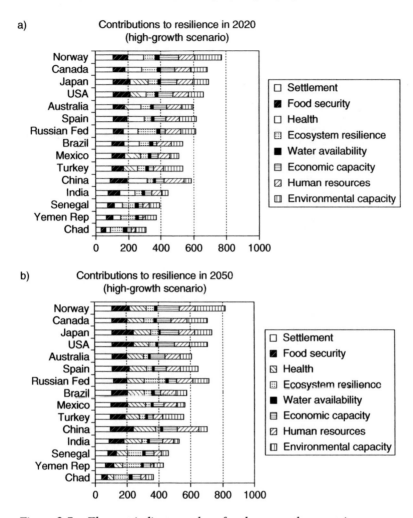

Figure 2.7 Element indicator values for the example countries

Interestingly, Australia shows hardly any change in resilience in any of the scenarios and becomes outranked by many countries, for example, consistently by Spain.

So what are the contributing factors in these phenomena? Figure 2.7 shows the contributing element indicator values to help analyze this. For example, on the one hand, China's investment in infrastructure alleviates the settlement sensitivity and leads to China becoming considerably more resilient in the high-growth scenario. On the other hand, for the currently highest-ranking resilient countries, reduced resilience in ecosystem

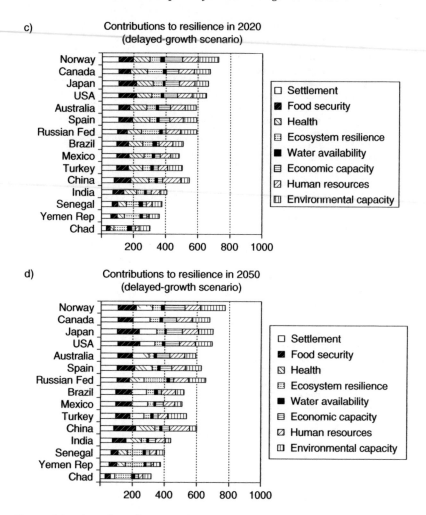

Figure 2.7   (continued)

sensitivity and water availability over time (due to increasing population and land-use changes) is compensated less by economic growth and infra-structure investment than in China.

The analysis allows some insight into decision options that could prove more effective in increasing resilience. In the next section, we discuss the additional potential options and insights for decision-makers.

Deterministic modeling does not take into account in its evaluation of results the uncertainties of model inputs (that is, the initial base year proxy values), the uncertainties of the forcing functions (that is, the changes over time expressed as a scenario description), and the impacts of the model structure. Moreover, in deterministic modeling the importance of parameter contribution (in our case, proxy contribution) to model output can be analyzed only through a decomposition process that implicitly assumes equal weights of those contributing parameters. This is clearly not the situation with VRIM analyses, given its hierarchical structure. Nor is it the case when decisions are being made.

Deterministic results may be understood as initial guidance for decision-makers about relatively important elements of a country's or state's vulnerability–resilience to climate change. Along with other, more detailed information, the results can add to the basis for policy or other development decisions in various elements.

BEYOND PROJECTIONS

To help analyze the consequences of the assumptions underlying the projections and the impacts of model structure on the uncertainty of the resilience indicator values, we placed the model in a Monte Carlo framework. In a Monte Carlo analysis repeated simulations (calculations) are performed with random combinations of randomly sampled parameters from predefined probability distributions.

To explore the impact of the model's structure, we first sampled from very narrow distributions (2 percent coefficient of variation) around each proxy value, at each point in time, for each country and for each scenario. We thus generated data sets of 1000 iterations of proxy values and resilience indicator values. We then calculated the squared Pearson correlation coefficients between the sampled proxies and the resilience indicators (see Gardner et al. 1983; Rose et al. 1991; Moss et al. 2001; Brenkert and Malone 2005; Malone and Brenkert 2008).

Results show that over time (only one time period is shown in Figure 2.8), for each country and scenario, the 18 proxy values contribute in a similar fashion to the uncertainty of the resilience indicator. Results also show that the hierarchy of the model matters. The sensitivity elements explain five-eighths of the total variance of the resilience, and the coping and adaptive capacity the remaining three-eighths, reflecting the shares of elements within indicators. That the variance (uncertainty) of the resilience is explained 100 percent indicates that no significant spurious correlations occurred among the sampled proxies.

The scenario descriptions were used to identify alternative options in development and assumed decision-making regarding pathways into the future (alternative forcing functions in the model). However, the question

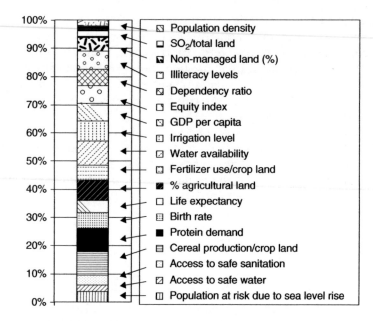

*Figure 2.8   Results of the analysis of the model structure (2% variance
           results and legend)*

remains as to what decision-making alternatives are available, at any
one time, which could lead to different outcomes. We may analyze this
as follows: the scenario pathways taken by individual proxies are proxies
themselves of the range of alternatives a decision-maker may have at a
given time. If we sample in the Monte Carlo framework from probability
distributions, based on the changes over time calculated in the deterministic solutions, we capture through our sampling from those ranges the
different pathways the proxies may take. We therefore sample each of
the proxies from distributions representing the 30-year change over time.
The upper and lower limits of the triangular distributions are the values
these proxies have either 15 years before, or after, the time of calculations.
The midpoint of the triangular distribution is determined by the deterministic proxy value results. The projected changes differ for each time period
and among the scenarios and by the region a country falls within. When
changes are large, the variances of the proxies for that point in time are
large. Conversely, when changes are slow, the uncertainty or variance is
less.

We then calculated the squared Pearson correlation coefficients between
the sampled proxies and the calculated vulnerability–resilience indicators.

Proxies with the highest explanatory power of the variance of the calculated indicators may be called leading indicators (Moss et al. 2001).

The results of the uncertainty analysis will address three questions:

- How does uncertainty affect the participation of indicators; is the model able to respond to anticipated changes in proxy values? If so, the type of approach outlined above can illuminate important factors in determining the future vulnerability and resilience of a particular location, state or entity.
- How do changes play out differently in different countries? Countries will change uniquely, depending on investments in infrastructure, their geographic locations (which determine their exposure to hazards), availability of water, and soil quality.
- How do changes play out in different scenarios?

Figure 2.9 shows the results for 2020 and 2050 of the high-growth and delayed-growth scenarios, for the 15 example countries. For each country, it shows the percentage contribution of each of the 18 proxies to the uncertainty of the resilience indicator. In high-growth scenarios, as compared to delayed growth, GDP per capita plays a larger role in determining the pathways of the projections. This is especially the case in developing countries. This confirms the A1v2 scenario description of economic growth, with convergence among countries as a main characterization of that scenario. Water availability and agricultural land pressures become apparent in developed countries. Changing sulfur emissions also explain part of the variance of the resilience indicator, especially in the United States, and to a lesser degree in Japan, Canada and Norway. The uncertainties around fertilizer use play an important role in the uncertainty of the resilience indicator, especially for Canada. Increases in resilience in Russia by the year 2050 could be explained by anticipated fast growth in GDP per capita and reduction in sulfur emissions.

In the delayed-growth scenario, crop production, fertilizer use and water availability contribute a much larger percentage of the explanation of the variance in the resilience. Only after 2050 does GDP per capita contribute to a large extent in the developing countries.

The uncertainty analysis adds to an understanding of the changes in resilience, as a consequence of assumed changes in the scenario assumptions, and further highlights differences among countries. The projected indicator values from the VRIM can in turn provide feedback to the integrated assessment models relative to factors such as pollution impacts, human health, labor productivity and land use. As a result, a more integrated assessment model can emerge.

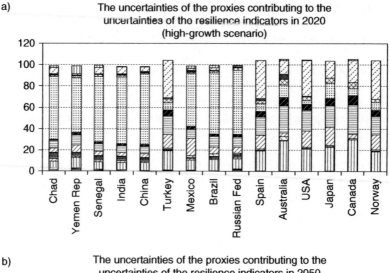

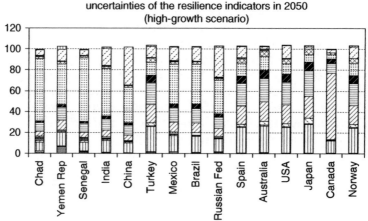

Note: Legend as in Figure 2.8.

Figure 2.9   Uncertainty analysis results for the example countries

DISCUSSION

What can decision-makers do with the results of the VRIM model runs? If national development goals include building resilience to climate change, then these results can provide meaningful insights in several ways. First, the overall ranking of a country compared to other countries can indicate

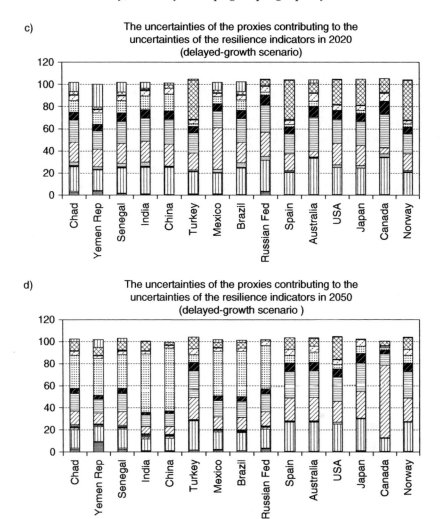

Figure 2.9   (continued)

whether vulnerability is a serious problem or confirm existing knowledge. Second, the decomposition into various elements of vulnerability–resilience points to places that need attention – especially those areas of weakness. For instance, Chad decision-makers may decide to focus on providing clean water and sanitation for reasons that include climate change vulnerability. In contrast, Senegal and Yemen may examine ways to reduce the vulnerability of areas prone to sea surges for very different reasons. The successes of other countries, with similar situations, may prompt consideration of alternative approaches. Third, decision-makers can use the results of the uncertainty analysis to see areas that may become problematic in the future. For example, monitoring the impacts of fertilizer use might be important for countries such as Canada. Again, this is a message about vulnerability and resilience to climate change that may be integrated with other development concerns to craft specific actions now and provide plans for the future.

The quantitative, comparative approach of the VRIM provides summarizing insights to country-level policy-makers who wish to include climate change in their general developmental planning. The use of the model can be downscaled to provide more fine-grained insights into states or other geographic area divisions – such as watersheds or farming areas – to highlight different policies and analyses that may be needed within a country. The process of gathering data and making projections using the VRIM may be a heuristic process in itself. Moreover, the model results can enable meaningful discussion and analysis of the issues in resilience–vulnerability to climate change in different locations.

NOTE

1. This study was undertaken as part of an Environmental Protection Agency (EPA)-sponsored project with Stratus Consulting. The Joint Global Change Research Institute (JGCRI) task was to assess socio-economic vulnerability in India and Indian states.

REFERENCES

Brenkert, A.L., M.E. Ibarrarán, E.L. Malone and L. Herrara (2006), 'Vulnerabilidad y resilencia ante el cambio climático: un análisis exploratorio para México', Presented to Políticas Publicas para Crecimiento y Desarrollo, IBERGOP, 28 August.

Brenkert, A.L. and E.L. Malone (2005), 'Modeling vulnerability and resilience to climate change: a case study of India and Indian states', *Climatic Change*, 72: 57–102.

Edmonds, J., M. Wise, H. Pitcher, R. Richels, T. Wigley and C. MacCracken (1997), 'An integrated assessment of climate change and the accelerated introduction of advanced energy technologies: an application of MiniCAM 1.0', *Mitigation and Adaptation Strategies for Global Change*, 1: 311–39.

Freedom House (2008), *Freedom in the World*, Washington, DC: Freedom House.

Gardner, R.H., B. Roder and U. Bergstrom (1983), 'PRISM: a systematic method for determining the effect of parameter uncertainties on model predictions', Studsvik Energiteknik AB report/NW-83/555, Nykoping, Sweden.

Malone, E.L. and A.L. Brenkert (2008), 'Uncertainty in resilience to climate change in India and Indian states', *Climatic Change*, **91**(3–4): 451–76.

McCarthy, J.J., O.F. Canziani, N.A. Leary, D.J. Dokken and K.S. White (2001), *Climate Change 2001: Impacts, Adaptation, and Vulnerability*, Contribution of Working Group II to the Third Assessment Report of the Intergovernmental Panel on Climate Change, Cambridge: Cambridge University Press.

Moss, R.H., A.L. Brenkert and E.L. Malone (2001), 'Vulnerability to climate change: a quantitative approach', Report, PNNL-SA-33642, Pacific Northwest National Laboratory, Washington, DC.

Nakicenovic, N. and R. Swart (2000), *Special Report on Emissions Scenarios*, Cambridge: Cambridge University Press.

O'Brien, K., R. Leichenko, U. Kelkar, H. Venema, G. Aandahl, H. Tompkins, A. Javed, S. Bhadwal, S. Barg, L. Nygaard and J. West (2004), 'Mapping vulnerability to multiple stressors: climate change and globalization in India', *Global Environmental Change*, **14**: 303–13.

Pitcher, H. (1997), *Sustainability: An Exploratory Analysis using the MiniCAM Integrated Climate Model*, Washington, DC: Pacific Northwest National Laboratory.

Prescott-Allen, R. (2001), *The Wellbeing of Nations: A Country-by-Country Index of Quality of Life and the Environment*, Washington, DC: Island Press.

Rose, K.A., E.P. Smith, R.H. Gardner, A.L. Brenkert and S.M. Bartell (1991), 'Parameter sensitivities, Monte Carlo filtering, and model forecasting under uncertainty', *Journal of Forecasting*, **10**: 117–33.

United Nations Development Programme (2005), *Human Development Report 2005: International Cooperation at a Crossroads: Aid, Trade, and Security in an Unequal World*, New York: Oxford University Press.

Watson, R.T., M.C. Zinyowera and R.H. Moss (eds) (1996), *Climate Change 1995: Impacts, Adaptations, and Mitigation of Climate Change: Scientific-Technical Analyses*, Cambridge: Cambridge University Press.

YCELP and CIESIN (Yale Center for Environmental Law and Policy, and Center for International Earth Science Information Network) (2002), *Environmental Sustainability Index: An Initiative of the Global Leaders of Tomorrow Environment Task Force, World Economic Forum*, New Haven, CT: YCELP.

3. Climate change and natural disasters: economic and distributional impacts

María E. Ibarrarán and Matthias Ruth

INTRODUCTION

Every year, a large number of potentially damaging natural events take place around the world – notably, there are windstorms, floods, droughts, cold spells, heatwaves, landslides and earthquakes.[1] Recently, however, there has been an increase in the frequency and intensity of these climatological events. It is estimated that this increase is related to global climate change (Easterling et al. 2000; IPCC 2001) and that the near future will see an increase in the devastating effects of such weather events. Simultaneous with these natural occurrences, it is expected that population growth and unsustainable economic growth will put ever larger numbers of people and their assets at risk, while reducing environmental buffering capacities such as appropriate vegetation cover on steep slopes, intact wetlands in coastal zones, or coral reefs.

Potentially damaging natural events occur all over the planet fairly randomly, and need not cause harm or destruction unless certain conditions hold. Natural events become disasters depending on their strength, the location where they hit, and the vulnerability of local ecosystems, populations, infrastructures and economic activities (Rasmussen 2004). Even though natural disasters affect both developing and industrialized countries at roughly the same rate, the extent to which they affect a given population – and the way that population copes with it – is what makes these two sets of countries different. Usually richer countries suffer less death from disasters than developing countries because they have resources and institutions available to mitigate disasters and to adapt to their resulting effects (IPCC 2001; Kahn 2005). In both sets of countries, however, natural disasters impact different population groups and economic sectors in diverse ways. Natural disasters tend to exacerbate existing differences across a population, often increasing poverty levels and income disparity.

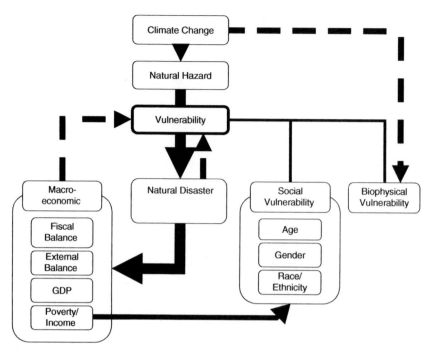

*Figure 3.1   Natural disasters, group-specific vulnerability and
macroeconomic performance*

This in turn can result in the worsening of individual and overall conditions for development. Natural disasters mostly have local and regional effects and seldom affect overall macroeconomic variables in major ways. They may, however, harm the social fabric by affecting particular groups.

The purpose of this chapter is to present a review of the literature and case studies addressing differential impacts of climate change-related natural disasters on a society and its economy. As illustrated in Figure 3.1, this chapter presents three central arguments. First, that climate change may increase the probability of natural hazards by enhancing the frequency and intensity of extreme weather events. Second, that it may also increase biophysical vulnerabilities that result from temperature and precipitation modifications, environmental, location and geophysical conditions. Finally, although natural hazards generally occur, they only become disasters when there is some sort of vulnerability.

Two aspects of vulnerability are distinguished here: biophysical and social. Vulnerability may ultimately be reflected through the macroeconomic performance which, in turn, may affect social and biophysical vulnerability (for example subsistence agriculture on marginal lands will further degrade the land, increasing both aspects of vulnerability). Macroeconomic performance is altered basically because people and/or economic activity are affected to some relatively large extent. The less prepared an economy, or a particular societal group, is to face the effects of natural disasters, the more affected it will be. Therefore, we look at the effects of natural disasters on two macroeconomic indicators, poverty and income distribution. We then disentangle these effects on particular social groups. We also explore potential feedback loops between macroeconomic performance and vulnerability, which are linked through a series of complex relationships.

The following section begins by describing what natural disasters are, where they typically occur, and how they affect different regions. It discusses the changes in frequency and intensity of extreme weather events that may result from climate change and the vulnerability those events impose. The third section concentrates on macroeconomic impacts of natural disasters (mainly on gross domestic product, fiscal and external balances), and their effect on income level and income distribution within and across countries. The fourth section analyzes, in more detail, the most affected members of society as a result of such natural disasters and, eventually, climate change. It discusses specific-group vulnerability and then provides insights on how socio-economic destitution affects macroeconomic performance and how this feeds back into more vulnerability to natural disasters. The final section draws some general conclusions and discusses their policy implications.

NATURAL DISASTERS: DEFINITION AND DISTRIBUTION

Natural disasters happen when large numbers of people or economic assets are damaged or destroyed during a natural hazard event (Dilley et al. 2005). The strength of the event – together with the vulnerability of the population, their coping ability and economic activity – determine the severity of any natural disaster. Hence, moderate natural events may map into severe natural disasters due to the vulnerability of a particular population. Conversely, severe natural events may result in moderate natural disasters due to preparedness of the population and its institutions.

Natural Hazards

According to the Centre for Research on the Epidemiology of Disasters (CRED), natural disasters are defined as events that have natural causes and lead to ten or more fatalities, affect 100 or more people, or result in a call for international assistance or the declaration of a state of emergency (CRED 2004). Natural disasters are usually discussed in terms of their relative destructiveness and compared in terms of human fatalities, injuries and displacement, direct economic losses, and indirect costs from infrastructure loss and capital needed to replace it. These latter costs refer to the foregone production derived as a result of disasters. Secondary costs, namely the macroeconomic implications of such disasters, are rarely calculated; and non-monetary costs – beyond loss of life or health – are hardly ever assessed. Non-monetary costs include stress to individuals and communities, deterioration of family relationships and damage to the social fabric.

Geographic differences in the occurrence of weather-related and geophysical hazards are used to map the expected effects on different regions of the world. For example, the Hazard Management Unit (HMU) at the World Bank determines risk levels for individual countries and regions from hazard exposure and historical vulnerability for population and gross domestic product (GDP) per unit area. Countries are likely to be hurt by natural events if a significant proportion of their land area can be affected. This often results in both population and economic losses (Dilley et al. 2005). Generally, there is a broad pattern in the occurrence of these events: most of the hydrometeorological hazards happen on the eastern coast of the Pacific Ocean; droughts are more present in the semi-arid regions north and south of the Equator; and regions with coastlines obviously experience more tropical storms and hurricanes than inland locations.

While natural processes determine the occurrence and severity of hazards, human activities may either exacerbate or ameliorate their ramifications. For example, certain patterns of economic behavior (such as deforestation in Haiti) can aggravate hazards (such as the triggering of landslides) (Lonergan 1998; Homer-Dixon 1994; Bilsborrow 1992). Similarly, rural-to-urban migration and increasing urbanization in the Caribbean can lead to severe water shortages; while urban encroachment along the coastlines of the United States can make ever larger amounts of infrastructure prone to sea level rise (Ruth 2006). As an example of the latter problem, 13 million now live in coastline counties in Florida, as opposed to 200 000 a century ago. This aggressive coastal development increases the area's vulnerability to natural disasters (De Souza 2004).

Conversely, mitigation and adaptation efforts may reduce the level of risk exposure and vulnerability. The United States Geological Survey jointly with the World Bank estimated that natural disaster-related economic losses worldwide could have been reduced by $280 billion had $40 billion been invested in mitigation and prevention efforts (Benson and Clay 2003a). Finally, institutional development may also be seen as a form

of increased capacity to cope with natural disasters and reduce vulnerability (Kahn 2005).

On a larger scale, Webster et al. (2005), Emanuel (2005) and Trenberth
(2005) have all found a positive relationship between increase in atmospheric temperature and the intensity of hurricanes in the North Atlantic
Basin. Recent – but yet still unpublished – research also hints that higher
temperatures may increase the frequency of such events. Higher atmospheric temperatures have been attributed to anthropogenic releases of
greenhouse gases into the atmosphere related to economic activity (IPCC
2001), and this is certainly expected to continue into the future. Thus,
extreme weather events that have led to natural disasters in the past are
likely to become more common in the future.

The urgency to mitigate climate change is justified to prevent an increase
in the frequency and severity of natural disasters and their negative consequences. In addition, there is a need to address the fact that climate change
has a clear regressive effect on world development, impacting poorer countries more than rich ones. Reasons for this disparate impact are discussed
below.

MACROECONOMIC EFFECTS OF DISASTERS

In addition to the short- and long-term dramatic impacts on individuals, households and communities, natural disasters have direct economic
effects. These disasters may set back development goals and achievements.
In Central America, for example, natural disasters have caused more than
56 thousand deaths, and $22 billion in economic damage since the early
1970s; the equivalent of 37 percent of the current aggregate GDP of those
countries (Martine and Guzman 2002).

A comparison of the effects of natural disasters on different countries is
difficult because of their differences in population, income level, and the
number and intensity of disaster events each suffers. For example, monetary
damages tend to be higher for industrialized and larger countries because
of the accumulated value of monetarized assets at risk there. The highest
overall average cost is reported for the US, followed by China and India
(see Kahn 2005). The average number of deaths for all events is higher in
developing countries. The average deaths from earthquakes are highest, followed by those related to floods and landslides (see Rasmussen 2004). Since
the 1970s, damage for developing countries was on average 0.69 percent
of GDP, compared to 0.08 percent for advanced economies. By contrast,
in certain Latin American and Caribbean countries the losses as a share of
GDP range from over 1 percent in most cases, to 20 percent on Barbados,

32 percent in Nicaragua and 85 percent on St Kitts & Nevis (Charveriat 2000). Similar variability in values is seen throughout Asia and Africa.

The remainder of this section analyzes the macroeconomic impacts of natural disasters within and between countries. It then addresses the specific effects of natural disasters on poverty and income distribution.

Within-Country Effects

Natural disasters tend to corrode or destroy physical and social infrastructure, change the environment and cause economic stress. To the population, such disasters cause the loss of property, impact livelihoods, and disrupt family and social relationships. Moreover, natural disasters affect the performance of the economy by changing the level and structure of public expenditure. This usually hurts the current level of public services and future public investment, and reduces transfers, particularly to the disenfranchised and poor. Sometimes this sets back long-term development projects that ultimately affect those with lower income levels.

Overall, macroeconomic studies have found that natural disasters may lead to an immediate contraction in economic output, a worsening of a country's balance of trade, a deterioration of the fiscal balances, and an increase in poverty, usually accompanied by an increase in income disparities (Rasmussen 2004). Each of these macroeconomic impacts is closely related to each other.

Reductions in the growth of GDP typically take place in the year that the event occurs, with the potential for sharp increases in subsequent years (Charveriat 2000). For the Latin American and the Caribbean region (Economic Commission for Latin America and the Caribbean – ECLAC), the median real decline in GDP growth typically is in the order of 2 percent in response to an average disaster, followed by an annual increase of 3 percent during the two subsequent years. Worldwide, the size of the effect on output growth depends in part on the overall size of the economy, the degree of integration of an affected area or sector with the rest of the economy, and the ability to adapt to varying production conditions (Benson and Clay 2004).

The growth rate of GDP falls because there is usually a significant fall in production, particularly in the case of hurricanes, floods or droughts. These events are perceived as, primarily, affecting the agricultural sector and primary activities such as forestry and fisheries. In addition, hurricanes and floods may have effects on other sectors such as tourism that rely heavily on the existence of natural capital. The manufacturing sector may be affected as well, in part because of a decrease in activity due to the disruption of transportation and a reduction in production capacities.

Transportation is commonly affected because natural disasters tend to hurt roads and bridges. Production capacity falls because of a delay in inputs such as water, energy and materials, plus the direct effect on workers and their productivity. Finally, the export sector is hurt because of the effects that both the primary and the secondary sectors suffer (Charveriat 2000; Albala-Bertrand 1993; Downing et al. 1999).

Gross formation of capital tends to fall in the year of the disaster but then increases due to new investment for reconstruction. Inflation rates tend to increase since the prices of goods and services go up as a result of disruptions in production and transportation.

If countries have access to additional resources and room either to increase or to reallocate expenditure, the fiscal balance suffers because of necessary diversions of government expenditure for aid and reconstruction (Benson and Clay 2003b). At the same time, tax revenue typically falls. The International Monetary Fund (IMF 2003) found that particular natural disasters in Africa caused an increase in the fiscal deficit of 3 percent of GDP in the year of the disaster.

Trade balances often suffer for at least two reasons. Exports may fall if either the production of exports is affected, or the infrastructure to put the products into the international market is damaged. Furthermore, imports of reconstruction materials and consumption goods usually rise in response to falling domestic production. ECLAC (2000) found that in the case of Latin America, the deterioration of the balance of payments was equivalent to a third of the estimated damage (Crowards 2000). Balance-of-payment impacts are particularly large for countries with high dependence on the primary sector for exports and domestic consumption (Benson et al. 2001), a situation common for many African countries. The current account is affected by trade imbalance and international help in the form of loans that increase long-term foreign debt (Charveriat 2000; Albala-Bertrand 1993; Downing et al. 1999).

The effect of natural disasters on selected components of GDP ultimately traces back to a fall in GDP per capita and to lower real income levels. When income levels fall, there is an increase in poverty since people have fewer resources available to fulfill their needs. If the relative income level of different groups is affected, income disparities accentuate. Usually when the income level drops it is also redistributed, and disparity increases because more resources flow to the rich (the capital assets they hold are now scarcer and the value of these assets is increased) and less to the poor. Thus, natural disasters tend to increase poverty and worsen income disparity.

In addition to a fall in income that has effects on welfare itself, the poor are often more affected because they tend to settle in the most vulnerable areas and have inadequate housing and working facilities (World Bank 2003). They are more vulnerable because they have fewer assets and access to insurance and credit markets to smooth income losses and consumption needs (IMF 2003). Additionally, natural disasters have a negative impact on living standards that may be felt outside the region directly affected. There can be regional, national and very often international effects, mainly through migration.

Differential Effects across Countries

As discussed above, not all countries suffer equally from the effects of natural disasters. Even though the probability of getting hit by a natural disaster is not statistically different for developing and industrialized countries, developing countries are more affected in terms of deaths and injury. According to Kahn (2005) this may be precisely due to their development level, since usually they have not made (or rather they cannot afford to make) the required investments to protect themselves from such natural events. Thus they are unable to protect their population; that is, poverty makes the population of certain areas more vulnerable to nature's events.

Benson and Clay (2004) state that short-run macroeconomic effects are more commonly seen in the case of small island economies and rural and agricultural settings. This is the case of Dominica, for example, where in 1979 Hurricane Allen caused its GDP to drop by 20 percent. Larger countries, in terms of land area, that face natural disasters tend to suffer less of an overall economic impact in the short term. Longer-term impacts can be difficult to determine at a national level even though negative impacts are usually present. This is quite evident in the case of Bangladesh. The change in GDP is rarely negative even under extreme weather-related events. Agricultural GDP shows more variability, but aggregate GDP is quite stable. However, distributional impacts may be quite strong, generating winners and losers (Benson and Clay 2004). This cannot be seen directly from macroeconomic variables such as the change in GDP.

Many countries have been able to build up their capacity to buffer natural disasters, and so reduce their vulnerability, through infrastructure, development and institutions. However, this is not always the case. Vulnerability is a changing feature of an economy. It can be affected by a change in the rate of economic growth and may be due to socio-economic change. Malawi, for example, is a case where vulnerability has increased and now it is more prone to drought due to a deteriorating natural environment. Vulnerability has increased due to unsustainable agricultural practices and weaknesses of the agricultural sector. Further, factors include deindustrialization and the return of competition from other countries into the regional economy, political instability and governance issues, public finance volatility, and the effect of HIV/AIDS on the population (Benson and Clay 2004). Output of maize has had great variability, sometimes falling up to 60 percent in response to drought.

Other empirical evidence suggests that, for example, as GDP per capita grows, there are fewer fatalities, controlling for the strength of the natural event (Kahn 2005). This raises an equity concern related to the distribution of the negative effects of natural disasters and eventually of climate change, as long as it seems to increase the intensity and frequency of natural hazards: they both hit poorer nations the hardest. Since natural disasters and climate change have a far greater effect on poorer nations than on rich ones, they have a clear regressive effect on world development.

The differential impact of natural disasters on different countries may also be explained by the fact that the higher income level of industrialized nations eventually translates into better institutions with a higher capability of addressing the effects of natural disasters. These stronger institutions were approximated by Kahn (2005). Overall Kahn's results show that better institutions insulate populations from the effects of disasters, that is, proxies for institutional quality lower deaths from natural disasters. Additionally, controlling for income, less democratic nations and more unequal nations face higher number of deaths. Finally, corruption indices are negatively correlated with income per capita. Corruption may increase deaths because of the failure to enforce building and zoning codes fully, and the poor quality of infrastructure.

Effects of Disasters on Poverty and Income Distribution

Even though statistical analysis of 57 countries listed in the EM-DAT data set indicates that rich and poor nations are similarly prone to natural hazards (Kahn 2005), vulnerability clearly varies significantly among and within countries. Accordingly, poor people usually rank among the most susceptible to such hazards. Studies continually show that the poor suffer higher mortality rates after natural disasters (Winchester 2000; Pelling 1997; Kahn 2005). This may be due to two factors. Firstly, the poor have fewer resources for preventative and adaptive measures; that is, they lack the endowments that provide resources to cope with the effects of natural disasters. Secondly, their social networks are less likely to contain connections to influential people, such as moneylenders or government officials.

The first of these factors relates to the fact that assets and income are a critical part of social vulnerability. Among the poor, reliance upon a single source of income is correlated with lower income (Kelly and Adger 2000). This increases the likelihood that a natural disaster will seriously and adversely affect their livelihood. With lower incomes and reduced assets, the poor then lack the savings to manage unplanned expenses associated with natural disasters, both preventative and recuperative. Items which could mitigate injury and property damage – such as quality health care, sturdy housing, adequate food and water supplies, and communication devices, are generally not accessible to the poor (Adger and Kelly 1999; O'Brien and Leichenko 2000; Wisner 1997; Pelling 1997; Blaikie et al. 1994; Winchester 2000). Additionally, due to a low income level and a lack of an endowment, the poor do not have the savings to purchase productive, stable land. Thus, marginal populations may be forced to live in marginal areas (Wisner 1997; O'Brien and Leichenko 2000; Vaux and Lund 2003; Lavell 1994; Chan and Parker 1996; Blaikie et al. 1994). Winchester (2000) found that in India, 20 years after the 1977 cyclone, more of the poor South Indian agricultural laborers had migrated to vulnerable coastal regions that were less expensive but more prone to damage from natural disasters. Susceptibility of disasters can even increase as poor groups tend to overexploit natural defenses (such as wetlands or forests) for their livelihood (Blaikie et al. 1994).

A second reason for disproportional impacts of disasters on the poor lies in their limited access to credit markets and government officials. This limited access can deprive them of the most critical forms of resilience, such as private and public insurance (Chan and Parker 1996; Pelling 1997; Blaikie et al. 1994). Insurance serves to protect against large swings in income. In Bangladesh, for example, a country that is particularly vulnerable to sea level rise from climate change, researches found a low ability to insure against catastrophe. On the other hand, government recovery and assistance plans act as a form of public insurance, though the poor may be left out of these programs as a result of systematic exclusion or oversight (Wisner 1997; Blaikie et al. 1994; Adger 1999). Furthermore, the poor may not be part of a government's social insurance program because they are concentrated in economic sectors that either cannot afford or choose not to contribute. These areas include the informal sector, small businesses and self-employment. Without private or public insurance, the poor often turn to informal insurance agreements. However, these plans may also fail after shocks because providers are often hit by the disaster as well (Lustig 2000) and financial resources may be diverted to rebuild infrastructures rather than compensate for the loss of livelihoods.

Social networks can provide essential information resources prior to the occurrence of a disaster and a source of support in the recovery period (Wisner 1997). The wealthy may be better able to work their way through the government system and receive a larger share of assistance. This can be facilitated through their network; ties to government officials provide early warning or public assistance after an event. Pelling (1997) found that wealthier neighborhoods in Guyana had better infrastructure and maintenance of government provisions such as sewers, sources of drinking water and municipal waste disposal. Incidents of sickness, and reported responses to flood, were less serious in these areas than in their lower-income regions. Finally, ties to local lenders allow the wealthy to obtain scarce loans after a natural disaster (Wisner 1997; Winchester 2000). Access to all of these resources reduce the social vulnerability of the wealthy, while the lack of access increases the vulnerability of the impoverished.

Income distribution – or rather its concentration – plays a role in determining the death toll from natural disasters. Controlling for differences in GDP, countries with a higher Gini coefficient experience a higher death toll from natural disasters. Thus, improving income distribution is crucial because a more equitable income distribution is usually, though not always, related to a decrease in the number of poor within a population.

Other dimensions, not necessarily related to income, are population density and land area. Countries that have a high population density, such as Japan, are more prone to have a higher toll from natural disasters that hit a highly populated area. Iceland, in contrast, can be affected disproportionately more than other countries with the same income level because of its small area.

GROUP-SPECIFIC VULNERABILITY TO CLIMATE CHANGE

Here we draw on research from a variety of disciplines to synthesize the effect of natural hazards on the livelihood, health and general well-being of the poor based on their age-cohorts, gender, ethnicity and race. Several empirical studies directly examine group-specific differences in vulnerability in relation to the impacts of climate change (for example Bunyavanish et al. 2003; Cutter et al. 2003; Bohle et al. 1994). Most studies dealing with group-specific vulnerabilities are of a qualitative nature – owing to the environmental, social, economic and technological complexities that determine the extent to which a social group experiences risks, is vulnerable and resilient. Some of this large body of literature isolates the effects of extreme events on marginal populations. Additionally, since risks, vulnerabilities and resilience are most apparent in periods of natural disasters, and since climate change increases the severity and frequency of extreme events, these studies help ascertain climate impacts on marginal populations (IPCC 2001; Cubash et al. 2001). We use these studies as a guide to disaggregate the vulnerability for the subgroups of the poor.

Defining Social Vulnerability

Among several options, here we choose to describe two major approaches to vulnerability. Bohle et al. (1994) break down vulnerability into environmental hazards and social inequalities. The poor are often more exposed to harmful environmental perturbation (risk of exposure); they are also more vulnerable because they possess limited coping capacity (risk of inadequate capacities). They suffer the most from the impact of an extreme event because they are far more constrained in their potential for recovery (risk of potentiality). Vulnerability, composed of the latter risk factors, is therefore a product of human ecology (the relationship between people and the environment), expanded entitlements (property rights, endowments, social entitlements and empowerments) and political economy (class and other macro-structure in which resource endowments and patterns of entitlements are embedded).

Cutter et al. (2003) create a model that combines the geographic distribution of hazards with the social characteristics of people. They define social vulnerability as the product of social inequalities that eventually shape the susceptibility of various subgroups to harm and govern their ability to respond. These inequalities are often expressed in the lack of, or limited access to, resources or political power and representation. Social vulnerability also incorporates place inequalities, defined as the characteristics of communities and the built environment. These could include the level of urbanization, growth rates and economic vitality. Furthermore, vulnerable groups will have limited social capital, including social networks and connections, and may hold beliefs and customs that increase their susceptibility. As mentioned in previous sections, groups with high social vulnerability may have increased biophysical or environmental vulnerability as well. Since it is often difficult to quantify many of these concepts, social vulnerability is usually described by using the specific characteristics of a subgroup. The variables commonly used to represent these groups are age, gender, socio-economic status and special needs – such as the needs of the physically or mentally challenged, immigrants, homeless, transients and seasonal tourists.

Empirical Evidence

With this brief overview of how social vulnerability is perceived, we move on to describe specific ways in which particular groups among the poor are vulnerable in the face of natural disasters and climate change. The literature suggests that, generally, ethnic or racial minorities, females, the elderly and/or the very young suffer the most.

Gender

In studies of heatwaves in the United States, no significant difference was found between women's and men's mortality rates (Semenza et al. 1996). Yet, this fact masks the higher vulnerability of women during natural disasters. While women may not be biophysically more vulnerable to natural disasters, and thus do not suffer higher mortality rates, the difference lies in their social vulnerability (Rashid 2000; Cannon 1994; Enarson 2000). All else being equal, women are more likely to be poor than men (Gordon et al. 2003). This gender–poverty gap is the result of lower empowerment. Indeed, wealthy, developed nations occupy the top rankings in indices of gender empowerment that aggregate a woman's right to make economic and political decisions. Empowerment reduces their vulnerability.

Restrictions on women's livelihood have effects on gendered vulnerability in both developing and developed nations. Schroeder (1987) cites four broad categories that affect women's vulnerability in developing nations: lack of access to means of production; lack of access to alternative sources of food; lack of assets; and restricted access to the labor market. Within these categories, he mentions specific examples for women, such as lower wages, restrictions on education, and virilocal marriage practices which displace them from their social networks. These factors inhibit women from fully contributing to their own, or their families', welfare. Further, they reduce the resources available to women to cope with disaster. Across developed nations, gender differences in employment opportunities and pay are also one of the greatest contributors to increased poverty rates among women.

As discussed above, the poor often lack multiple sources of income. For women, this is of greater importance because their labor tends to be in particularly disaster-prone sectors (Denton 2002). As opportunities for women's paid labor are reduced due to natural disasters, the amount of unpaid work in the home increases, further exacerbating this problem (Enarson 2000). Household chores become more difficult and numerous (Rashid 2000). In the developing world, tasks such as cooking, cleaning, fetching water, care giving, and balancing work and family require more effort when tools are washed away and sources of water become contaminated (Rashid 2000; Enarson 2000). Women of developed nations face an increase in these tasks because of tragedy, lack of child care, and the loss of conveniences like electricity and permanent housing. Furthermore, the deaths of family members (loss of social network), and the breakdown of law and order after a natural disaster, might lead to violence against women, thus making them even more vulnerable.

Poor women are especially dependent upon aid for recovery after disasters because they lack the endowments available to their wealthier counterparts. However, institutional discrimination may reduce the amount of aid that reaches them. Aid is sometimes distributed to male heads of household (Enarson 2000). Such cases have been documented in both developed and developing countries. Enarson (2000) documents these occurrences in California and Malawi. When men leave their families, as is not infrequent after a natural disaster, women receive no public assistance. One notable report found that the United States Small Business Administration disproportionately favored male-headed businesses in granting recovery loans (Enarson 2000).

Thus, the greatest source of gendered vulnerability is through the other half of the feedback loop. Research reveals that women in both developed and developing countries are disproportionately poor, adding all the risk factors that accompany that low socio-economic status (Chan and Parker 1996; Enarson 2000).

Race and Ethnicity

In most regions, racial and ethnic minorities tend to have a lower socio-economic status (Fothergill 1999; Chan and Parker 1996). Studies consistently show these minorities have higher death rates from natural disasters (McGeehin and Mirabelli 2001; Fothergill et al. 1999). Jones et al. (1982) found that non-white residents had heatstroke mortality rates three to six times higher than white residents after a US heatwave. Higher vulnerability for racial and ethnic subgroups is usually the result of discrimination, both intentional and through negligence. Deliberately discriminatory practices, like insurance redlining and neighborhood segregation, place minorities in precarious housing situations with few resources for disaster mitigation (Fothergill et al. 1999). As with females, racial and ethnic minorities tend to depend upon the government for aid. Government workers may participate in discrimination because of a lack of knowledge about cultural norms – that is, warning signs may be in the wrong language, or aid may structured around a nuclear household unit. As an example of the latter, the Federal Emergency Management Agency (FEMA) could not sufficiently assist Haitians living in Florida after a natural catastrophe because several families tended to live in one household (Fothergill et al. 1999). Examples of discrimination in emergency response have also been documented (Beady and Bolin 1986). Knowing about previous discrimination may also affect minorities' current view of government services and so discourage them from seeking available help (Langer 2004).

Meadows and Hoffman (2003) provide a clear example of the interaction of poverty and race-based vulnerability. Historic inertia also plays a role. In South Africa black farming communes were relegated to sloped, marginal land during apartheid. Today this land is more degraded, from a lack of investment due to discriminatory lending practices, and more intensive farming because of poverty. Conversely, land given to whites had higher commercial value and continues to be productive because they are able to afford inputs. Consequently, Meadows and Hoffman predict that black farming communities will be hit harder in a climate change-induced drought.

Age

While the elderly and very young are physiologically more vulnerable to natural disasters, they are more socially vulnerable as well (McGeehin and Mirabelli 2001; Blaikie et al. 1994; Scheraga and Grambsch 1998; Ngo 2001). This physical vulnerability is channeled into overall vulnerability depending on the resources they have to mitigate risk.

There is empirical evidence that, in general, the elderly display disproportionately higher injury rates after natural disasters (Ngo 2001). Studies on heatwave mortality also show that persons over the age of 65 have higher rates of heatstroke and are more likely to exhibit characteristics of risk (Kilbourne et al. 1982; Jones et al. 1982). Older persons are more vulnerable because they have diminished coping skills. Their bodies adapt to temperature changes more slowly and are less able to perceive excess heat, preventing them from taking adaptive measures (Scheraga and Grambsch 1998; McGeehin and Mirabelli 2001). Reduced mobility may also inhibit them from leaving a dangerous situation. Finally, they are also more susceptible to disease because of pre-existing health conditions (Ngo 2001).

This physical vulnerability can be overcome with adaptive measures; but frequently these measures are only accessible to the wealthy. For example, the elderly are more likely to lack the private transportation necessary to leave a dangerous area. The wealthy may be able to hire a taxicab. The poor, though, must rely upon neighbors or relatives. Because the ride could constitute a considerable burden, many of the elderly may be discouraged from requesting assistance. Thus, the elderly's vulnerability is highly dependent upon their economic status (Langer 2004). Controlling for other variables, the elderly show disproportionate rates of poverty, because they do not generate income any more and have very low endowments, if any. Poor older persons in developed nations are more likely to live isolated and alone. Lack of personal contact and distrust of strangers decreases their access to assistance (Scheraga and Grambsch 1998; Langer 2004). The elderly are also less likely to take advantage of public recovery and prevention programs, perceiving them as welfare (Langer 2004; Ngo 2001). In developing countries, they are somewhat relegated because of their lower income capability and the extra work they impose on others. Also, the government may more often than not ignore their needs.

Children, in contrast, are not typically thought to be a marginalized population, but they lack the power to make critical decisions that affect their well-being. Children suffer from the same physiological effects as their elderly counterparts. The young are more susceptible to disease because their respiratory and immune systems are not yet fully developed (Bunyavanich et al. 2003). Children also have diminished abilities to care for themselves (Blaikie et al. 1994). Adults are responsible for adjusting physical conditions for the very young. Barriers to communication, lack of mobility and reduced ability to employ coping mechanisms – like ingesting fluid or changing attire – increase youth vulnerability (Blaikie et al. 1994; Blum et al. 1998). Children also have greater sustentative needs. If food or water sources become scarce during a drought, it may have more serious consequences for poor children, especially in cultures where children eat last (Bunyavanish et al. 2003). If a disproportionate number of children are poor, like the elderly, their vulnerability is more likely to go unmitigated (Gordon et al. 2003).

Poverty and Vulnerability Feedbacks

Climate change has been linked to an increase in frequency and intensity of extreme natural disasters. There is empirical evidence that the macroeconomic impact of these disasters will fall largely upon the poor (Deininger and Squire 1996). Given that the poor are more vulnerable, climate change has the potential to create a vicious cycle of poverty and vulnerability.

While growth tends to increase the incomes of the poorest groups, thereby reducing poverty, economic declines have an opposite impact. Additionally, shocks also tend to increase income inequality (Deininger and Squire 1996). Reardon and Taylor (1996) find empirical evidence for this phenomenon in Burkina Faso. The poor use livestock sales to augment their income from agriculture. Droughts lead to further sales, making them more vulnerable to the next drought. After the 1984 drought, the authors find that the richest third of the population suffered a 58 percent drop in income, while the poor suffered a 69 percent drop accompanied by larger livestock sales. Lustig (2000) estimates that for every percent decrease in gross domestic product in Latin American countries, there is a corresponding 2 percent increase in poverty, but this is mainly due to the downward mobility of the middle class. Incomes of the top 10 percent rose during this period. Other studies find that the wealthy may also fall into poverty as a result of natural disasters. In South India, Gaiha and Imai (2004) show that all segments of the population, landless and landholders, upper and lower castes, are vulnerable to poverty after crop shocks. Regardless of the distribution of a shock's impact, the gross increase in poverty increases social vulnerability within a population. Social vulnerability can aggregate over time, especially with increased frequency of natural disasters. This, in turn, forces groups into a permanent state of poverty and exposure.

POLICY IMPLICATIONS

Several lessons can be drawn from this research. First, given that the poor are more vulnerable to natural disasters, and that climate change tends to increase the frequency and intensity of many of these disasters, climate change has the potential to create a vicious cycle of poverty and vulnerability. Second, that investment in disaster prevention, awareness and mitigation will be progressive in terms of inequality and poverty reduction. Empirical evidence presented here shows that the macroeconomic impact of these disasters falls largely upon the poor. However, a review of the literature also indicates that through physical, economic and institutional development a country – a group of people – may somewhat insulate itself to a greater degree from the negative effects of natural disasters.

Additionally, even though catastrophes can be somewhat unexpected and uncertain in their occurrence and effects, they need to be considered as events that are likely to happen and therefore require advanced planning. Past experiences highlight the need to prepare for disasters, giving special attention to their effects on poverty and their distributional impacts. This implies that the monetary and physical resources to face such catastrophes should be available beforehand and, when feasible, reflected within the national budgets. Moreover, subgroup vulnerability should be addressed and built into natural disaster prevention programs to avoid further gaps among the poor, thus increasing overall social and economic resilience to disasters. For example, this could be done by granting relief to women, when appropriate, rather than men. Well-planned evacuation programs could help mobilize the elderly and the very young, and particular policies could address minorities, making sure not to discriminate against the non-minority poor.

Finally, adaptation has to be implemented on two levels. Household and community-level strategies may be put in place to reduce risk. Such strategies may include moving out of hazard-prone zones, investing in hazard-resistant technology, and diversifying income sources.

At the public level, a short-term policy is to design a contingency fund within the budget to provide aid when a disaster takes place. A tricky balance may need to be struck between providing insurance (or government assistance) in case a disaster hits, and not encouraging through the supply of such provisions moral hazards and adverse behavior, such as settlements in flood-prone regions, or farming on steeply sloped lands. Other public-level policies that could be accomplished in the medium term may be relocating settlements and building physical infrastructure to mitigate the effects of natural disasters and contain their magnitude. In the long run, policies such as diversification and the relocation of economic activity and the generation of resources to face future disasters may be vital. In this sense, physical and institutional awareness, as well as financial preparedness, are crucial in order to respond to emergencies and to allow for rehabilitation and reconstruction in a timely fashion.

ACKNOWLEDGEMENTS

We thank Sanjana Ahmad and Marisa London who contributed to earlier versions of this chapter. We also want to thank Haewon Chon, Dana Coelho and Julia Miller for feedback on the material presented here. This research was partially funded by Universidad de las Americas, Puebla, Mexico, and the Roy F. Weston Chair in Natural Economics at the School of Public Policy, University of Maryland, USA.

NOTE

1. In the remainder of this chapter we will not address earthquakes when discussing natural disasters because they are not related to climate change. However, they do impose a high toll of death and injury, and have similar macroeconomic implications; specific group vulnerabilities hold.

REFERENCES

Adger, W.N. (1999), 'Social vulnerability to climate change and extremes in coastal Vietnam', *World Development*, **27**(2): 249–69.
Adger, W.N. and P.M. Kelly (1999), 'Social vulnerability to climate change and the architecture of entitlements', *Mitigation and Adaptation Strategies for Global Change*, **4**(3–4): 253–66.
Albala-Bertrand, J.M. (1993), *Political Economy of Large Natural Disasters*, Oxford: Clarendon Press.
Beady, C. and R. Bolin (1986), 'The role of the black media in disaster reportings to the black community', Natural Hazard Working Paper, Institute of Behavioral Science, University of Colorado, Boulder, CO.
Benson C. and E. Clay (2003a), 'Understanding the economic and financial impacts of natural disasters', Disaster Risk Management Series No. 4, World Bank.

Benson, C. and E. Clay (2003b), 'Economic and financial impacts of natural disasters: an assessment of their effects and options for mitigation', Overseas Development Institute, London.

Benson, C. and E. Clay (2004), Beyond the damage: probing the economic and financial consequences of natural disasters, Presentation at ODI, 11 May, http://www.odi.org.uk/speeches/disasters_2004/presentation.pdf.

Benson, C., E. Clay, F.V. Michael and A.W. Robertson (2001), 'Dominica natural disasters and economic development in a small island state', Disaster Risk Management Working Paper Series No. 2, World Bank, Washington, DC.

Bilsborrow, R.E. (1992), 'Population growth, internal migration, and environmental degradation in rural areas of developing countries', *European Journal of Population/Revue européenne de Démographie*, **8**(2): 125–48.

Blaikie, P., T. Cannon, I. Davis and B. Wisner (1994), *At Risk: Natural Hazards, People's Vulnerability, and Disasters*, London: Routledge.

Bohle, H.G., T.E. Downing and M.J. Watts (1994), 'Climate change and social vulnerability: toward a sociology and geography of food insecurity', *Global Environmental Change*, **4**(1): 37–48.

Bunyavanich, S., C. Landrigan, A. McMichael and P. Epstein (2003), 'The impact of climate change on child health', *Ambulatory Pediatrics*, **3**(1): 44–52.

Cannon, T. (1994), 'Vulnerability analysis and the explanation of "natural" disasters', in A. Varley (ed.), *Disasters, Development and Environment*, Chichester: John Wiley and Sons, pp. 13–30.

Centre for Research on the Epidemiology of Disasters (CRED) (2004), 'EM-DAT: the OFA/CRES International Disaster Database', http://www.em-dat.net.

Chan, N.W. and D.J. Parker (1996), 'Response to dynamic flood hazard factors in Peninsular Malaysia', *Geographical Journal*, **162**(3), 313–25.

Charveriat, C. (2000), 'Natural disasters in Latin America and the Caribbean: an overview of risk', Working Paper No. 434, Inter-American Development Bank, Washington, DC.

Crowards, T. (2000), 'Comparative vulnerability of natural disasters in the Carib-bean', Staff Working Paper No. 1/00, Caribbean Development Bank, Barbados.

Cubash, U., G.A. Meehl, G.J. Boer, R.J. Stouffer, M. Dix, A. Noda, C.A. Senior, S. Raper and K.S. Yapp (2001), 'Projections for future climate change', in J.T. Houghton, Y. Ding, D.J. Griggs, M. Noguer, P.J. van der Linden, X. Dai, K. Maskell and C.A. Johnson (eds), *Climate Change 2001: The Scientific Basis. Contributions of Working Group I to the Third Assessment Report of the Intergovernmental Panel on Climate Change*, Cambridge: Cambridge University Press, pp. 525–82.

Cutter, S., B. Boruff and W.L. Shirley (2003), 'Social vulnerability to environmental hazards', *Social Science Quarterly*, **84**(2): 242–61.

De Souza, R.M. (2004), 'In harm's way: hurricanes, population trends, and environmental change', Population Reference Bureau, http://www.prb.org.

Deininger, K. and L. Squire (1996), 'A new data set measuring income inequality', *World Bank Economic Review*, **10**(3): 565–91.

Denton, F. (2002), 'Climate change vulnerability, impacts and adaptation: why does gender matter?', *Gender & Development*, **10**(2): 10–20.

Dilley, M., R.S. Chen, U. Deichmann, A.L. Learner-Lam and M. Arnold (2005), 'Natural disaster hotspots: a global risk analysis', Disaster Risk Management Series No. 5, World Bank, Washington, DC.

Downing, T.E., A.A. Olsthoorn and R.S.J. Tol (1999), *Climate Change and Risk*, Routledge: London and New York.

Easterling, D.R., G.A. Meehl, C. Parmesan, S.A. Changnon, T.R. Karl and L.O. Mearns (2000), 'Climate extremes: observations, modeling, and impacts', *Science*, **289**: 2068–74.

Economic Commission for Latin America and the Inter-American Development Bank (ECLAC) (2000), 'A matter of development: how to reduce vulnerability in the face of natural disasters', Port-of-Spain, Trinidad and Tobago.

Emanuel, K. (2005), 'Increasing destructiveness of tropical cyclones over the past 30 years', *Nature*, **436**: 686–8.

Enarson, E. (2000), 'Gender and natural disasters', ILO In Focus Programme on Crisis Response and Reconstruction, Working Paper 1.

Fothergill, A., E.G.M. Maestas and J.D. Darlington (1999), 'Race, ethnicity and disasters in the United States: a review of the literature', *Disasters*, **23**(2): 156–74.

Gaiha, R. and K. Imai (2004), 'Vulnerability, shocks and persistence of poverty: estimate for semi-arid rural South India', *Oxford Development Studies*, **32**(2): 261–81.

Gordon, L., M. Dunlop and B. Foran (2003), 'Land cover change and water vapour flows: learning from Australia', *Philosophical Transactions of the Royal Society*, **358**: 1973–84.

Homer-Dixon, T.F. (1994), 'Environmental scarcities and violent conflict: evidence from cases', *International Security*, **19**(1): 5–40.

Intergovernmental Panel on Climate Change (IPCC) (2001), 'Summary for policymakers', in J.T. Houghton, Y. Ding, D.J. Griggs, N. Noguer, P.J. van der Linden, X. Dai, K. Maskell and C.A. Johnson (eds), *Climate Change 2001: The Scientific Basis. Contribution of Working Group I to the Third Assessment Report of the Intergovernmental Panel on Climate Change*, Cambridge: Cambridge University Press, pp. 1–2.

International Monetary Fund (IMF) (2003), 'Fund assistance for countries facing exogenous shocks', http://www.imf.org/external/np/pdr/sustain/2003/080803.pdf.

Jones, T.S., A.P. Liang, E.M. Kilbourne, M.R. Griffin, P.A. Patriarca, S.G. Wassilak, R.J. Mullen, R.F. Herrick, H.D. Donnell Jr, K. Choi and S.B. Thacker (1982), 'Morbidity and mortality associated with the July 1980 heatwave in St Louis and Kansas City, Mo.', *Journal of the American Medical Association*, **247**(24): 3327–31.

Kahn, M. (2005), 'The death toll from natural disasters: the role of income, geography and institutions', *Review of Economics and Statistics*, **87**(2): 271–84.

Kelly, P.M. and W.N. Adger (2000), 'Theory and practice in assessing vulnerability to climate change and facilitating adaptation', *Climate Change*, **47**(4): 325–52.

Kilbourne, E.M., K. Choi, T.S. Jones and S.B. Thacker (1982), 'Risk factors for heatstroke', *Journal of the American Medical Association*, **247**(24): 3332–6.

Langer, N. (2004), 'Natural disasters that reveal cracks in our social foundation', *Educational Gerontology*, **30**: 275–85.

Lavell, A. (1994), 'Prevention and mitigation of disasters in Central America: vulnerability to disasters at the local level', in A. Varley (ed.), *Disasters, Development and Environment*, Chichester: John Wiley and Sons, pp. 49–63.

Lonergan, S. (1998), 'The role of environmental degradation in population displacement', *Environmental Change and Security Project Report*, Issue 4: 5–15.

Lustig, N. (2000), 'Crisis and the poor: socially responsible macroeconomics', *Economia*, **1**(1): 1–30.

Martine, George and Jose Miguel Guzman (2002), 'Population, poverty, and vulnerability: mitigating the effects of natural disasters', *ECSP Report*, Issue 8: 45–68.

McGeehin, M.A. and M. Mirabelli (2001), 'The potential impacts of climate variability and change on temperature-related morbidity and mortality in the United States', *Environmental Health Perspectives*, **109**(2): 185–9.

Meadows, M.E. and T.M. Hoffman (2003), 'Land degradation and climate change in South Africa', *The Geographical Journal*, **169**(2): 68–177.

Ngo, E. (2001), 'When disasters and age collide: reviewing vulnerability of the elderly', *Natural Hazards Review*, May: 80–89.

O'Brien, K. and R. Leichenko (2000), 'Double exposure: assessing the impacts of climate change within the context of economic globalization', *Global Environmental Change*, **10**(3): 221–32.

Pelling, M. (1997), 'What determines vulnerability to floods: a case study in Georgetown, Guyana', *Environment and Urbanization*, **9**(1): 203–26.

Rashid, S.F. (2000), 'The urban poor in Dhaka City: their struggles and coping strategies during the floods of 1998', *Disasters*, **24**(3): 240–53.

Rasmussen, Tobias N. (2004), 'Macroeconomic implications of natural disasters in the Caribbean', IMF Working Paper WP/04/224.

Reardon, T. and J.E. Taylor (1996), 'Agroclimatic shock, income inequality, and poverty: evidence from Burkino Faso', *World Development*, **24**(5): 901–14.

Ruth, M. (ed.) (2006), *Smart Growth and Climate Change: Regional Development, Infrastructure and Adaptation*, Cheltenham, UK and Northampton, MA, USA: Edward Elgar.

Scheraga, J.D. and A.E. Grambsch (1998), 'Risks, opportunities, and adaptation to climate change', *Climate Research*, **10**: 85–95.

Schroeder, R.A. (1987), 'Gender vulnerability to drought: a case study of the Hausa social environment', Natural Hazard Research, Working Paper 58.

Semenza, J.C., C.H. Rubin, K.H. Falter, J.D. Selanikio, W.D. Flanders, H.L. Howe and J.L. Wilhelm (1996), 'Heat-related deaths during the July 1995 heatwave in Chicago', *New England Journal of Medicine*, **335**(2): 84–90.

Trenberth, K.E. (2005), 'Uncertainty in hurricanes and global warming', *Science*, **308**: 1036–9.

Vaux, T. and F. Lund (2003), 'Working woman and security: Self Employed Women's Association's response to crisis', *Journal of Human Development*, **4**(2): 265–87.

Webster, P.J, G.J. Holland, J.A. Curry and H.R. Chang (2005), 'Changes in tropical cyclone number, duration, and intensity in a warming environment', *Science*, **309**(5742): 1844–6.

Winchester, P. (2000), 'Cyclone mitigation, resource allocation and post-disaster reconstruction in South India: lessons from two decades of research', *Disasters*, **24**(1), 18–37.

Wisner, B. (1997), 'Environmental health and safety in Urban South Africa', in B. Johnston (ed.), *Life and Death Matters*, Walnut Creek, CA: Altamira, pp. 265–86.

World Bank (2003), 'Caribbean economic overview 2002: macroeconomic volatility, household vulnerability, and institutional policy responses', Report No. 24165-LAC, Washington, DC.

PART II

Differential Impacts

4. Health impacts of heat: present realities and potential impacts of a climate change

Laurence Kalkstein, Christina Koppe, Simone Orlandini, Scott Sheridan and Karen Smoyer-Tomic

INTRODUCTION

In many mid-latitude locations it is recognized that heat is the most important weather-related killer – outpacing hurricanes, tornadoes, snow and ice, and lightning. In the US, about 1500 people are killed by heat during an average summer (Harvard Medical School 2005). During extreme heat events, such as the one that occurred in Europe in 2003, excess deaths were in the tens of thousands (Valleron and Mendil 2004). The scope of the problem is immense and large population centers around the world, from Shanghai to New Delhi to London to Toronto, are not immune (Tan et al. 2003).

The impact of a climate change could make matters worse. Several studies show that, if the climate changes as forecast by a number of climate models, the frequency of extreme heat events may double, or even triple, in many cities over the remainder of this century (Hayhoe et al. 2004b). This could lead to a dramatic increase in deaths from heat-related causes. It should be noted, however, that heat intensity is not the only major factor contributing to increased negative health responses. Probably more important is the variability of the weather. Clearly more people die from heat-related causes in cities like Philadelphia, Toronto and Chicago, than they do in Phoenix and Miami, where summer conditions are considerably warmer. This is due to the unexpected nature of extreme heat events at many mid-latitude locations, where benign weather is punctuated by heat events of great magnitude (WHO et al. 1996). Thus, if climate change brings about an increase in temperatures but a lower variability in summer weather (for example, if Philadelphia's summer climate approaches Miami's), heat-related mortality may not rise in a warmer world. However, if variability stays high, as many climate models indicate, heat-related problems will likely increase in a warmer world.

How Does the Body Respond to Heat?

Human beings respond dramatically to the atmospheric environment because of the need to balance their heat budget. This involves all the complex conditions of heat exchange between the human body and the thermal environment (Parsons 2003). Accordingly, thermal stress can have adverse effects on human health. This issue has been addressed in numerous epidemiological studies in which the thermal environment was related to heat- and cold-related mortality (for example, Basu and Samet 2002; Hajat et al. 2002; Kunst et al. 1993; Kyselý and Huth 2004). In these studies different methods are used to assess the thermal environment. The methods range from simple one-parameter indices (for example, mean, minimum, maximum temperature), to indices that consist of more than one parameter (for example, temperature and humidity), to more complex indices such as the synoptic approach or assessment procedures based on thermo-physiological modeling of the human body.

Since humans adapt physiologically (acclimatization) to meteorological situations, there is a change in the physiological response we as humans have to thermal stress (Fanger 1972). This response reduces the effective heat load, or cold stress, a human has to bear by increasing the effectiveness of the thermoregulatory system. Additionally, the thermal load is reduced due to short-term behavioral adaptation. Many epidemiological studies show that humans, to a certain extent, adapt and acclimatize to their local climate. This fact can be seen in the regional and temporal variability of the thermal thresholds beyond which human health declines. Generally speaking, the more severe or unusual the thermal condition the greater the human mortality. In many studies, a so-called U- or V-shaped relationship between mortality and the thermal environment is established.

In addition to the absolute level of the parameter used to assess the thermal environment, the persistence of a thermal stress situation is important. Heat-related health impacts are in general greater the longer a heat situation persists (Smoyer et al. 2000). Some of the heat-related mortality is caused by the so-called 'harvesting effect', where a number of susceptible individuals die from the heat early in the summer season, leaving fewer susceptible individuals to die later in the season. Harvesting can account for 20–40 percent of the total deaths during an excessive heat event (Kalkstein 1998).

Of great interest is a study of different European time series of mortality and meteorological parameters using a physiologically based method that includes short-term behavioral adaptation and short-term acclimatization. This study showed that all of the analyzed time series had the highest mortality with values between 13 percent and 34 percent above the baseline during a 'strong heat load' situation (Koppe 2005). Smaller thermal loads were associated with average to slightly above average mortality; this clearly demonstrates the notion of a 'threshold' level of heat load beyond which mortality rises rapidly. In this study, the harvesting phenomenon was more pronounced in the warmer sections of Europe.

HEAT RESPONSE, SOCIAL IMPLICATIONS, AND POTENTIAL CLIMATE CHANGE IMPACTS

Not all populations are equally vulnerable to extreme heat. Risk factors are physiological, demographic and social. Physiological risk factors include a wide range of underlying health conditions and the use of certain medications that impede the body's ability to maintain homeostasis (for example, in the case of extreme heat or cold, core body temperature). The very young (especially infants), the chronically ill and elderly have less of an ability to maintain thermal equilibrium. Accordingly, socio-economic risk factors for these groups are more complex.

The greatest social risk factor for extreme heat is poverty. Access to sufficient financial resources is essential for securing adequate housing and equipment. For example, air conditioning and the means to pay for its operation and maintenance are generally necessary to protect from extreme heat. Similarly, insulated housing, heating equipment and the funds for fueling it are needed for protection against extreme cold. Nations with more distributive economic systems may provide high-quality housing for impoverished households, while other nations may provide only basic housing with insufficient heating and cooling equipment, leaving residents at risk of extreme temperatures.

Access to health care is essential in maintaining good health and in lessening a group's susceptibility to extreme heat. Although universal health care is available in most industrialized nations, disparities in quality of care exist by socio-economic status. In the US, the wealthy can afford high-quality health care, many employers offer affordable health insurance, and the very poor may qualify for government-provided health care. The working poor, as well as some moderate-income families, may have insufficient or unaffordable health insurance and thus lack access to adequate health care. This, in turn, increases their vulnerability to extreme heat; a problem likely to be exacerbated if the climate changes in the future in accordance with the forecast of recent models.

With poverty comes a host of other conditions that are added risk factors to adverse health outcomes of extreme heat. For example, in Table 4.1, in perceived high crime areas people without air conditioning may not open their windows. This failure exposes them to dangerous indoor temperatures. Low-income individuals who suffer from mental illness, substance abuse or senior dementia are particularly at risk from social isolation – a known risk factor in heat-related mortality (Klinenberg 2002). These individuals are also more likely to inhabit substandard housing. In addition, low socio-economic status groups often have higher exposure to environmental toxins and air pollution. In addition they are more likely to live in socially marginalized, deprived areas with less access to health-promoting amenities ranging from healthy food retail outlets to physical activity centers. Thus the combined impacts of limited financial resources, stressful neighborhood environment conditions and limited health-promoting amenities all underlie their vulnerability to extreme temperatures, and impede resilience. The web of poverty, and the conditions that accompany it, set the stage for increased risk to extreme heat.

Climate change is expected to increase occurrences of high summer temperatures in many mid-latitude areas. While warmer winter conditions are expected to occur in many of these regions, research has shown that this does not necessarily decrease cold-related mortality (Kalkstein 2007). The societal implications of extreme heat and cold vulnerability under climate change are complex because accompanying climate change are several complex factors, all of which vary within and among countries. These factors include global changes in urban morphology, socio-economic characteristics and demographic structure. For example, increased standard of living in many countries leads to urban sprawl and the loss of green space, exacerbating urban heat islands and requiring more energy resources for heating, cooling, lighting larger dwellings and transportation. Impoverished populations are also extending into the suburbs, thus reducing access to social services and requiring more funds for transportation. The higher energy demands of these societal changes also increase emissions of greenhouse gases. Demographically, the populations of most nations are aging, while experiencing a reduction in family size and fragmentation of extended family networks. While the high-risk group of the very young may decrease in size, elderly populations (and with them, the chronically ill) are growing. Compounding the vulnerability of aging populations are changes in family structure and care-giving norms. This results in an increasing number of elderly without family support. Increasingly, public resources will be needed to provide health care and social services to this growing vulnerable population, regardless of the impacts of climate change.

The impacts of climate change are not experienced equally. Financial

Table 4.1   *Heat-related mortality projections for the 1990s, 2050s and 2090s for five California cities, as calculated by Hayhoe et al. (2004a)*

	1990s	2050s		2090s	
	Acc	UnAcc	Acc	UnAcc	Acc
Los Angeles					
Actual	165				
PCM B1	158	357	304	394	319
PCM A1	158	818	719	948	790
Had B1	153	351	275	667	551
Had A1	153	432	339	1429	1182
San Francisco					
Actual	41				
PCM B1	35	84	84	134	134
PCM A1	35	146	146	447	447
Had B1	39	92	92	153	153
Had A1	38	75	75	271	271
San Bernardino/Riverside					
Actual	32				
PCM B1	28	50	50	83	83
PCM A1	28	57	57	104	104
Had B1	28	60	60	82	82
Had A1	33	73	73	135	129
Sacramento					
Actual	10				
PCM B1	14	18	11	29	17
PCM A1	14	25	15	86	52
Had B1	15	43	26	51	31
Had A1	25	42	25	148	89
Fresno					
Actual	13				
PCM B1	10	19	5	30	7
PCM A1	10	26	6	72	17
Had B1	12	14	4	18	5
Had A1	14	42	10	74	18

Note: UnAcc refers to unacclimatized values; Acc are acclimatized values.

resources facilitate adaptation to extreme heat, and impoverished groups will need to allocate more of their already limited resources to stay cool during increasingly hot summers. In some areas, winter temperatures are expected to rise, thus reducing the financial burden of heating costs. However, the economic and health implications of added financial demands for basic heating and cooling are likely to be both pervasive and hard to predict.

A Quantitative Evaluation of Climate Change-Induced Heat Mortality: The California Example

Summer temperatures in California under scenarios of future climate change are projected to increase by two degrees, to 7°C, depending on the emission scenario used and the sensitivity of the climate model. Increases will be accompanied by longer, more frequent and more severe extreme heat conditions (Hayhoe et al. 2004b). Estimates of increases in heat-related mortality for these scenarios were developed for five California urban areas (Table 4.1), and indicate that mortality totals are likely to rise dramatically, even if the population acclimatizes somewhat to the warmer conditions. The models used, the PCM and Hadley models, were run assuming business as usual (A1, higher emissions in the future) and reduced emissions (B1). In virtually all cases, even if emissions are reduced, the number of deaths is expected to increase markedly.

In another study that attempted to determine the potential impacts of a climate change, the very hot summer in Europe of 2003 was used as an analog for five US cities (New York, Philadelphia, Detroit, St Louis and Washington). This study attempted to determine how mortality might increase in these cities if such a heatwave occurred here (Kalkstein et al. 2008). The premise was that heatwaves similar to the European 2003 event are more likely to occur in a warmer world. Results indicate that excess heat-related mortality for the analog summer is two to over seven times the long-term average in US cities – with New York showing the greatest increases. In all cities, calculated excess heat-related mortality for the analog summer exceeds the hottest recorded summer in the past 35 years. These numbers should be treated with care, since they do not consider potential changes in urban structure, demographics and intervention strategies within the cities.

MITIGATING THE PROBLEM

Because of the recent recognition that heat is a major killer, and due to the possibility of a warmer world in the future, an increasing number of cities are implementing hot weather health warning systems (HHWSs). These systems are designed to inform the public and important stakeholders about hazardous heat. Although they are an important part of adaptation to extreme heat, they cannot solve the problem of vulnerability to extreme heat on their own. Potential solutions for decreasing the impact of heat for all income groups include planning solutions like those already under-way in cities as diverse as Chicago, Toronto and Shanghai. These include 'cool city' initiatives to reduce the urban heat island, such as using lighter-colored building materials, increasing urban green spaces, tree planting programs and green roof projects (for example, replacing tar surfaces with gardens). Government-sponsored or public–private partnerships provide a member of these alternatives to increase product and housing efficiency (especially of heating and cooling equipment). These are other ways of off-setting the increased financial burden of reducing vulnerability to extreme heat and cold for low-income households, as well as for reducing green-house gas emissions.

However, interest in the development of HHWSs has been quite recent. For example, before the intense event of 2003, very few systems existed in Europe (Koppe and Becker forthcoming). Like numerous other environ-mental forcing factors, a disaster must occur before decision-makers will begin to work to mitigate the problem.

An HHWS is designed to alert both decision-makers and the general public of impending dangerous hot weather, and to serve as a source of advice on how to avoid negative health outcomes associated with hot weather extremes (WHO et al. 1996). The development of a high-quality HHWS requires a number of steps and pathways to be completed, includ-ing accurate weather forecasting, dissemination of the watch or warning, identification of vulnerable population groups, interaction with stakehold-ers, implementation of a mitigation procedure and a check of effectiveness, among others.

An effective HHWS can employ a myriad of meteorological procedures and its physical nature may vary based on local population, political con-structs of the area and available resources. Still there are several system aspects that must be universal. First, all systems must be custom-developed for each local area, and their construction should consider local meteorol-ogy, demographics and urban structure (Sheridan and Kalkstein 2004; Kalkstein et al. 2008). A common mistake often made by national weather service offices is to develop a one-size-fits-all set of systems, for a large number of urban areas, within different cultural and climate zones. For example, in the US a system was designed in the 1990s to call an excessive heat warning whenever the apparent temperature was forecast to exceed 41°C for three consecutive hours on two consecutive days, no matter where it occurred (NOAA 1996). Such a system does not take into account the relative, rather than absolute, nature of weather's impacts upon a particular area. Second, all systems should be based upon thresholds that are related to actual heat – health outcomes. HHWSs trigger mechanisms should be geared to the point when human health actually deteriorates, and this threshold varies greatly from place to place. It can also vary within one particular place. For example, a meteorological situation leading to excess morbidity or mortality could be different early in the summer season as opposed to later within the season, at the same place. For this reason, some new generation systems actually have changing thresholds within the same urban area as the summer season progresses. Third, the HHWS nomenclature should be clearly understood by the public, local stakeholders and decision-makers. Thus, on a national level, it is best to have the same names for warnings, alarms and alerts, and the same sort of understandable criteria. Fourth, all systems should be paired with a quality notification and response program. This involves interaction with the media, and messages to the public, as to how they should react to the extreme weather. Finally, all systems should be evaluated to determine their effectiveness. A good example of a detailed evaluation plan has been put forth by the Italian Department of Civil Defense (Protezione Civile Nazionale 2005), which determines the accuracy of the Italian systems in forecasting deadly heat events, and checks to see if the systems actually save lives.

The development of most HHWSs begins with the establishment of certain thresholds of human health tolerance to the extreme weather. If these thresholds are exceeded, this would trigger the issuance of a warning or alert. The benchmark for issuing a warning varies from place to place, based upon differential local responses to extreme weather. However, in most cases, prior to HHWS development, correlations between negative human health outcomes (morbidity, mortality, heat load on the body) and extreme weather are developed to permit an estimate of those health outcomes based on forecast data.

In most locales, it is the national weather service office (NWS) that is responsible for issuing advisories and warnings for heat. Forecasts issued by the NWS are then used as the primary input into the HHWS where, most frequently (but not always), algorithms based on the human heat–health responses attempt to estimate the degree of negative health impact of the weather. If the negative impact is significant, the responsible agency (whether it is the NWS or a local health department) issues a warning or alert.

If a good-quality HHWS is paired with proper intervention procedures, along with increasing public awareness and the ability of responsible agencies to respond rapidly, it is likely that such a system will provide quality adaptation measures, even if the climate warms as many expect.

Asthma and Climate Change: Another Set of Challenges

Of course, many health issues are closely related to weather, and may be exacerbated if a climate change occurs. A number of reports on time trends in asthma prevalence have shown a substantial increase in cases since the early 1960s. However, accumulating evidence indicates that rising trends in prevalence of asthma among adults and older children may have plateaued, or even decreased, after increasing for decades. This is especially true in countries with existing high rates of occurrence (von Hertzen and Haahtela 2005). Younger childhood data are less reassuring, and show continued increases (Asher et al. 2006). Allergic rhinitis is an increasing global health problem, affecting between 10 and 25 percent of the population. It significantly alters the social life of patients and affects school learning performance as well as work productivity. Thus it results in a significant economic effect on society in terms of both direct and indirect costs.

Data about the influence of weather on asthma are poor and controversial. Weather affects asthma directly, acting on airways, or indirectly by influencing airborne allergens and the level of pollutants. The complexity of the aerosol reaching the airways and the several compounds that play a role in this relationship might explain the controversial results of studies conducted so far. Decreases in air temperature represent an aggravating factor of asthmatic symptoms, regardless of the geography or the climate of areas under study. Furthermore, studies based on a synoptic method support findings derived from analyses with only air temperature as the meteorological variable. While results about effects of cold air on asthma are consistent, the role of humidity, wind and rainfall is still debated and studies including these variables showed inconclusive and inconsistent results. This is believed to be due to the fact that their impact on the diffusion of allergens and pollution is greater than that of air temperature (Cecchi et al. 2006b).

Upper respiratory infections also play a key role in exacerbating the presence of chronic pulmonary diseases, producing the typical increase of hospitalizations and medical calls in cold months. The reasons for the seasonal pattern of infections are generally behavioral because people spend longer periods of time in confined and crowded places, allowing for wider diffusion and transmission of viruses. Recent findings, however, also suggest an impairment of natural immunity mechanisms of airways induced by cold air breathing (Beggs 2004).

While the impact of weather and climate change on the prevalence of allergic diseases is still speculative, the influence on aeroallergens is suggested based on recent studies showing impacts on pollen amount, pollen allergenicity, pollen season, plant and pollen distribution, and other plant attributes (Fitter and Fitter 2002). Analysis of data from the International Phenological Gardens in Europe (a network of sites covering 69–42° N and 10° W–27° E) shows that spring events, such as flowering, have advanced by six days, and that autumn events have been delayed by 4.8 days, compared with the early 1960s. On average the length of the growing season in Europe increased by 10–11 days during the last 30 years up to the year 2000. Trends in pollen amount over the latter decades of the twentieth century increased based on local rises in temperature (Menzel 2000). Substantial increases in pollen production resulted from exposure to increased CO_2 concentrations under experimental conditions (Rogers et al. 2006); this might provide a reliable model for evaluating the effects of global warming. Duration of the pollen season is also extended with warmer temperatures, especially in summer and in late-flowering species. In addition, there is evidence of significantly stronger allergenicity in pollen from trees grown at increased temperatures (Ahlholm et al. 1998). These associations with changes in temperature vary across plant species (annual more than perennial species, with insect-pollinated species advancing more than wind-pollinated ones).

Changes in climate appear to have altered the spatial distribution of pollens. New patterns of atmospheric circulation over Europe might contribute to episodes of long-distance transport of allergenic pollen, increasing the risk of new sensitizations among allergic population (Cecchi et al. 2006a). There is growing evidence that climate change might also facilitate the geographical spread of particular plant species to new areas which become climatically suitable. However, the effect of the expected rate of warming could be less pronounced than effects of land use change, socio-cultural changes and international transport.

The socio-economic burden of allergic diseases is increasing worldwide, especially in developing countries. However, the influence of climate change on prevalence and symptoms of respiratory allergy is still unpredictable. Two opposite effects could be at work if the climate warms. On the one hand, global warming could increase the length and severity of the pollen season. On the other, it could reduce the effects of cold air on asthma and rhinitis, also making patients less susceptible to upper respiratory infections.

CONCLUSIONS

Although the majority of research suggests that both heat-related illnesses and asthma prevalence may increase if the climate warms, there are still many uncertainties that cannot be accounted for in the models or the historical record. Demographic changes, the effectiveness of mitigation measures, urban structure changes and adaptation will all play roles in determining how humans respond to climate change. Thus, any 'predictions' must be viewed with caution. However, heat-related mortality is already the leading weather-related killer in the Western world and asthma prevalence is increasing among younger individuals. Thus, regardless of climate change impacts, it is important that we become more aware of the vagaries of weather upon the human body, and develop means to lessen the negative health outcomes.

REFERENCES

Ahlholm, J.U., M.L. Helander and J. Savolainen (1998), 'Genetic and environmental factors affecting the allergenicity of birch (*Betula pubescens* ssp. *czerepanovii* [Orl.] Hämet-Ahti) pollen', *Clinical & Experimental Allergy*, **28**: 1384–8.

Asher, M.I., S. Montefort, B. Björkstén, C.K.W. Lai, D.P. Strachan, S.K. Weiland, H. Williams and the ISAAC Phase Three Study Group (2006), 'Worldwide time trends in the prevalence of symptoms of asthma, allergic rhinoconjunctivitis, and eczema in childhood: ISAAC Phases One and Three repeat multicountry cross-sectional surveys', *Lancet*, **368**: 733–43.

Basu, R. and J.M. Samet (2002), 'Relation between elevated ambient temperature and mortality: a review of the epidemiological evidence', *Epidemiologic Reviews*, **24**: 190–202.

Beggs, P.J. (2004), 'Impacts of climate change on aeroallergens: past and future', *Clinical & Experimental Allergy*, **34**: 1507–13.

Cecchi, L., M. Morabito, M.P. Domeneghetti, A. Crisci, M. Onorari and S. Orlandini (2006a), 'Long-distance transport of ragweed pollen as a potential cause of allergy in central Italy', *Annals of Allergy, Asthma & Immunology*, **96**: 86–91.

Cecchi, L., M. Morabito, S. Orlandini (2006b), 'Asthma and weather', *Giornale Europeo di Aerobiologia, Medicina Ambientale e Infezioni Aerotrasmesse* (*European Journal of Aerobiology and Environmental Medicine*), **2**: 80–86.

Fanger, P.O. (1972), *Thermal Comfort*, New York: McGraw-Hill.

Fitter, A.H. and R.S.R. Fitter (2002), 'Rapid changes in flowering time in British plants', *Science*, **296**: 1689–91.

Harvard Medical School (2005), *Climate Change Futures: Health, Ecological and Economic Dimensions*, Cambridge, MA: The Center for Health and the Global Environment, Harvard Medical School.

Hajat, S., R.S. Kovats, R.W. Atkinson and A. Haines (2002), 'Impact of hot temperatures on death in London: a time series approach', *Journal of Epidemiology and Community Health*, **56**: 367–72.

Hayhoe, K., D. Cayan, C.B. Field, P.D. Frumhoff, E.P. Maurer, N.L. Miller, S.C. Moser, S.H. Schneider, K.N. Cahill, E.E. Cleland, L. Dale, R. Drapek, R.M. Hanemann, L.S. Kalkstein, J. Lenihan, C.K. Lunch, R.P. Neilson, S.C. Sheridan and J.H. Verville (2004a), 'Emissions pathways, climate change, and impacts on California', *Proceedings of the National Academy of Sciences*, **101**: 12422–7.

Hayhoe, K., L.S. Kalkstein, S. Moser and N. Miller (2004b), *Rising Heat and Risks to Human Health*, Cambridge, MA: Union of Concerned Scientists Publications.

Kalkstein, A.J. (2007), 'Geographical variations in seasonal mortality across the US: a bioclimatological approach', PhD Dissertation, Arizona State University.

Kalkstein, L.S. (1998), 'Climate and human mortality: relationships and mitigating measures', in A. Auliciems (ed.), *Advances in Bioclimatology*, Berlin and Heidelberg: Springer.

Kalkstein, L.S., J.S. Greene, D. Mills and A. Perrin, J. Samenow and J.-C. Cohen (2008), 'Analog European heatwaves for US cities to analyze impacts on heat-related mortality', *Bulletin of the American Meteorological Society*, **89**: 75–86.

Klinenberg, E. (2002), *Heatwave: A Social Autopsy of Disaster in Chicago*, Chicago: University of Chicago Press.

Koppe, C. (2005), 'Gesundheitsrelevante Bewertung von thermischer Belastung unter Berücksichtigung der kurzfristigen Anpassung der Bevölkerung an die lokalen Witterungsverhältnisse', *Berichte des Deutschen Wetterdienstes*, No. 226, Offenbach: Deutscher Wetterdienst.

Koppe, C. and P. Becker (forthcoming), 'Comparison of operational heat health warning systems in Europe', *EuroHEAT*.

Kunst, A.E., C.W.N. Looman and J.P. Mackenbach (1993), 'Outdoor air temperature and mortality in the Netherlands: a time-series analysis', *American Journal of Epidemiology*, 137: 331–41.

Kyselý, J. and R. Huth (2004), 'Heat-related mortality in the Czech Republic examined through synoptic and "traditional" approaches', *Climate Research*, **25**: 265–74.

Menzel, A. (2000), 'Trends in phenological phases in Europe between 1951 and 1996', *International Journal of Biometeorology*, **44**: 76–81.

National Oceanic and Atmospheric Administration (NOAA) (1996), 'Heatwave Workshop: Report', Silver Spring, MD: Department of Commerce.

Parsons, K.C. (2003), *Human Thermal Environments: The Effects of Hot, Moderate, and Cold Environments on Human Health, Comfort and Performance*, 2nd edn, London: Taylor & Francis.

Protezione Civile Nazionale (2005), 'Sistema Nazionale di Allarme per la Prevenzione dell'Impatto delle Ondate di Calore' ('National civil protection'), Rome: Dipartimento di Epidemiologa ASL RME.

Rogers, C.A., P.M. Wayne, E.A. Macklin, M.L. Muilenberg, C.J. Wagner, P.R. Epstein and F.A. Bazzaz (2006), 'Interaction of the onset of spring and elevated atmospheric CO_2 on ragweed (*Ambrosia artemisiifolia* L.) pollen production', *Environmental Health Perspectives*, **114**(6): 865–9.

Sheridan, S.C. and L.S. Kalkstein (2004), 'Progress in watch warning system technology', *Bulletin of the American Meteorological Society*, **85**: 1931–41.

Smoyer, K.E., D.G.C. Rainham and J.N. Hewko (2000), 'Heat-stress-related mortality in five cities in Southern Ontario: 1980–1996', *International Journal of Biometeorology*, **44**: 190–97.

Tan, J., L.S. Kalkstein, J. Huang, S. Lin, H. Yin and D. Shao (2003), 'An operational heat/health warning system in Shanghai', *International Journal of Biometeorology*, **48**: 157–62.

Valleron, A.J. and A. Mendil (2004), 'Epidemiology and heatwaves: analysis of the 2003 episode in France', *Comptes rendus biologies*, **327**, 125–41.
von Hertzen, L. and T. Haahtela (2005), 'Signs of reversing trends in prevalence of asthma', *Allergy*, **60**: 283–92.
WHO, WMO and UNEP (1996), *Climate Change and Human Health*, Geneva: World Health Organization.

5. Gender and climate change vulnerability: what's the problem, what's the solution?

Anthony G. Patt, Angie Dazé and Pablo Suarez

INTRODUCTION

While gender issues are increasingly recognized in the global arena, the policy environment of climate change adaptation initiatives has not kept pace with new findings. The policy environment still fails to recognize fully the gender-specific characteristics of vulnerability and adaptive capacity. Women are usually subject to cultural norms and practices that differentiate them from men, such as poverty and marginality. Gender can play a major role in people's ability to prepare for, and respond to, climate-related threats.

The Beijing Platform for Action, adopted at the Fourth World Conference on Women (1995), and the conclusions reached at the Economic and Social Council (ECOSOC) (1997/2) call on the United Nations and its member states, international organizations and non-governmental organizations (NGOs) systematically to integrate gender perspectives into all policy areas. These areas include disasters and environmental management. The Millennium Declaration, through its third commitment (or Millennium Development Goal), recognizes the importance of promoting gender equality and women's empowerment as an effective pathway for combating poverty, hunger and disease, and for stimulating truly sustainable development.

Gender equality does not mean the pursuit of identical outcomes for males and females, but rather equality in rights, resources and voice. The *World Development Report* of 2006 defines gender equality as equal access to the 'opportunities that allow people to pursue a life of their own choosing and to avoid extreme deprivations in outcomes' (World Bank 2005). One of the priorities in the Hyogo Framework for Action 2005–15 was that 'gender perspectives should be integrated into all disaster risk management policies, plans and decision making processes, including those related to risk assessment, early warning, information management, and education and training' (UNISDR 2005). This attention to gender is a new phenomenon. With its emphasis on the physical processes associated with global warming and the North–South cleavage, the early phases of the climate change debate (including the United Nations Framework Convention on Climate Change – UNFCCC – process) did not pay much attention to issues of gender (Denton 2004). Yet gender, like poverty, is a cross-cutting issue and needs to be recognized as such. While socio-economic studies of climate change tend to neglect the differences in impacts between men and women, diverse voices have called for analysis, advocacy and action to put in place implementable policies that take gender fairness into consideration (see for example Masika 2002). This may be particularly difficult at a time when women are underrepresented in policy-making processes. According to Röhr (2006), between 1996 and 2005 the delegation of states participating in the UNFCCC Conference of the Parties (COP) were profoundly gender biased. There, the share of women only ranged between 15 percent and 28 percent.

This chapter discusses gender as one of the key dimensions for analysis of the distributional impacts of climate change and for exploring opportunities to promote climate adaptation. We summarize the key gender-differentiated impacts of climate change, review the behavioral literature on gender and decision-making (including new results from an experimental study), and present two case studies – from Bangladesh and Tajikistan – which highlight the role of gender in climate vulnerability and adaptation. We conclude with recommendations for researchers and practitioners.

GENDER AND DIFFERENTIAL VULNERABILITY

The term 'gender' refers to the socially constructed identities, roles and expectations associated with males and females. Over time, beliefs about gender have resulted in different valuations of men and women. These valuations often lead to denial of political representation and discrimination in the provision of diverse services such as education and even swimming lessons. Recent work in academic and policy realms has begun to highlight several aspects of the relationship between gender and climate change. For example, Lambrou and Piana (2006) briefly review mitigation measures, adaptation options and national regimes with a gender perspective, and argue for the pursuit of capacity-building efforts specifically aimed at women. Climate-related disasters such as floods, droughts, cyclones and extreme temperatures can have different and inequitable impacts on men and women, depending on their roles in the community and the productive process. Gender intersects with economic, ethnic and other factors, creating hazardous social conditions that can place groups of women at greater risk when disasters unfold (Wisner et al. 2004).

For example, women in Bangladesh are more calorie-deficient than men and consequently cannot recover as well from the negative effects of flooding on health (Cannon 2002). In a study of the 1991 Bangladesh cyclone that killed about 138 000 people, Bern et al. (1993) show that mortality was greatest among women over 40 years old. While the authors uncritically attribute the disproportionate death of women to differences in physical strength and endurance, many other studies identify various social and cultural issues as the main causes for such colossal and unequal human losses. In her study of the same cyclone, Ikeda (1995) shows how physical disadvantages interact with social norms and role behavior, putting women at a disadvantage in their rescue efforts by limiting their movement and their access to information about cyclone-induced floods. For example, rural women are expected to remain in family houses, and to wear a sari (a traditional cloth that makes running and swimming more difficult). Additionally, there are social prejudices against women learning to swim. This leads to a consequent reduction in the probability of their surviving a flood event (Cannon 2000). With climate change, flooding is expected to become much more severe in Bangladesh (Mirza 2002), and so the gender inequities discussed above may be exacerbated. In the realm of agriculture and food security, women are often in charge of crop pro-duction, securing the supply of wood for cooking fuel and collecting wild fruits or roots in times of scarcity. The expected impact on the resource base will inevitably add to their workload and impair their ability to feed their households. Water, sanitation and health challenges derived from climate change are also likely to add a disproportionate burden on women (Denton 2004). Haque (1995) recommends the inclusion of various dimen-sions of human response in the operational design of warning systems. Finally, in most cultures, women care for children and the elderly or sick. Shouldering this additional responsibility hampers their own rescue efforts in any type of extreme weather event.

Climate-related disasters can negatively affect women in unexpected ways in certain cultural contexts. Food insecurity, resulting from inad-equate rainfall, can accelerate the spread of HIV/AIDS in southern Africa. It is not uncommon for girl-children to be married off early in times of drought, usually to older men who have had numerous sexual partners. Women with no other subsistence options may resort to selling sex for gifts or money on an occasional or more continuous basis (Malawi Government 2001). Women can also be at greater risk of male violence in the aftermath of disasters; not just in rural Africa, but also in the developed world, as was seen in the aftermath of Hurricane Katrina (Picardo et al. 2007). Immediate harm can have lasting repercussions later. During and after severe droughts, it has been observed that often more girls than boys drop out of school. This increased drop out rate may be attributed to factors such as the need to reduce household expenses by saving on school fees, to allow for fetching water from more distant sources, or as a result of pregnancy and early marriage (see Eldridge 2002). Lower education levels in turn reduce the ability of girls and women to access information and resources, or make their voices heard in decision-making processes at the household or community level, augmenting the asymmetries in vulnerability.

Gender-differentiated roles do not always result in higher losses for women. Evidence from Central America, for example, indicates that immediate mortality caused by Hurricane Mitch was higher for men (Bradshaw 2004). A likely explanation is the fact that in that region men tend to be more engaged in outdoor activities, and when disasters strike are less risk averse. Like most other aspects of climate vulnerability and adaptive capacity, gender issues are place-sensitive. So, the differential impact on gender must be better understood in order to find better ways of improving collective decision-making to confront climate change.

GENDER AND DIFFERENTIAL ADAPTIVE CAPACITY

A growing body of research in psychology and economics shows that women and men make decisions differently, in ways that are important for sustainable development and climate change adaptation. To some extent this research confirms commonly held wisdom about differences between women and men, but with some new twists. In this section, we first present a brief review of the empirical literature on gender and decision-making, which focuses on observed behavior (rather than speculating about the causes of that behavior). Second, we report new data from an experiment we conducted with participants in Africa, examining the willingness of men and women to use and learn from outside advice. The results from experiments on gender and decision-making, including our own new results presented here, can begin to explain the differential vulnerability of women to both climate change and natural disasters, and point the way to a solution.

Risk Aversion and Overconfidence

One set of findings concerns the relative risk aversion of men and women. A risk-averse person would prefer to receive a guaranteed payment of €50 than to take a gamble paying €75 or €25 with equal probability. A risk-neutral person would be indifferent between the two options, and a risk-taking person would prefer the gamble.

In a meta-analysis of 150 studies over 30 years, Byrnes et al. (1999) found that men were more risk-taking than women. There are several explanations which support this finding. First, it appears that men view risks as challenges. Being more competitive, men seek to take on risks, in order to have the opportunity to win. Women, by contrast, see risky situations as threats, and structure their behavior to avoid them entirely (Arch 1993). Somewhat corroborating this explanation is the finding that men enjoy competition more than women (Gneezy et al. 2003). While women see competition as an often unavoidable ritual they must go through in order to get what they want, men like to compete, regardless of the prizes they may win (Eriksson and Villeval 2004). Hence, men take risks because they like them. As such they engage in competition because they like to win, not because of the relative rewards they may receive from winning a gamble or a competition.

A second reason why women may be more risk averse than men is that they are less overconfident. People who are overconfident view uncertainty as smaller, and hence believe that their own knowledge about a phenomenon is greater than it actually is. For example, when people are asked to provide best-guess estimates about a number of quantities for which they probably do not know the true answer (for example, the exact height of Mt Everest), and also their 98 percent uncertainty bounds for that same quantity (that is, the range of height within which they believe, with 98 percent confidence, the true value to lie), people typically draw the range far too narrowly, in that the true value lies outside of people's stated 98 percent confidence range as much as half of the time (Rabin 1998). Overconfidence can cause people to engage in behavior that is riskier than they otherwise would, because they underestimate the variance of outcomes. In a study of men and women investing in the stock market, Barber and Odean (2001) found that men exhibited greater overconfidence than did women. Men believed that they could predict the future of risky gambles better than women; a belief which led them to take on more risks, and suffer greater losses.

Patt (2001) made a related finding that is appropriate for the issue of development and adaptation. He studied the performance of subsistence farmers in Zimbabwe in a gambling experiment to see if they would change their behavior in ways appropriate to changes in the probabilities in a series of gambling games. The first gambling game that participants played involved placing five sequential bets on a roulette wheel that was half green and half red. If participants bet on green and won, they would win $3, whereas if they bet on red and won, they would win $2; the optimal strategy (that is, to maximize expected winnings) was thus to place all five of their bets on green, and none on red. On average people placed three green bets and two red bets, and there was no significant difference between men and women. The participants then played several other, more complicated, games involving probabilities. At the end of the experiment they returned to the first game, placing another series of five bets on red or green, with the same pay-offs. At this point there was a sharp difference between the men and the women. Close to 60 percent of the women adopted the optimal strategy of placing five green bets, whereas among the men, slightly more than 30 percent had learned this optimal strategy. Women's average winnings were, consistent with this behavior, higher. The women had, on average, learned to adopt the optimal strategy given the uncertainty inherent in the roulette wheel, whereas the majority of the men persisted in trying to predict each spin, and place their bet contingent on that prediction.

Learning and Trust

The type of overconfidence observed in Patt (2001) was that of believing one's own intuition strongly, and not being willing to alter that belief in the presence of new evidence. We conducted a second experiment in Zimbabwe that examines the relationship between this phenomenon and that of trust. The main intention of the experiment was to observe whether differences in social cues, relative to the relationship between an advisor and a decision-maker, would affect whether the decision-maker accepted and used the information the advisor was offering. The exact set-up of the experiment is described in detail in Patt et al. (2006), where we also reported the results of the different treatments relating to social cues. We did not report on the gender-related findings in that experiment, and do so for the first time here. We present them here first because they are interesting and important in their own right, and also because they illustrate the type of methodology that experimenters use to identify gender differences in behavior.

Experimental Design

The experiment made use of the Monty Hall Three Door Game (Friedman 1998). The experimenter showed one participant a card with three doors, informing her that opening one of the doors would reveal a prize, while two of the doors were losing choices. The participant indicated which door she wanted to open to try to win the prize. Before opening that door, however, the experimenter gave her a hint, by opening one of the other two doors and showing it to be a losing door. This left two doors unopened: the door that the participant had indicated, and one remaining door. The experimenter then gave the participant the choice to stay with her original pick, or to switch to the other remaining door. The mathematics of the game are such that switching doors will generate a winning outcome with a two-thirds probability, while staying with the original pick will win only one-third of the time. This is counter-intuitive to most people, and indeed most people stayed with their original choice, and lost (Granberg and Brown 1995).

In our version of the game there was a third person involved, and an advisor. The advisor was a member of the local community, who had learned that the best strategy in the game was always to switch doors. Except for in the control treatment, where no advice was offered, the experimenter introduced the advisor to the participant as someone who had seen the game played many times and based on that knowledge could offer advice on how to try to win. In many ways this is analogous to the case of experts offering advice on climate change adaptation. At the point where the experimenter offered the participant the opportunity to switch doors, the advisor stepped in, and suggested that it would be a good idea to switch doors, because that would increase the chances of winning. This advice, therefore, was correct. The participant then had the choice of following the advice or not. There were three treatments related to social cues. In the first treatment, simple advice, there was no discussion of rewards to the advisor. In the second treatment, aligned incentives, the advisor would receive a payment if the participant won the prize (regardless of whether the advice was followed). In the third treatment, prepayment, the participants decided whether to give some of the money they had already received (simply for agreeing to participate in the experiment) to the advisor; if they chose to pay the advisor, they would receive advice. If they chose not to pay the advisor, they would receive no advice.

Participants played the game twice. During the first play, about two-thirds of the participants observed that the choice to switch doors would generate a winning outcome, while the remaining one-third observed that the choice to stay with their original pick would generate a winning outcome. Thus, in two-thirds of the cases, the advice offered appeared to be correct. In analyzing participants' choices on the second play of the game, we can thus distinguish between those who observed apparently high-quality advice, and those who observed apparently low-quality advice.

Gender Differences in the Results

There were three gender-related differences in the results that are interesting. The first finding is that women are more likely to seek advice than are men. We analyzed the behavior of participants who were randomly assigned to the prepayment treatment (28 men and 33 women). Participants had received ZW$1000 (Zimbabwe dollars) as their initial payment for agreeing to participate, and were promised an additional ZW$1000 for each time they won the game.[1] To receive advice for both rounds of the game, participants in the prepayment treatment needed to pay the advisor ZW$100 before the first round. Of the men, 61 percent elected to make this relatively small payment to receive advice, whereas 91 percent of the women so chose – a difference significant at the 99 percent confidence level. This is consistent with findings that men view games such as these as personal challenges, whereas women are interested in maximizing their earnings (Bohnet 2006; Eriksson and Villeval 2004). It also is consistent with the stereotype that men will not ask for directions.

The second finding is that women are more likely to listen to advice than are men. Figure 5.1 shows the results from the first play of the game. Within the control treatment, where no advice was offered, a higher proportion (although statistically insignificant) of men switched doors than

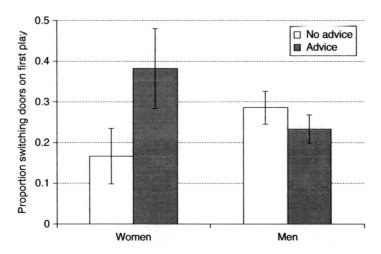

Note: Bars represent one standard error. Women were more likely to change decisions consistent with the advice that they were offered, whereas men were not.

Figure 5.1 Proportion of participants switching doors on the first play of the game

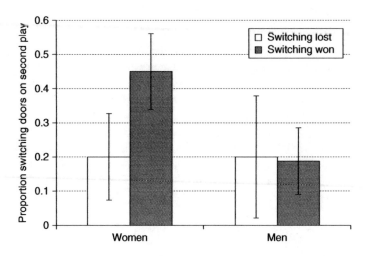

Note: Bars represent one standard error. Women were more likely to learn from the results of the first play of the game, whereas the results observed on the first play of the game had no effect on men's behavior.

Figure 5.2   Proportion of participants not receiving advice who switched doors on the second play of the game

did women. Within the treatments where advice was received, a higher proportion of women than men switched doors, a difference significant at the 99 percent confidence level. Indeed, offering men the advice to switch doors made them less likely to do so, although the difference was not significant. For the women, providing advice more than doubled the proportion switching doors, a difference significant at the 95 percent confidence level.

The third finding is that women learn from experience more than men. Figure 5.2 shows the proportions within each group switching doors on the second play of the game, limited to those participants in the control treatment, that is, not receiving advice. Given that people were generally reluctant to switch doors on the first play, subjects who learned from experience would be more likely to switch doors on the second play if they observed that switching would have worked on the first play, compared to those who observed that switching would not have worked. This was clearly evident among the women, who were more than twice as likely to switch doors on the second play if they had observed that strategy as correct on the first play. Among the men, there was no apparent difference in behavior on the second play, contingent on what they observed on the first. The fact that women learn faster than men to cope with a probabilistic decision-making problem, in the absence of assistance, is consistent with the results from Patt (2001).

CREATING AND RESPONDING TO SOCIAL BONDS

Perhaps the most fundamental difference between women and men, however, appears to be the extent to which they consider the social context of their actions. More than men, women make use of subtle social cues, often to the frustration of the experimenters trying to research them. For example, numerous researchers have studied the differences between women and men in the context of a social dilemma such as the 'Prisoner's Dilemma', to see if women are more or less likely to cooperate than men. Some of the researchers found women to cooperate less than men (Rapoport and Chammah 1965), others found women to cooperate more (Sibley et al. 1968), while others found no significant difference (Dawes et al. 1977). According to Croson and Gneezy (2004), who reviewed these studies, the different results were a function of small changes in the way that the experiment was structured, such as the opportunity for participants to communicate their intentions with each other. As a general rule, women become more and more cooperative, the more they are able to communicate with each other (Stockard et al. 1988).

Women may respond to evolving social bonds to a much greater extent than do men. Where social bonds are weak, men can be observed to be more cooperative, and more generous to the community, than women (Brown-Kruse and Hummels 1993). Where social bonds are stronger, however, the reverse is true, and women contribute more to the common good than men (Nowell and Tinkler 1994). Women are more aware of social bonds than men, and their decision-making responds to that heightened awareness. This translates into greater reciprocity, helping someone who has helped you, something observed across a variety of cultural settings (Croson and Buchan 1999). This in turn indicates that women's awareness of social bonds, and response to those bonds, can create the very conditions – greater interpersonal interaction and communication – under which women demonstrate greater cooperation and altruism to the community.

While women seem to respond to social bonds, and generate conditions of trust, men are more concerned with maintaining their status, or relative social standing. In particular, men hate to be taken advantage of, and will make decisions to minimize the chances that they will be visibly betrayed. Bohnet (2006) examined the relationship between gender, trust and betrayal, in a set of experiments where people could win or lose money both in pure lotteries, and as a result of others' actions. She found that women treated the two types of experiments similarly, and decided whether to trust, or not, based on the anticipated odds of winning or losing money. The risk of losing money because of another's actions was equivalent to losing money as a result of random chance. Men, by contrast, treated losing money because of another's action as more serious than as a result of random chance. Hence men were unwilling to trust another person if the risk of betrayal was present. While women respond to evolving social bonds (and in Bohnet's experiment there were no social bonds) through greater trust and greater generosity, men are worried about being taken advantage of, something not conducive to the creation of social bonds.

EVIDENCE FROM THE FIELD: CLIMATE ADAPTATION INITIATIVES IN BANGLADESH AND TAJIKISTAN

The humanitarian organization CARE has piloted an approach to community-level adaptation to climate change in vulnerable communities in Bangladesh and Tajikistan. In both countries, the objective of the project was to increase the capacity of communities to cope with the adverse effects of climate change. In Bangladesh, the project worked in 16 communities in the southwestern part of the country over a four-year period. The key climate-related vulnerability issues identified included flooding, salinity, waterlogging and cyclones. The project in Tajikistan is ongoing, with target communities located at three different altitudes in the northwestern mountainous region. In these areas, communities are struggling to cope with increasing snow, a shifting winter season, erosion and mudflows. In both countries, it was clear that there are institutional factors contributing to vulnerability, and that local governments and NGOs have an important role to play in supporting adaptation.

A Gender-Sensitive Approach to Community-Level Adaptation

The projects adopted a holistic approach to reducing vulnerability by working directly with households to support the implementation of practical strategies to support adaptation, while at the same time developing the capacity of local organizations to support the communities in coping. Recognizing the importance of an enabling policy environment for adaptation, each project also included an advocacy component targeted at changing policies and practices that contribute to vulnerability. Gender issues have been integrated into the approach at four key stages:

identification of key climate-related vulnerability issues, design of adaptive strategies, implementation of strategies and evaluation of project results.

The CARE approach to adaptation is grounded in a participatory assessment of vulnerability and adaptive capacity, which identifies the key vulnerability issues in the communities, examines the impacts of climate-related changes and hazards on household livelihoods, and analyzes existing capacity to adapt. Recognizing that vulnerability is gendered and that women and men employ different coping strategies, the vulnerability assessments were undertaken separately for groups of men and women. Conducting exercises with groups of women only was felt to encourage open dialogue on issues of concern, without the influence of male family and community members. Whenever possible, sessions for women's groups were facilitated by female field staff to increase the comfort level. Results allowed comparison of priority issues and coping strategies for men and women and, particularly in the case of Bangladesh, provided some interesting insights.

The results of the vulnerability assessment were then used to identify strategies to increase capacity to cope with existing climate-related vulnerability issues, and to improve capacity to adapt to future changes in climate. The strategies focused on household-level livelihood interventions as well as in the creation of an enabling environment for adaptation through capacity development for local NGOs and governmental institutions. Gender issues were considered in the selection of adaptation strategies in terms of prioritization of vulnerability issues to address, and in analysis of the feasibility of strategies with consideration of women's mobility and existing responsibilities. In Bangladesh, not surprisingly, women tended to prioritize adaptation strategies that could be implemented close to home – such as homestead gardening or duck rearing. Figure 5.3 shows a shift from raising chickens to raising ducks as an example of an adaptation strategy in light of increased flood risks.

Similarly, in Tajikistan, rather than building a community greenhouse the decision was made to provide selected households with cold frames, because it was felt that this would be more conducive to women's control of the planting and harvesting. The projects also made efforts to address the underlying causes of gender inequality through training and awareness-raising efforts for staff, partners and community members. However, recognizing that these are deeply rooted traditions that are unlikely to change in the short term, it is necessary to work within existing cultural and religious restrictions to the extent possible to ensure that women are empowered to participate in adaptation.

Project implementation was planned to promote effective participation of women, both at the project level and the community level. In selecting

Note: Poultry rearing is a common livelihood strategy in the pilot site in Bangladesh, particularly for women; however, recurrent flooding has resulted in loss of chicken stocks. CARE's partners worked with vulnerable women to introduce duck rearing as an alternative to poultry rearing, reducing the impact of flooding on household livelihood security.

Source: Photograph by A. Dazé.

Figure 5.3   Duck rearing as an adaptation strategy

target households, the project prioritized those headed by women. As a result, in Tajikistan, 40 percent of participating households are woman-headed. Learning and training sessions for women's groups were held at one group member's homestead, as opposed to in a public space, and the sessions were held at times that did not conflict with women's responsibilities in the home. The latter was done in order to reduce the likelihood that male members of the household would object to women participating. As a result, women comprised 58 percent of total project participants in Bangladesh. The projects made special efforts to recruit female field organizers, and encouraged partner organizations to do the same. CARE and partners set maternity leave and child care policies that would make it easier for women to work on the project.

A participatory approach to design and implementation requires a participatory approach to the evaluation of results. In Bangladesh, a series of participatory exercises was undertaken with selected target groups at the end of the project to assess the impact of the project strategies on reducing vulnerability, and to reflect on modifications to the approach that could increase impact. These end-of-project evaluations were again undertaken with separate groups of men and women (14 male groups and 14 female groups), and emphasis was placed on women's participation and mobility throughout the discussions. A team including project staff, representatives of partner NGOs and the project's external technical advisor qualitatively analyzed the raw data gathered through the sessions. This process allowed the team to draw some general conclusions regarding the approach and the results achieved.

The following sections reflect on CARE's experience in addressing climate-related vulnerability in Bangladesh and Tajikistan. The qualitative conclusions focus primarily on the results of the participatory evaluation exercises conducted in Bangladesh. The Tajikistan program is ongoing; however, preliminary results support the findings in Bangladesh.

EVIDENCE OF DIFFERENTIAL IMPACTS

Women's responsibilities in the family make them more vulnerable to environmental changes such as increasing salinity or drought, which will be exacerbated by the impacts of climate change. Women are primarily responsible for gathering water, fodder and fuel, and generally their workload increases with increasing environmental degradation. This has secondary impacts in that girl-children are more likely to be kept home from school to help out with the chores. Women's responsibilities in caring for children, the elderly and sick family members are undervalued, as they do not contribute directly to family income. This difference in family responsibilities translates to differing priorities in men and women when examining vulnerability issues. In Bangladesh, the results of the vulnerability assessment show that women's groups tended to prioritize health, housing and water, while men focused on income and food security.

Social and cultural practices contribute to women's vulnerability to climate-related disasters. Women in Tajikistan and Bangladesh are generally less mobile than men. Their responsibilities in the family and home tend to confine them to the homestead, save for trips to gather water, fodder and fuel. When it comes to involvement in economic or political activities in the community, it is most often the men who represent the household. This lack of mobility and participation means that women have less access to information regarding potential hazards and possible coping strategies.

As well, in times of crisis, women often stay behind to protect the home and assets, and this can lead to increased incidence of injury or death. This is linked to social norms as well; for example in Bangladesh women are often not comfortable in a shelter situation where community members are living in close proximity, so they may be reluctant to leave the home.

During natural disasters such as floods or cyclones, women take responsibility for keeping the family together and providing the daily essentials. When the home has been damaged, or in a shelter situation, simple tasks such as gathering water and cooking food can become much more difficult. When livelihood security is threatened, families are often forced to employ drastic coping mechanisms, including male migration for work, which is common in CARE target communities in both Tajikistan and Bangladesh. This leaves women single-handedly to care for the family and deal with post-disaster recovery.

GENDER AND DECISION-MAKING ON CLIMATE CHANGE ADAPTATION

One of the positive aspects of the community-based approach to adaptation is its emphasis on women's participation. In both Tajikistan and Bangladesh, the projects made a special effort to ensure that activities were appropriate for women in light of the local social and religious context, and that women received positive encouragement and support for participation. The organizing of women to participate in training sessions, to support each other in implementing adaptation strategies, and to participate in group marketing of produce and handicrafts, has increased social cohesion and provided opportunities for women to visit and share experiences. Women's groups also indicated that they feel empowered when they have access to information and new skills.

In Bangladesh, the project attempted to have equal representation of women on committees (for example, water management committees) formed through project activities, and promoted the representation of women in institutions such as the Union Parishads, the local government agencies that were targeted in capacity development activities. In most cases, the representation was not equal (for example, 40 percent of water management committee members were women). However, representation did increase over the life of the project. The question of representation versus participation remains; however, women's groups stated in the final evaluation that representation is important, and that after being given the opportunity to observe and learn, effective participation would come.

The examination of pre- and post-project coping mechanisms yielded some interesting insights relevant to the discussion about decision-making for adaptation. One of the coping mechanisms identified by women for surviving lean times was to skip meals or to eat non-traditional foods (for example, water hyacinth), in order to ensure that the rest of the family had enough. After the project, groups reported that this was no longer a common coping mechanism, which indicates that the strategies for improving food security did reduce vulnerability.

In the cultural and religious contexts of Bangladesh and Tajikistan, decision-making control for the family is rarely in the hands of women. Further, a lack of access to resources and information makes it difficult for women to innovate in their livelihood strategies. However, evidence from the two projects indicates that women felt empowered by the opportunity to contribute to family income, and that this was leading to increased recognition of their contribution by other family members. Results also indicate that when given the opportunity, and adequate support, women will choose to make decisions that are conducive to increasing adaptive capacity. For example, some women's groups in Bangladesh indicated that they are secretly saving part of their earnings from income-generating activities for coping in lean times of the year. Other groups noted that they are preserving food to be used in the flood season, and that this has reduced the impact of flooding on food security.

The adaptation strategies with the highest rates of adoption, particularly by women, tended to be those that could be undertaken within the homestead, such as duck rearing, which was adopted by over 1300 women, compared to approximately 800 men. In addition, these measures require a low initial investment, and therefore are considered to be lower risk. The risk element is important in that male family members are less likely to object to women starting up a new activity if there is a lower chance that it will be a losing enterprise. Also, low initial investment and low risk means that poorer households, many of which are woman-headed, are more likely to be able to adopt the strategies. Early results indicate that providing women with opportunities to generate food and income for the family increases the likelihood that they will be allowed to participate in decision-making, and that this may lead to decisions that will reduce household vulnerability.

CONCLUSION

We have argued that gender differences must be considered not just in terms of differential vulnerability, but also in terms of differential adaptive capacity. The first point is clear: women suffer the harm of climate-related natural disasters and slower-onset, chronic events such as food insecurity, disproportionately. The causes are varied, but often relate to women's roles in supporting the family, engaging in greater self-sacrifice in times of difficulty, and having less independence and control of resources. This reduces their ability to engage in self-protective behavior when it is most needed. The harm is both direct – injury, loss of life; and indirect – a lack of access to educational and economic opportunities.

The second point, less frequently argued in the literature, is a crucial element to finding solutions to general problems of vulnerability. Women make decisions differently than men in several fundamental ways. First, they are more sensitive to risk, viewing it as a problem to be managed, rather than a personal challenge to be conquered. Second, they have a more realistic appraisal of acting or failing to act. Third, women tend to seek out help, and listen to advice, more than men, something reported in the literature and further confirmed by the experimental results presented in this chapter. Fourth, women are more likely to change their behavior as a response to success and failure. Table 5.1 summarizes these differences. Empowering women to make more decisions for the family, in ways that are relevant for climate change vulnerability, may lead to more adaptive behavior and a reduced vulnerability to the effects of climate change.

But while empowering women to be the agents of adaptation in their communities may improve overall adaptive capacity and reduce vulnerability, it may not eliminate the differences in vulnerability between men and women.

The most important set of findings from the behavioral literature relates to social connectedness. Women make decisions that enhance the functioning of the group within which they are operating, and this can be an important element further improving adaptive capacity. But within well-functioning groups, women display greater altruism. This means that they may continue to assume a greater share of the risk for themselves in order to protect others. Women may continue to spend more time taking care of sick relatives, with less freedom for the avoidance of disasters.

Typically cultural factors are used to explain these features, especially in cultures where women have less freedom than men. The literature from psychology, however, suggests that there may be a component of differential vulnerability that relates to differences in how women and men make decisions, based on what they value. Given well-developed social connections and communication, women prioritize the good of their group – their family and their friends – much more so than do men. Women may suffer the effects of disasters more than men not just because cultural factors put them and keep them in harm's way, but because they themselves choose to prioritize the health and safety of others over their own health and safety.

Table 5.1   Adaptive behavior

Identified difference	Implications for adaptive decision-making
Women are more risk averse than men	Reducing vulnerability is a matter of risk management, and women's greater aversion to risk can promote increased willingness to take costly measures to minimize climate risks.
Women are less overconfident than men	Climate change is characterized by high uncertainty. People who are willing and able to envision a wider range of potential outcomes can adopt an adaptation strategy that is more robust to the occurrence of extreme events.
Women seek out help and listen to advice	Adapting to climate change often involves taking into account scientific information, rather than only one's own experiences. People who seek out help and listen to advice are going to more likely to apply scientific information successfully. People who refuse help in order to preserve personal challenges are likely to make poor decisions in cases where their own experience is of little practical guidance.
Women change their strategies in response to new information	Because of the high uncertainties involved, reducing vulnerability requires adaptive management: experimenting with new strategies, and learning from success and failure. People who are willing to change their strategies in response to new information will be more successful than those who try to persevere with their habitual behavior.

The practical experiences that are being gained in developing countries, highlighted by the examples from Bangladesh and Tajikistan, add support to both of these arguments. They show not only how women suffer differential harm, but also how they also develop practical solutions to cope with change. Supporting and promoting these solutions with government, NGO and donor projects can lead to real reductions in communities' vulnerability. Such projects can maintain sensitivity to the existing gender roles in society, while gently giving women the opportunity to control a greater fraction of resources, and to make independent decisions. In terms of empowerment, an essential component of quality of life, women will disproportionately benefit from such projects. In terms of identifiable and measurable indicators of vulnerability to climate-related events, however, both men and women benefit together.

ACKNOWLEDGEMENTS

We are grateful to the communities in Bangladesh, Tajikistan and Zimbabwe for their collaboration in this work and for the inspiration they provided. CARE Canada gratefully recognizes financial support from the Canadian International Development Agency (CIDA) for the implementation of the Bangladesh and Tajikistan projects. The United States National Oceanic and Atmospheric Administration Human Dimensions of Global Change research program, administered by the Office of Global Programs, provided funding for the experiment described in the first half of the chapter. Conversations with Minu Hemmati and Ulrike Röhr helped us understand the relevance of gender in climate change issues and identify relevant literature. All errors are those of the authors.

NOTE

1. At the time of the experiment, ZW$1000 was worth about US$0.75. It was difficult to estimate per capita income in the peri-urban areas from which we recruited participants, but it was probably less than ZW$3000 per day.

REFERENCES

Arch, E. (1993), 'Risk-taking: a motivational basis for sex differences', *Psychological Reports*, **73**(3): 6–11.
Barber, B. and T. Odean (2001), 'Boys will be boys: gender, overconfidence, and common stock investment', *Quarterly Journal of Economics*, **116**(1): 261–92.
Bern, C., J. Sniezek, G.M. Mathbor, M.S. Siddiqi, C. Ronsmans, A.M. Chowdhury, A.E. Choudhury, K. Islam, M. Bennish, E. Noji and R.I. Glass (1993), 'Risk factors for mortality in the Bangladesh cyclone of 1991', *Bulletin of the World Health Organization*, **71**: 73–8.
Bohnet, I. (2006), 'Why women and men trust others', J.F. Kennedy School of Government Working Paper, Harvard University.
Bradshaw, S. (2004), *Socio-economic Impacts of Natural Disasters: A Gender Analysis*, Santiago, Chile: United Nations.
Brown-Kruse, J. and D. Hummels (1993), 'Gender effects in laboratory public goods contributions: do individuals put their money where their mouth is?', *Journal of Economic Behavior and Organization*, **22**: 255–67.
Byrnes, J., D. Miller and W. Schafer (1999), 'Gender differences in risk taking: a meta-analysis', *Psychological Bulletin*, **125**: 367–83.
Cannon, T. (2000), 'Vulnerability analysis and disasters', in D.J. Parker (ed.), *Floods*, London: Routledge.
Cannon, T. (2002), 'Gender and climate hazards in Bangladesh', *Gender and Development*, **10**: 45–50.

Croson, R. and N. Buchan (1999), 'Gender and culture: international experimental evidence from trust games', *Gender and Economic Transactions*, **89**(2): 386–91.

Croson, R. and U. Gneezy (2004), 'Gender differences in preferences', University of Pennsylvania Working Paper Series.

Dawes, R., J. McTavish and H. Shaklee (1977), 'Behavior, communications, and assumptions about other people's behavior in a commons dilemma situation', *Journal of Personality and Social Psychology*, **35**: 1–11.

Denton F. (2004), 'Gender and climate change: giving the "Latecomer" a head start', *IDS Bulletin – Institute of Development Studies*, **35**(3): 42.

Eldridge, C. (2002), 'Why was there no famine following the 1992 Southern African drought? The contributions and consequences of household responses', *IDS Bulletin – Institute of Development Studies*, **33**(4): 79–87.

Eriksson, T. and M. Villeval (2004), 'Other-regarding preferences and performance pay: an experiment on incentives and sorting', IZA Discussion Paper 1191.

Friedman, D. (1998), 'Monty Hall's three doors: construction and deconstruction of a choice anomaly', *American Economic Review*, **88**(4): 933–46.

Gneezy, U., M. Niederle and A. Rustichini (2003), 'Performance in competitive environments: gender differences', *Quarterly Journal of Economics*, **118**(3): 1049–74.

Granberg, D. and T.A. Brown (1995), 'The Monty Hall dilemma', *Personality and Social Psychology Bulletin*, **21**(7): 711–23.

Haque, C.E. (1995), 'Climatic hazards warning process in Bangladesh: experience of, and lessons from, the 1991 April cyclone', *Environmental Management*, **19**(5): 719–34.

Ikeda, K. (1995), 'Gender differences in human loss and vulnerability in natural disasters: a case study from Bangladesh', *Indian Journal of Gender Studies*, **2**(2): 171–93.

Lambrou, Y. and G. Piana (2006), 'Gender: the missing component of the response to climate change', Food and Agriculture Organization of the United Nations, Gender and Population Division.

Malawi Government (2001), 'Sexual and reproductive health behaviours in Malawi: a literature review to support the situational analysis for the National Behaviour Change Interventions Strategy on HIV/AIDS and Sexual and Reproductive Health', National AIDS Commission and Ministry of Health and Population, Lilongwe, Malawi.

Masika, R. (ed.) (2002), *Gender, Development and Climate Change*, Oxfam Focus on Gender series, Oxford: Oxfam Press.

Mirza, M.M.Q. (2002), 'Global warming and changes in the probability of occurrence of floods in Bangladesh and implications', *Global Environmental Change – Human and Policy Dimensions*, **12**(2): 127–38.

Nowell, C. and S. Tinkler (1994), 'The influence of gender on the provision of a public good', *Journal of Economic Behavior and Organization*, **25**: 25–36.

Patt, A.G. (2001), 'Understanding uncertainty: forecasting seasonal climate for farmers in Zimbabwe', *Risk Decision and Policy*, **6**: 105–19.

Patt, A.G., H.R. Bowles and D. Cash (2006), 'Mechanisms for enhancing the credibility of an advisor: prepayment and aligned incentives', *Journal of Behavioral Decision Making*, **19**(4): 347–59.

Picardo, C.W., S.V. Burton and J. Naponick (2007), 'Gender-based violence experiences in reproductive-aged women displaced by Hurricane Katrina', *Obstetrics and Gynecology*, **109**(4): 63S.

Rabin, M. (1998), 'Psychology and economics', *Journal of Economic Literature*, **36**(1): 11–46.

Rapoport, A. and A. Chammah (1965), 'Sex differences in factors contributing to the level of cooperation in a Prisoner's Dilemma game', *Journal of Personality and Social Psychology*, **2**: 831–8.

Röhr, U. (2006), 'Gender relations in international climate change negotiations. Genanet – Focal Point Gender Justice and Sustainability', accessed 11 June 2007 at http://www.genanet.de/fileadmin/downloads/themen/Themen_en/Gender_climate_policy_en_updated.pdf.

Sibley, S., S. Senn and A. Epanchin (1968), 'Race and sex of adolescents and cooperation in a mixed-motive game', *Psychonomic Science*, **13**: 123–4.

Stockard, J., A. van de Kragt and P. Dodge (1988), 'Gender roles and behavior in social dilemmas: are there sex differences in cooperation and its justification?', *Social Psychology Quarterly*, **51**: 154–63.

UNISDR – United Nations International Strategy for Disaster Risk Reduction (2005), 'Hyogo Framework for Action 2005–2015: building the resilience of nations and communities to disasters', World Conference on Disaster Reduction, 18–22 January, Kobe, Hyogo, Japan.

Wisner, B., P. Blaikie, T. Cannon and I. Davis (2004), *At Risk: Natural Hazards, People's Vulnerability and Disasters*, London: Routledge.

World Bank (2005), *World Development Report 2006: Equity and Development*, Washington, DC: World Bank.

6. Income distribution effects of policies to mitigate greenhouse gases: the case of Mexico

Roy Boyd and María E. Ibarrarán

INTRODUCTION

Much of the economic literature on energy policy and climate change concerns the relationship between them, and finding mechanisms that reduce the cost of emission reduction without losses in economic efficiency. Understanding how to lower the marginal social cost of energy production and consumption, involves discussing investment in new energy sources, pollution permit schemes, environmental taxes and trade-related energy policies.

Energy and environmental policies, however, have an inequitable impact on the distribution of income. As we point out in our book *Hacia el Futuro: Energy, Economics and the Environment in 21st Century Mexico* (Ibarrarán and Boyd 2006), such equity issues cannot be ignored since all viable policies need to be thought of as fair and acceptable to the constituency of policy-makers. While all consumers can be expected to regard an increase in environmental quality as a positive change, the popularity of any environmental policy depends upon whether it is perceived as spreading costs equitably across income groups. This is especially true in developing countries where a large portion of the general population lives at or below the poverty line, and where environmental improvement is often at odds with economic development.

Mexico is a country with severe income inequality, vast energy resources and increasing environmental problems. Historically, the distribution of income in Mexico has been highly skewed with relatively large Gini coefficients (0.52 in 1996, versus 0.41 for the United States in 1997; CIA 2002), and pockets of severe poverty. The share of income by each decile has varied little since 1998 (see Table 6.1). The social, economic and political problems caused by such inequality have been daunting. Traditionally, policy-makers have responded to these problems by providing assistance

Table 6.1   Distribution of total quarterly income for households (2002 prices)

Decile	1992	1994	1996	1998	2000	2002
I	1.6	1.6	1.8	1.5	1.5	1.6
II	2.7	2.8	3.0	2.7	2.6	2.9
III	3.7	3.7	4.0	3.6	3.6	3.9
IV	4.7	4.6	4.9	4.7	4.6	4.9
V	5.7	5.7	6.0	5.8	5.7	6.1
VI	7.1	7.1	7.4	7.2	7.1	7.4
VII	8.9	8.7	9.0	8.9	8.8	9.3
VIII	11.4	11.3	11.5	11.5	11.2	11.9
IX	16.0	16.1	16.0	16.0	16.1	16.4
X	38.2	38.4	36.4	38.1	38.7	35.6
Total	100.0	100.0	100.0	100.0	100.0	100.0

Source: INEGI (various years).

in the petroleum and electricity markets. Energy expenditure makes up a substantial portion of low-income consumers' budgets; and policies such as maintaining low gasoline prices and subsidizing electricity rates have long been used to assist those in the lowest income brackets.

Recently, policy-makers have addressed other competing concerns regarding energy use. First, there is a renewed emphasis on deregulation of prices to promote economic efficiency. In Mexico, prices of many refined products, including electric power, are administered (that is, fixed) by the state to achieve development, industrialization and distributive goals. Second, the use of energy is often connected with increased levels of greenhouse gas emissions related to climate change, air pollution and environmental degradation. Notable researchers, such as Jacobson et al. (2005), argue that the poor suffer disproportionally from energy-related pollution. Thus, the adoption of energy-saving investments, and the expansion of clean burning alternatives (such as natural gas), will promote economic efficiency and address environmental issues, while meeting distributional concerns (see Paavola and Adger 2006).

This chapter focuses on the equity impacts of various proposed energy and environmental policy options in Mexico. Here we summarize the distributional implications of several policies analyzed in detail in *Hacia el Futuro: Energy, Economics and the Environment in 21st Century Mexico* (Ibarrarán and Boyd 2006). In the next section, we use the dynamic computable general equilibrium (CGE) model of Mexico and simulate the impact of these alternative policies on economic growth, carbon emissions, capital stock and the economic welfare of diverse income groups. Accordingly, there are a number of alternative simulations of the Mexican economy over the period from 2000 to 2020. The third section describes the policies to be examined and the results of the actual simulation runs. Specifically, it contains an analysis of a host of issues including investment in natural gas, deregulation of electricity prices, technological change, and carbon taxes. Finally, the fourth section presents the conclusions and policy implications of our analysis. In each case we calculate how the policies affect income and wealth among four income groups and examine how this effect could evolve over the 20-year period covered by the analysis.

THE GENERAL EQUILIBRIUM MODEL

Over the last century, most of the empirical work done in economics has relied upon partial equilibrium analysis. This type of analysis concentrates on a single market and quantifies the changes in supply, demand, prices, quantities and welfare brought about by exogenous shocks and/or parametric changes. This framework is well suited for markets with limited size or weak linkages to other economic sectors. However, other economic problems are not conducive to analysis within such a simplified framework. Often, the economic sector analyzed is large, and changes in that sector create repercussions throughout the economy. Such problems are more appropriately dealt with by using a general equilibrium analysis. In this type of analysis, all sectors in the economy are seen as one linked system where a change in any part affects prices and output economy-wide.

Mathematically, an interlinked economy cannot be described in one or two equations, but rather by a large system of simultaneous equations. In an economy with N markets, we require $N-1$ equations to solve for all of the prices and outputs in the system. While the theory behind general equilibrium can be described fairly easily, the computations involved are complex and fairly difficult to solve. Indeed, it was not until the advent of high-speed computers, and efficient solution algorithms, that large economy-wide general equilibrium problems could be solved at all.

The use of general equilibrium analysis to calculate the impact of various economic policies dates back to the early work of Harberger (1962, 1964). Such analyses were generally limited to two or three sectors until the introduction of the more complicated CGE models in the early 1970s. The policies analyzed through these models include changes in various kinds of taxes and tariffs, technological changes, natural resource and employment policies. Both efficiency and distribution impacts are presented in these studies (see Shoven and Whalley 1972).

Extension from a static CGE model to a dynamic one is fairly straight-forward. Although computationally more complex, a dynamic CGE model only differs from its static counterpart by the inclusion of a driving force to move the economy from period to period. In most dynamic models this force is provided by growth in the underlying labor force and/or a change in the level of technology in one or more sectors of the economy. These changes are facilitated by new investments and the growth of the capital stock in the economy.

As with the static model, the actual output for each sector in a specific base year is replicated through the calibration process. In addition, the economy is now expected to grow, and in the initial benchmark has to be run with all sectors, quantities and factors of production – each is required to grow at the same steady state rate. When a counterfactual shock is given to a dynamic CGE model two things occur. First, the affected prices and quantities traverse to a new growth path in the years following the shock. Second, the new growth path itself returns to a steady state but with eco-nomic variables at a level different than what they would have been in the benchmark case. Generally, interest in these dynamic models is on that new path and how much higher or lower it is than the original benchmark path.

Analytical treatment of aggregate economic growth has its origin in the work of early theorists such as Ramsey (1928), Solow (1956) and Koopmans (1965). Nonetheless, due to their heavy computational require-ments, true dynamic extensions of CGE models are a fairly recent devel-opment. In the past few years, authors such as Summers and Goulder (1989), Jorgenson and Wilcoxen (1990) and Rutherford et al. (1997) have all begun to use dynamic CGE models to explore a variety of policy issues using a single consuming agent.

New models have recently been developed in order to address the appropriate energy policies and carbon taxes necessary to prevent global warming. A comparison of many of these models is found in Goulder (1995b). They all estimate the economic impact of imposing a tax on carbon emissions. Most of these models have been applied to industrial-ized nations, especially the United States (see for example, Goulder 1995a, 1995b; Jorgenson and Wilcoxen 1995). However, there are also some applications to India, Indonesia and Pakistan (Shah and Larsen 1992). Other important studies on this topic are found in Nordhaus (1993a, 1993b), Bovenberg and Van der Ploeg (1994), Bovenberg and de Mooji (1992, 1994), Poterba (1991, 1993) and Manne and Rutherford (1994). Boyd et al. (1995) have also developed a model to analyze the net benefit of energy taxation and energy conservation as policies to reduce CO_2 emissions.

Researchers have also studied the impact of environmental taxes in Mexico. Notably, Romero (1994) and Fernández (1997) studied the impact of an environmental tax reform using static computable general equilibrium models. In his study, Romero found that under a 20 percent *ad valorem* carbon tax scenario, total emissions decrease by 13 percent. However, the effect on the consumer price index is very small, and for the year 2001 gross domestic product (GDP) is only 0.6 percent lower than under a no-tax scenario. Sectors harmed most by a carbon tax include oil, mining, construction and chemicals. The long-run demand of oil in each sector declines by 13 percent as a response to such a tax, and the long-run capital stock falls by almost 1 percent, even as the price of capital goods increases slightly, and the return rate to capital increases. The wage bill drops from 1 to 2 percent overall, but there tends to be high variation among sectors. Wages drop by 14 percent in the transportation sector and 18 percent in the chemicals sector, but increase by 23 percent in the mining sector due to increased hiring. However, the tax policy analyzed in Romero's study is not revenue-neutral (that is, the total tax receipts are allowed to vary from the base case).

Fernández (1997) introduced an environmental tax to the manufacturing sector and evaluated the policy outcome both with and without revenue neutrality. The baseline case used considers a maximum tax of 5 percent on the most highly polluting manufacturing industries – basic petrochemical products. The remaining tax rates for the rest of the industries within the manufacturing sector are then defined as depending on the pollution intensity of each sector relative to the heaviest polluter. Results indicate that introduction of an environmental tax on manufacturing reduces pollution significantly, decreases output of the heavily polluting sectors, and reallocates resources from the private to the public sector.

We now turn to the problem of modeling the general equilibrium effects of energy and environmental policies. Since the energy sector is strongly linked to a number of other sectors throughout the Mexican economy, changes there can have important economic repercussions nationwide. Consequently, such policies are best dealt with by using a general equilibrium analysis. In this framework, all sectors in the economy are seen as one linked system where a change in any part affects national prices and output economy-wide.

Here we look at a model that has nine producing sectors and ten production goods (given that oil and natural gas are produced jointly in one sector; see Table 6.2). For the purposes of this chapter, the model also has four household (income) categories (see Table 6.3). There are seven

Table 6.2   Producing sectors and production goods

Producing sectors	Production goods
1. Manufacturing	Manufacturing goods
2. Coal mining	Coal
3. Chemicals and plastics	Chemicals and plastics
4. Other agriculture	Other agriculture
5. Services	Production services
6. Transportation	Transportation for production
7. Electricity	Electricity
8. Oil and gas	Crude petroleum
	Natural gas
9. Refining output	Refining output

Table 6.3   Household categories based on income

Category	Income
Agent 1	Bottom 2 deciles: 1–2
Agent 2	Deciles 3–5
Agent 3	Deciles 6–8
Agent 4	Top 2 deciles: 9–10

consumption sectors: food, energy, autos, gasoline, consumer transport, consumer services and housing (including household goods such as furnishing and other consumer durables). There is also a foreign sector and a government sector in this model.

The economic variables determined by the model are: investment, capital accumulation, production by each sector, household consumption by sector, imports and exports, relative prices, wages and interest rates, government budget expenditure and revenues, and total wage income. The level of depreciation and the initial return to capital are taken as exogenous, as is the rate of labor force growth. These assumptions are made to make the model more tractable. However, little is gained by letting the model solve for those endogenously since these numbers are very realistic assumptions.

In each year that the model is solved for, producers maximize profits in a competitive environment. Profit maximization, based on the described production technology, yields output supply and factor demands for each production sector and factor market in the model. Output and input prices are treated as variables. Taxes are included in final consumption prices. It bears noting, however, that the goods produced in the model's production sectors are not the same final goods consumed by consumers. For example, agricultural products must be combined with transportation services, manufacturing and chemicals, before they can be consumed by individuals as food. Hence, in our model, we use a matrix to map from the vector for production of goods to that for goods consumption.

On the demand side, the model reflects the behavior of domestic consumers and foreigners (those who can also invest through their savings), as well as the government. Domestic consumers are assigned to four groups (agents) according to income and a demand equation is specified for each group. Each demand equation has a corresponding different consumption bundle depending on its income. All four groups are endowed with labor. Since only the wealthy actually have (formal) savings in Mexico, we assume here (in accordance with the latest data from INEGI) that only the top two groups (agents 3 and 4) own capital. The gross income of each group rises by the rate of population growth plus the rate of technological change. This is taken as capital-augmenting. These resources are rented out to firms in order to finance the purchase of domestic or foreign goods and services, save or pay taxes to the government.

The government is modeled with an expenditure function similar to that of households. Revenues derived from all taxes and tariffs are spent accordingly. Within this function the government spends its revenues on goods and services from various private production sectors.

Taxes in the model are expressed *ad valorem* and include personal income taxes, labor taxes, capital taxes, property taxes, revenue taxes (such as payments from oil and gas activities), value added taxes, sales taxes, import tariffs and export taxes. Taxes on final goods, such as gasoline, differ from other consumer goods because of special rates levied by the government. Similarly, final goods such as electricity differ in treatment due to existing government subsidies. When applicable, taxation is based on marginal rates. Subsidies, on the other hand, are essentially treated as negative taxes where the government transfers funds back to a sector in proportion to its output. If these subsidies are abolished, the government has more revenue (see Ibarrarán and Boyd 2006).

The model is calibrated for 2000 using different data sources. Data on consumer expenditures on final goods by income category are from the *Encuesta Nacional de Ingresos y Gastos de los Hogares* (various years), published by the Instituto Nacional de Estadística, Geografía e Informática (INEGI). Data on imports and exports are from *International Financial Statistics* (IMF various years), published by the International Monetary Fund (IMF), *The Mexican Economy* (1995), published by the Banco de México, and the *Anuario Estadístico de los Estados Unidos Mexicanos* (1996), published by INEGI. Data on inputs, outputs, and use of labor and capital by production sector comes from data compiled by INEGI and supplied by the Secretaría de Medio Ambiente y Recursos Naturales (SEMARNAT). These same sources, along with the *Anuario Estadístico de los Estados Unidos Mexicanos*, were used to calculate the transformation matrix and find investment levels by sector. All results on fossil fuel consumption (both aggregate and sectoral), fuel prices, fuel imports and exports, and government consumption of various fuels, were provided by the Secretaría de Energía (SE), Petróleos Mexicanos (PEMEX) and INEGI.

MODEL SIMULATIONS : BENCHMARK CASE

We then run a number of simulations to see the impact of economic efficiency and climate change mitigation policies. First, we run the model in the 'benchmark' to test how well it is capable of reproducing the initial data set. We then allow for oil depletion in the model and run the program again to see the impact of this change. This is referred to as scenario 1 in the tables, and it is the relevant base case against which all other results are compared. Following scenario 1, we run several further scenarios designed to quantify the economic impact of correcting for market (or policy) failures and internalizing externalities (due to excessive use of fossil fuels). Initially, in scenario 2 we simulate the effect of price deregulation in the electric power sector. Then, in scenario 3 we examine the impact of additional investment in both the petroleum and electric power sectors. Scenario 4 shows the combined impact of electricity price deregulation and capital-enhancing technological change in the energy sectors. This is followed, in scenario 5, by a simulation of electricity deregulation of prices with an energy-efficient technological change in all of our model's sectors. The impact of a carbon tax designed to mitigate global warming is modeled in scenarios 6 and 7. Finally, in scenario 8 we combine the impact of investment in the energy sector, a carbon tax and capital-enhancing technological change in all sectors. All results are provided in Tables 6.4–6.7. The discussion below focuses on the distributional implications of our model and its implications for other aspects of the economy.

The model is first run in a 'benchmark' using an updated 2000 Mexican social accounting matrix (SAM). In this benchmark, imports, exports, consumption, government expenditure, production and carbon emissions in all sectors rise steadily by the initial rate of growth. Further, all prices expressed in 2000 decline each period by the rate of discount. Put more precisely, the values of all future outputs measured in 2000 prices decline by the discount rate. In our model this is accomplished by letting current

Table 6.4   Assumptions for scenarios

Scenario	Assumptions
Scenario 0	The benchmark case
Scenario 1	The benchmark case plus oil depletion
Scenario 2	Scenario 1 plus deregulation of energy prices
Scenario 3	Scenario 1 plus new investment in PEMEX and CFE producing capital-enhancing technological change in energy sectors
Scenario 4	Scenario 1 plus deregulation of energy prices and capital-enhancing technological change in energy sectors
Scenario 5	Scenario 2 plus energy efficient technological change in all sectors
Scenario 6	Scenario 4 plus a carbon tax
Scenario 7	Scenario 5 plus a carbon tax
Scenario 8	Scenario 3 plus a carbon tax and capital-enhancing technological change in all sectors

Table 6.5   Comparison of scenarios

Scenario 1 is compared to scenario 0
Scenario 2 is compared to scenario 1
Scenario 3 is compared to scenario 1
Scenario 4 is compared to scenario 1
Scenario 5 is compared to scenario 4
Scenario 6 is compared to scenario 4
Scenario 7 is compared to scenario 6
Scenario 8 is compared to scenario 6

prices decline in each period after the initial one. In addition, income, household welfare and capital stock grow by this same initial rate. In the literature, the original 'benchmark' equilibrium is often referred to as 'steady-state' equilibrium since no forces act to move the economy off from this growth rate in all sectors.

To see the effects of changes in government tax and subsidy policies, as well as in investments in oil and natural gas, fossil fuel depletion, emission levels, technology changes and carbon taxes, we run the model again, altering various subsidies, sector growth rates, and employment and technology parameters. These changes are based on proposed tax and subsidy policies, reasonable expectations regarding changes in oil stocks, and plausible increases in the efficiency of the refinery, manufacturing and electricity sectors. By running the model with these changes and comparing their results with both the benchmark case and with each other, we

Table 6.6 Quantities: CGE results data for Mexico for 2020 (hundreds of billions of 2000 dollars)

	Scenario 0	Scenario 1	Scenario 2	Scenario 3	Scenario 4	Scenario 5	Scenario 6	Scenario 7	Scenario 8
GDP	11.2585	11.0544	11.0614	11.1798	11.1562	11.2954	11.1348	11.2423	13.1870
Oil output	0.4304	0.2708	0.2702	0.3565	0.3559	0.2552	0.3039	0.2267	0.3217
Power output	0.1979	0.1925	0.1916	0.2226	0.2215	0.2148	0.2132	0.1862	0.2481
Consumption	7.5271	7.6342	7.6303	7.6565	7.6520	7.6821	7.6581	7.6715	8.8420
Imports	3.3175	3.3173	3.3173	3.3177	3.3177	3.3175	3.3175	3.3168	3.3155
Exports	3.6073	3.4755	3.4710	3.5567	3.5522	3.4755	3.5032	3.4424	3.7308
Exports oil	0.3899	0.2451	0.2448	0.3234	0.3230	0.2321	0.2760	0.2074	0.2803
BoP surplus	0.2897	0.1582	0.1537	0.2390	0.2345	0.1580	0.1857	0.1256	0.4154
Cumulated welfare agent 1	3.4175	3.4060	3.4026	3.4207	3.4171	3.4179	3.4147	3.4101	3.8403
Cumulated welfare agent 2	10.2034	10.1732	10.1637	10.2172	10.2076	10.2098	10.1999	10.1858	11.4841
Cumulated welfare agent 3	15.9316	15.8119	15.8026	15.8450	15.8357	15.8409	15.8387	15.8331	17.2150
Cumulated welfare agent 4	26.5939	26.3226	26.3447	20.3116	26.3335	26.3482	26.3698	26.3949	27.5731
Terminal capital stock	29.5613	28.2687	28.1667	28.5702	28.4689	29.0199	27.9907	28.1188	27.7904
Cumulated govt. revenue from PEMEX	0.0637	0.0572	0.0574	0.0546	0.0548	0.0554	0.0524	0.0541	0.0507
Cumulated govt. revenue from CFE	0.0080	0.0082	0.0082	0.0080	0.0080	0.0085	0.0080	0.0082	0.0097
Cum. govt. revenue from other sources	0.8367	0.8475	0.8473	0.8593	0.8592	0.8634	0.8811	0.8785	1.2762
CO_2 emissions (hundreds of millions of metric tons)	6.6766	4.5415	4.5299	5.8088	5.8016	4.1913	4.9790	3.7496	5.4411
Price of emissions (dollars per metric ton)	–	–	–	–	–	–	$104.46	$480.86	$95.66

Table 6.7 Summary CGE Results Data for Mexico 2020 (% changes from respective scenarios)

	Scenario 1	Scenario 2	Scenario 3	Scenario 4	Scenario 5	Scenario 6	Scenario 7	Scenario 8
GDP	−1.81	0.06	1.13	0.92	1.25	−0.19	0.97	18.43
Final level of investment	−11.18	0.76	3.75	2.99	4.01	−4.32	0.00	19.03
Oil output	−37.09	−0.21	31.64	31.43	−28.30	−14.62	−25.38	5.87
Power output	−2.72	−0.48	15.64	15.06	−3.02	−3.78	−12.64	16.39
Consumption	1.42	−0.05	0.29	0.23	0.39	0.08	0.17	15.46
Imports	−0.01	0.00	0.01	0.01	−0.01	−0.01	−0.02	−0.06
Exports	−3.65	−0.13	2.34	2.21	−2.16	−1.38	−1.73	6.50
Exports oil	−37.13	−0.15	31.92	31.77	−28.14	−14.56	−24.85	1.55
BoP surplus	−45.41	−2.82	51.12	48.30	−32.65	−20.84	−32.33	123.72
Cumulated welfare agent 1	−0.34	−0.10	0.43	0.33	0.02	−0.07	−0.14	12.46
Cumulated welfare agent 2	−0.30	−0.09	0.43	0.34	0.02	−0.07	−0.14	12.59
Cumulated welfare agent 3	−0.75	−0.06	0.21	0.15	0.03	0.02	−0.04	8.69
Cumulated welfare agent 4	−1.02	0.08	−0.04	0.04	0.06	0.14	0.10	4.56
Terminal capital stock	−4.37	−0.36	1.07	0.71	1.94	−1.68	0.46	−0.72
Cumulated govt. revenue from PEMEX	−10.20	0.32	−4.55	−4.22	1.02	−4.41	3.19	−3.19
Cumulated govt. revenue from CFE	2.33	0.00	−2.27	−2.27	6.98	0.00	2.33	20.93
Cum. govt revenue from other sources	1.29	−0.02	1.40	1.38	0.50	2.55	−0.30	44.84
CO_2 emissions	−31.98	−0.25	27.90	27.75	−27.76	−14.18	−24.69	9.28

are able to examine the economy-wide results on the production of CO_2 emissions, petroleum and electricity output, the value of the capital stock, consumer welfare, the distribution of income and economic growth in Mexico for the period from 2000 to 2020.

Welfare per individual grows at the rate of technical progress (the overall growth rate less the population growth rate). Thus, the benchmark case entails no change in the distribution of income or the relative share of income received by any one segment of Mexico's wage-earning populous. The benchmark case may then be thought of as a 'balanced-growth' scenario starting in the year 2000. This means that the total production of oil starts at a level of 2.8 million barrels per day in 2000, and ends at 8 million barrels per day in 2020. In this initial run we assume that investment in the oil sector will continue at its current level and that new production will not be constrained by concerns regarding depletion. Hence, in examining the effects of depletion, carbon taxes, new investment, and new technology in Petróleos Mexicanos (PEMEX) – or the effects of new technology and subsidy removal in Comisión Federal de Electricidad (CFE) – we can measure them in terms of the deviations they cause from the steady-state case.

Scenario 1: Introducing Depletion

In scenario 1, the level of oil produced is allowed to rise according to the overall rate of economic growth until the year 2004. From then on, the amount of oil production is held constant at 4 million barrels per day. This is done since the depletion of existing stocks of petroleum make it impossible for extraction to rise with the rest of the economy without massive investment by PEMEX in drilling and oil exploration activities. Furthermore, by capping oil production at this amount our model simulations correspond closely to PEMEX's current long-run planning goals (see Secretaría de Energía 2000). This assumption provides a more reliable benchmark with which to measure the impacts of technological change, carbon taxes, subsidy removal and new investment in the energy sector. As in scenario 0, the overall growth of the economy is set at 2.9 percent.

Scenario 1 assumes that existing subsidies in CFE (that is, the national electric corporation) remain in place and that there is an increase in investment in natural gas consistent with current policy proposals. In addition, it assumes that there is no capital-augmenting technological change occurring, either in oil exploration or electricity generation, beyond that already assumed in the benchmark case above.

Tables 6.4–6.7 provide results from scenario 1 and contrast these results with earlier ones from the benchmark case. Looking first at aggregate natural resource use, we are not surprised to find that crude oil production declines substantially – by about 37 percent from its final total in the steady-state benchmark case. This decline is not restricted to oil production. Because oil is the chief contributor in the generation of CO_2 emissions, these also decline precipitously by some 32 percent. Furthermore, since oil plays such a central role in the Mexican economy, there is a marked drop in GDP, the final (that is, 2020) level of investment and the final value of the capital stock. This value, along with the welfare and government expenditure numbers, are discounted back to 2000 dollars for purposes of consistency. Boosted by significant government investments, the production of natural gas does not follow the general trend but actually increases modestly.

Faced with lower incomes and decreased returns to capital, all agents, particularly agents 3 and 4 (that is, the higher-income groups who do all of the formal saving in the Mexican economy), find saving for the future less attractive and accordingly increase their level of current consumption. In spite of this increase in consumption there is a decrease in welfare for all four income groups in the model. This is because welfare is a function of leisure and savings (that is, future consumption) as well as present consumption, and these are both negatively affected by the fall in the level of income. Furthermore, the decrease in the level of welfare is not constant across income groups. As shown in Tables 6.4–6.6 those in higher-income groups suffer the greatest loss since the negative effects on savings affect the highest two income groups the most. These groups account for all of the formal savings in Mexico and when investment earnings go down they take the lion's share of the losses.

Scenario 2: Depletion and Deregulation of Electricity Prices

Prices in the energy sector have been set as a result of policies designed to promote industrialization and distributional goals, and not based on supply and demand. Electricity prices in particular were subsidized to benefit consumers. In scenario 2, we eliminate this policy of subsidies. The results are quite similar to scenario 1 – which is contrasted in Tables 6.4–6.7. Here again we run the dynamic CGE model assuming a moderate rate of growth and depletion of oil. The only difference is that we now eliminate all of the $1.1 billion worth of electricity subsidies presently in place. For a number of years CFE has given power subsidies to sectors such as agriculture and transportation. In addition, it has given considerable subsidies to both low-income residential and rural area consumers. Because of the high costs to the government, and disparities created by its incentives, the Mexican government has lowered its subsidy payments.

Currently, subsidies average about 20 percent of the value of total output in the electricity sector. However, the government is highly selective in the industries that it continues to heavily subsidize. For example, most service industries are not subsidized and the total amount of government subsidies going into the electric power sector amount to no more than 0.35 percent of aggregate GDP. Consistently, the summary tables for this chapter show that if all present subsidies were removed there would be little economy-wide effect. When scenario 2 is compared to scenario 1 there is a slight, but not statistically significant, change in the aggregate variables. But this is only one part of the story. As economic sectors go in this model, the power sector is not all that large. It is, nevertheless, an important sector since it plays a crucial role in various types of productive activity. It is also highly important for consumer welfare since consumers are dependent on power for a variety of household needs.

Efficiency gains here come at the cost of distributional equity. Economic welfare declines for most consumers and the bulk of this decline is concentrated in the lower income groups. This is due to the fact that subsidies are, by and large, given to lower-income groups. Indeed, almost all consumer subsidies are given to those in the bottom five income deciles (that is, agents 1 and 2) and no subsidies are given to consumers in the top two income deciles (that is, agent 4). Furthermore, much of the remainder of these subsidies goes to agriculture which provides staple foods for the poor. Thus, in spite of its obvious efficiency and environmental benefits, elimination of distorted energy prices may cause income distribution concerns among policy-makers.

Scenario 3: Capital-Enhancing Investment in the Energy Sector

In scenario 3, there is oil depletion. Now, however, the model allows for an increase in the production of both CFE and PEMEX as the result of increased government investment in capital stock. In technical terms we impose what is called a capital-enhancing technological change. Under such a change capital inputs are allowed to become more efficient while labor inputs are assumed to remain at the same level of efficiency. It is very important to note that this change (which averages 3 percent per annum over the 11-year period from 2003 to 2020) is separate and distinct from the 2.9 percent improvement spoken about above. That earlier change was due to an overall increase in labor productivity throughout the Mexican economy. By contrast, this change involves the enhancement of capital in the oil and gas, and electrical power industries only.

The impact of these changes on the Mexican economy is shown in Tables 6.4–6.7. These tables reveal that, relative to scenario 1, GDP, oil output, carbon emissions, power output and the final value of the capital stock have all risen significantly. The GDP is a net figure since investment is deducted from the GDP calculations of our computer model. The amount of investment was determined outside the model by calculating the funds needed to generate the 3 percent technological change in the capital used in energy production. We assumed a 5 percent rate of return for those funds. This is exactly what we would expect in the presence of technological change. In the case of electricity, a large increase occurs because electric power benefits from technology change at several stages of the production process. First, and most obviously, electricity production increases when productivity increases within that industry itself. This increase can be thought of as a 'direct effect' of technological change. Second, electricity benefits when there is an increase in productivity and a decrease in the cost of oil and gas extraction. These lower costs are due to capital efficiency gains and translate into lower energy input prices for CFE. Further, they have the added result of causing the power industry to operate in a more energy-intensive manner. This increase can be thought of as an 'indirect effect' of change in input technology. Combined, the 'indirect' and 'direct' effects serve to amplify the total change brought about in the power sector, and lead to significant increases in CFE output. The resulting increases are readily apparent in the simulation results.

Aggregate consumer welfare goes up relative to its scenario 1 level. Technological advancement, with its positive impact on productivity, leads to a generally higher level of consumer well-being. Further, the increase in welfare appears fairly balanced, with most groups benefiting. This increase, however, is slightly regressive with respect to income distribution, as the highest-income groups exhibit slight losses. This is due to the fact that a technological change of this nature mainly helps manufacturing items, and not the service and financial service items consumed by the wealthy.

Scenario 4: Investment and Deregulation of the Electricity Sector

In scenario 4 we assume that all electric subsidies are removed as in scenario 2 and that we now have capital-enhancing technological change as in scenario 3. Here, the capital stock, GDP, investment, aggregate government revenues, and the welfare levels of agents 1 to 3, all go down slightly compared to scenario 3 – where electricity subsidies remains in place. Interestingly, the welfare of the wealthiest consumers goes up here compared to scenario 3 since they do not profit from power subsidies. When we compare scenario 4 to scenario 1, we find that all income groups experience welfare gains. Thus, according to our simulations, the combination of increased investment in energy capital and elimination of electric subsidies is both a progressive and Pareto improving move. In a wider context, however, our results are not so straightforward. A quick glance at Tables 6.6 and 6.7 shows that the level of CO_2 emissions rises significantly from scenario 1 to scenario 4, and – due to the significant amount of other pollution accompanying higher CO_2 emissions – the external costs of these emissions to consumer welfare is significant, even without considering global warming impacts. Hence, it is more accurate to say that in going from scenario 1 to 4 all agents will experience a definite welfare gain in terms of traditional national income accounting variables. They will also experience a correlatively significant decline in the welfare associated with environmental quality. Furthermore, because the lower-income groups are located closer to the pollution sources, the environmental impact is regressive. Still, it is extremely difficult to quantify accurately the net effect on aggregate welfare and real income distribution.

Scenario 5: Energy-Efficient Technological Change

Scenario 5 is very similar to scenario 4 in all respects except in the type of technological change that is modeled. In scenario 5 we assume that there has been an equivalent investment in energy-efficient technology among those sectors that burn fossil fuel. An energy-efficient technological change is precisely what proponents of tax incentive programs have in mind.

The results of this scenario are given in Tables 6.4–6.7. In all our tables the results of this exercise are contrasted with the results of scenario 4 to see the impact of different varieties of technological change. As we see there, compared with scenario 4, the use of petroleum drops sharply. Electricity use also declines slightly, compared with scenario 4, but is significantly higher than in scenario 1. Accompanying the decline in fossil fuel extraction, there is a significant drop in CO_2 emissions relative to scenario 4. Furthermore, since the increase in energy efficiency occurred economy-wide, rather than in just a few industries, the level of GDP and of the capital stock increase slightly over that in the previous scenario. Economic growth occurs in a cleaner manner than before, and economic welfare is up slightly among all groups. As eluded to earlier, this is probably a significant understatement of welfare gains. Aggregate emissions here have dropped substantially compared with scenario 4, bringing down medical and other costs associated with a variety of different pollutants (for example, SO_2, particulates, ozone and nitrous oxides). This kind of energy-efficient technological change has distinct environmental advantages over change aimed solely at increasing capital output in industrial sectors.

Scenario 6: Capital-Enhancing Technological Change and Carbon Taxes

In scenario 6, all assumptions are the same as in scenario 4 except we now levy a carbon tax on petroleum, coal, and natural gas. Since the carbon content of these fuels is different they are taxed at different rates with the highest tax on coal and the lowest on natural gas. Specifically, over the period from 2005 to 2020 graduated taxes were as follows: 50 percent on coal, 25 percent on petroleum and 12.5 percent on natural gas.

The results reveal that the aggregate level of CO_2 emissions drops off significantly from scenario 4 levels. This decrease in total emissions has positive impacts on Mexico's local environmental quality. Still, there are definite costs, in terms of both economic efficiency and equity. The negative impacts on economic efficiency are readily apparent since GDP, investment and the terminal capital stock all decline relative to their value in scenario 4. With respect to economic equity, it appears that the carbon tax is also somewhat regressive. Specifically, the two lower-income agents lose welfare compared to gains by the two higher-income agents. This relates to the fact that, in Mexico, lower-income groups devote a higher proportion of their total income to energy expenses than the higher-income groups. However, the aggregate level of air pollutants declined in a manner likely to offset any regressive equity effect – especially in large urban areas like Mexico City.

Scenario 7: Energy Efficiency and Carbon Taxes

Scenario 7 combines the effects of a carbon tax with an energy-efficient technological change affecting all sectors. In this model simulation, we imposed a carbon tax on coal, natural gas and petroleum at the exact same levels used in scenario 6, and levied tariffs of equal magnitude on the importation of these goods. In addition to this carbon tax, the assumption was made that increased investment would lead to greater efficiency in burning those fuels (see scenario 5). Thus scenario 7 represents the effort by policy-makers to cut back fully on fossil fuel emissions through both economic and technological means. Accordingly, it is instructive to compare this scenario to scenario 6 where only taxation and tariffs are employed.

The results of the simulation are set forth in Tables 6.4–6.7. As these tables reveal, the combination of a carbon tax with energy-efficient technological change yields dramatic results relative to emissions. Notably, there is a dramatic decline in the consumption of fossil fuels, and CO_2 emissions, from the levels in scenario 6. Similarly, dramatic changes are seen in measuring changes between scenario 7 and scenario 4. For example, when compared with scenario 4, the production of oil declines by over 36 percent and the total emissions of CO_2 decline by over 35 percent. Thus, if policy-makers were concerned only with curtailing greenhouse gases, this action would be the most effective.

The summary tables show GDP increases slightly with more efficient fuel use as does the terminal level of the capital stock. The level of welfare of agents 1 to 3 declines slightly; however, these numbers do not include the medical, and other, savings realized when the level of aggregate emissions drop, particularly in urban areas.

Scenario 8: Adding a Carbon Tax and an Overarching Capital-Enhancing Technological Change

In scenario 8 we ran the dynamic CGE model with a broad-based carbon tax identical to that imposed in scenario 6. In addition, we allowed for technological improvement in all of our production sectors. Specifically, we imposed a 'Harrod neutral' or capital-specific technological enhancement on each of the production sectors over the 20-year time horizon studied. In accordance with Organisation for Economic Co-operation and Development (OECD) estimates (for developing countries) the technological change for each sector was assumed to be 3.1 percent for the ten years from 2005 to 2015. These results are provided in Tables 6.6 and 6.7.

The impact of this technological change is both clear and dramatic. The balance of payments, GDP, investment, PEMEX and CFE revenue, and consumer welfare all increase significantly over scenario 6 and scenario 7 totals. Unfortunately for environmental policy, the aggregate level of CO_2 emissions rises over 9 percent above its total in scenario 6. These numbers show the trade-offs between environmental quality and economic growth that policy-makers will face in the coming years. With other types of pollution (for example, SO_2 pollution of the air, and organic pollution of the water) technological change can sometimes act as an agent to enhance changes in the environment. In the case of CO_2, however, output-enhancing technological change can only decrease pollution to the degree of total energy use. While this may be possible in a static setting, it is more problematic when economic growth is a top priority of policy-makers and it needs to be targeted in the manner exhibited in scenario 7. Otherwise environmental costs are likely to be quite high.

The impact of broad technological change on consumer welfare is highly progressive with lower-income agents benefiting by larger percentages than their higher-income counterparts. This is partly due to changes occurring in the relative prices for the consumption goods. By and large, the largest portions of low-income consumers' budgets are spent on basic necessities such as food, energy and housing, while higher-income groups tend to spend more on consumer services. In the wake of a technological change, the production of food and housing climbs dramatically and prices fall relative to the prices of services. This, in turn, tends to benefit the poorest agents more than the richer ones.

CONCLUSIONS

For about the last century the petroleum industry has been an important voice in establishing policy in Mexico. Indeed, government entities like PEMEX and CFE were largely established to promote economic growth and distributional equity. Examples of government-driven policies include low energy prices and electricity subsidies. In this chapter we examined energy policy alternatives currently being faced by the Mexican government.

Proportionally, the greatest amount of energy is consumed by the lowest-income groups. Accordingly, our model simulations found that increased investments and exploration in natural gas yields progressive effects. Investments in energy-saving technologies have the greatest, positive, impacts on those in the lower-income deciles. The same cannot be said, however, for deregulation of electricity prices and carbon taxes. Existing subsidies to electricity were designed to benefit agricultural production and consumption by low-income groups. Simulations which model removal of those subsidies show that the benefits go largely to the wealthy. Similarly, carbon taxes affect lower-income groups more severely.

The direct impacts of any energy policy are often accompanied by environmental impacts and can have important distributional consequences. Largely attributable to residential location, Mexico's lower-income groups are disproportionally affected by the negative externalities associated with air pollution. Energy policies associated with lower CO_2 emissions levels – as well as other local pollutants such as CO, SO_2, O_3, NO_2, PM10, PM2.5 and lead – are generally progressive relative to income distribution. Seen in this light, increased investment in energy efficiency and clean-burning natural gas are desirable from an equity standpoint. This, in turn, reinforces their progressive direct impacts. Increased investment in energy capital, on the other hand, leads to higher emissions levels. The resulting regressive environmental impacts work against its progressive direct effects. Finally, deregulation leads to generally higher electricity prices and, therefore, lower emission levels. From an environmental standpoint these impacts can be viewed as progressive and, to some degree, they offset its regressive direct consequences.

REFERENCES

Banco de México (1995), *The Mexican Economy*, Mexico City: Banco de México.

Bovenberg, L. and R. de Mooji (1992), 'Environmental taxation and labor market distortions', Working Paper, Ministry of Economics Affairs, The Hague.

Bovenberg, L. and R. de Mooji (1994), 'Environmental levies and distortionary taxation', *American Economic Review*, **84**(4): 1085–9.

Bovenberg, A.L. and F. van der Ploeg (1994), 'Environmental policy, public finance and the labour market in a second-best world', *Journal of Public Economics*, **55**(3): 349–90.

Boyd, R., K. Krutilla and W. Viscusi (1995), 'Energy taxation as a policy instrument to reduce CO_2 emissions: a net benefit analysis', *Journal of Environmental Economics and Management*, **29**: 1–24.

CIA (2002), *CIA World Fact Book*, United States Central Intelligence Agency, Washington, DC: US Government Printing Office.

Fernández, O. (1999), 'Efectos de la aplicación de un impuesto ecológico neutral en México: análisis mediante un modelo de equilibrio general computable', in A.M. García (ed.), *Instrumentos económicos para un comportamiento empresarial favorable al ambiente en México*, Mexico City: El Colegio de México/Fondo de Cultura Económica.

Goulder, L. (1995a), 'Effect of carbon taxes in an economy with prior tax distortions: an intertemporal general equilibrium analysis', *Journal of Environmental Economics and Management*, **29**: 271–97.

Goulder, L. (1995b), 'Environmental taxation and the "double dividend": a reader's guide', *International Tax and Public Finance*, **2**: 157–83.

Harberger, A. (1962), 'The incidence of the corporation income tax', *Journal of Political Economy*, **70**: 215–40.

Harberger, A. (1964), *Taxation, Resource Allocation and Welfare, The Role of Direct and Indirect Taxes in the Federal Reserve System*, Princeton, NJ: Princeton University Press.

Ibarrarán, M.E. and R. Boyd (2006), *Hacia el Futuro: Energy, Economics and the Environment in 21st Century Mexico*, Dordrecht: Springer.

International Monetary Fund (IMF) (various years), *International Financial Statistics*, Washington, DC: International Monetary Fund Printing Office.

INEGI (1996), *Anuario Estadístico de los Estados Unidos Mexicanos, 1996*, Mexico City: Instituto Nacional de Estadística, Geografía e Informática.

INEGI (various years), *Encuesta Nacional de Ingreso y Gastos de los Hogares*.

Jacobson, J.O., N.W. Hengartner and T.A. Louis (2005), 'Inequity measures of evaluations of environmental justice: a case study of close proximity to highways in New York City', *Environment and Planning A*, **37**(1): 21–43.

Jorgenson, D.W. and P. Wilcoxen (1990), 'Intertemporal general equilibrium modeling of US environmental regulation', *Journal of Policy Modeling*, **12**(4): 715–44.

Jorgenson, D.W. and P. Wilcoxen (1995), 'Reducing US carbon emissions: an econometric general equilibrium assessment', in D. Gaskins and J. Weyant (eds), *Reducing Global Carbon Dioxide Emissions: Costs and Policy Options*, Stanford, CA: Stanford University Energy Modeling Forum, pp. 85–99.

Koopmans, T. (1965), *On the Concept of Optimal Economic Growth: The Economic Approach to Development Planning*, Amsterdam: North-Holland.

Manne, R. and T. Rutherford (1994), 'International trade in oil, gas, and carbon emission rights: an intertemporal general equilibrium model', *Energy Journal*, **15**(1): 57–76.

Nordhaus, W. (1993a), 'Reflections on the economics of climate change', *Journal of Economic Perspectives*, **7**(4): 11–25.

Nordhaus, W. (1993b), 'Optional greenhouse-gas reductions and tax policy in the "DICE" model', *American Economic Review*, **83**(2): 313–17.

Paavola, J. and W.N. Adger (2006), 'Fair adaptation to climate change', *Ecological Economics*, **56**(4): 594–609.

Poterba, J.M. (1991), 'Tax policy to combat global warming: on designing a carbon tax', in R. Dornbusch and J. Poterba (eds), *Economic Policy Responses to Global Warning*, Cambridge, MA: MIT Press, pp. 71–97.

Poterba, J.M. (1993), 'Global warming policy: a public finance perspective', *Journal of Economic Perspectives*, **7**(4): 47–63.

Ramsey, F. (1928), 'A mathematical theory of saving', *Economic Journal*, **38**: 543–59.

Romero, J. (1994), 'Energía, emisiones y precios relativos', in A. Yúnez-Naude (ed.), *Medio ambiente: problemas y soluciones*, Mexico City: El Colegio de México, pp. 111–22.

Rutherford, T., D. Montgomery and P. Bernstein (1997), 'CETM: A Dynamic General Equilibrium Model of Global Energy Markets, Carbon Dioxide Emissions, and International Trade', University of Colorado Paper 97-3.

Secretaría de Energía (2000), *Programa Nacional de Energía 2001–2006*, Mexico City: Secretaría de Energía.

Shah, A. and B. Larsen (1992), 'Carbon taxes, the greenhouse effect, and developing countries', Policy Research Working Papers No. 957, World Bank.

Shoven, J. and J. Whalley (1972), 'A general equilibrium calculation of the effects of differential taxation of income form capital in the US', *Journal of Public Economics*, **1**: 281–322.

Solow, R. (1956), 'A contribution to the theory of economic growth', *Quarterly Journal of Economics*, **70**(1): 65–94.

Summers, L. and L. Goulder (1989), 'Tax policy, asset prices, and growth: a general equilibrium analysis', *Journal of Public Economics*, **38**(3): 256–96.

7. Climate change and cities: differential impacts and adaptation options in industrial countries

Matthias Ruth, Paul H. Kirshen and Dana Coelho

INTRODUCTION

As the number of people in urban areas increases, along with the volume and intensity of their economic activities, there is a corresponding increase in environmental impacts. With these social and economic changes, the resilience of urban systems is impacted (Rotmans 2006). These impacts are chiefly determined by the interplay of historical, ethnic, economic, locational and environmental policies. They are rarely, if ever, spread uniformly across society. Not all inhabitants of cities have equal abilities to cope. Thus these differential impacts present equity and justice concerns in relation to adaptation costs (Adger 2001). The differential impacts and abilities to adapt influence the larger social, economic and environmental changes in urban areas. Because those changes are non-trivial with respect to their magnitude, as well as the moral and ethical obligations they may create, assessments of life in, as well as the planning and management of, cities need to be sensitive to these differential impacts.

Traditional urban analysis has focused on the individual drivers of urban change and their impacts on people, the economy and the environment (for example, Robson 1969; Dear and Dishman 2002). Urban systems analysis is often rich in empirical detail and theoretical conceptualization relative to temporal and spatial dimensions of urban change (for example, Black and Henderson 1999; Fujita et al. 1999; Brenner 2000). However, the interconnection among the various drivers and repercussions – social, economic and environmental – have rarely been the object of analysis.

The need for heightened attention to the complexity of urban change and the differential impacts of the combined social, economic and environmental changes in the urban context are increasingly recognized. For example, researchers and decision-makers are generally concerned with climate change impacts. In its Third Assessment Report, the Intergovernmental Panel on Climate Change (IPCC) recognized, at length, that the impacts of climate change would be felt differently across regions and across the socio-economic spectrum (IPCC 2001, Chapter 7). Settlements in regions that are already water-deficient (including much of North Africa and the Middle East), and/or have economies that rely heavily on natural resources (such as coastal resources for fishing and tourism, forests and agriculture), are particularly vulnerable when the climate changes to warmer weather. In addition, many settlements in the more northern regions are vulnerable to fires (for example, boreal regions in Canada, Alaska and Russia) and/or damage to transportation and other infrastructure systems from the melting of permafrost. These findings are corroborated in the Fourth Assessment Report. The Report's 'Summary for Policymakers' from Working Group II recognizes urban areas' vulnerabilities to extreme weather events and identifies them as being more important than mere gradual climate changes (IPCC 2007a). The distinction was also made that, while total monetary damages (for example, property and physical infrastructure loss and damage) will be greater in more industrialized regions, total human stresses (for example, displacement and loss of life) will be greater in less developed areas (IPCC 2007a; Kates 2000). Due to both the complexity of climate change, and its potential impacts on human settlements, the IPCC focuses on vulnerabilities of distinct regions, groups and types of infrastructures. Vulnerability here is defined as 'the degree to which a system, subsystem or system component is likely to experience harm due to exposure to a perturbation or a source of stress' (Turner et al. 2003; Clark et al. 2000).

Much of the work on differential impacts shows greater vulnerability by inhabitants of cities in the developing world than in industrialized countries (for example, Cross 2001; ISDR/EIRD 2004; O'Brien and Leichenko 2003; World Tourism Organization 2003). Similarly, extensive evidence exists of higher adverse impacts of climatic change on people in coastal cities than those further inland. This is particularly the case in developing countries which are highly dependent on coastal natural resources for harvest or to attract tourism (for example, ADRC et al. 2004; Adger et al. 2005; Freer 2006; Mendelsohn et al. 2000; Pielke et al. 2005). In contrast to previous studies, this chapter addresses some of those differential impacts on industrialized nations. The discussion here is based on insights from a combination of theoretical, empirical, simulation-based and stakeholder-guided assessments. It begins by discussing expected climate change impacts in urban areas in the industrialized world as drawn from literature and recent case studies. Thereafter, it explores the causes behind differential urban vulnerabilities based upon analyses of urbanization, urban infrastructure and metabolism, and environmental quality. This is followed by a discussion of available options to manage best the inevitable differences in urban areas so as to reduce vulnerabilities. Finally, the chapter concludes with a brief summary, and proposed agenda, for further research in this topic area.

CLIMATE CHANGE IMPACTS AND VULNERABILITIES IN URBAN AREAS

Climate change impacts on urban areas highlight existing, or emerging, disparities across spatial and socio-economic dimensions. For example, the disaster and controversy surrounding Hurricane Katrina, in August 2005, evidences that climate change – and its associated potential for more severe weather events – places urban populations at risk (Petterson et al. 2006). Currently, few case studies, or even broader-ranging empirical analyses, exist on the relationships between climate impacts and the locational or socio-economic aspects of vulnerability. There are only a few exceptions, as described in the following sections. Table 7.1 summarizes some of the manifestations of climate change impacts in urban areas. Since a research agenda on the differential impacts of climate change is just emerging, some of these manifestations are speculative and will require careful empirical analysis and hypothesis testing. Accordingly, the intent here is to stimulate such research rather than provide definitive answers.

Climate's Long-Term Impacts on Metro Boston (CLIMB)

Recently an analysis was conducted on the distributional impacts of coastal flooding in metro Boston. This analysis was based upon the results of the Climate's Long-Term Impacts on Metro Boston (CLIMB) study. The methodology and results are summarized in Ruth and Kirshen (2001) and Kirshen et al. (2008), and are available in full in Kirshen et al. (2005). The metro Boston area, as analyzed (for example, Figure 7.1), includes the major cities of Boston and Cambridge and the other 99 municipalities within approximately 20 miles of Boston. The area is bordered on the east by Boston Harbor (the confluence of three major rivers) and on the south, west and north by the circumferential Route 495. This is an area covering 3683 square kilometers. Metro Boston's population is approximately 3.2 million and is expected to increase to 4 million by 2050. Land use varies from densely populated urban areas in the east, suburbs in the center, undeveloped farmland, and some urban sprawl on the fringes. It is an area

Table 7.1   Examples of potential climate-induced impacts and vulnerabilities

Characteristic / Impact	Location		Socio-economics	
	Physical characteristics	Infrastructures and institutions	Income	Gender, race, age
Coastal flooding	Low areas inundated, more coastal flooding	More economic damage to infrastructure and coastal development	Lower-income communities less able to flood-proof, evacuate or relocate; mitigation and adaptation costs constitute a disproportionately large share of disposable income, flood-prone land often inhabited by low-income groups because less expensive	Inadequate access to early warning and evacuation, especially for the young and the very old who tend to have limited mobility options
Energy demand and reliability of delivery	Disruption of exposed transmission and distribution lines; loss of power has multiple negative impacts on vulnerabilities	Higher impact of extreme weather events on areas that rely on centralized power supply and lengthy transmission infrastructure	Lower-income communities less able to invest in air conditioning, new/more efficient end use devises, on-site power generation (e.g., heat pumps, solar cells); mitigation and adaptation costs constitute a disproportionately large share of disposable income	Women, minorities and the elderly suffer a disproportionate increase in expenditure as a share of disposable income
Water quality	Activities on land close to water bodies are negatively affected	Reduced recreational value of coastal, lacustrine and riverine land; reduced productivity of agriculture and fisheries;	Lower income communities experience reduced ability to upgrade water purification or purchase bottled water; increased incidence of	Elderly and very young more prone to water- and food-borne diseases; consumption of contaminated fish higher among poorly educated

Table 7.1   (continued)

Characteristic / Impact	Location		Socio-economics	
	Physical characteristics	Infrastructures and institutions	Income	Gender, race, age
		groundwater resources damaged from saltwater intrusion; biodiversity loss	water-borne disease; mitigation and adaptation costs constitute a disproportionately large share of disposable income; less ability to go to high-quality recreational areas	immigrant groups, significant risk to women of child-bearing age and young children
Transportation, communication	Loss of transportation/ communication lines and modes because of flooding or disruption of energy supply	Loss of mobility/ accessibility leads to a loss of business activity and social interaction	Poor have fewer transportation and communication options; mitigation and adaptation costs constitute a disproportionately large share of disposable income	Women, some minorities, and the young and elderly have fewer transportation/ communication options to begin with and are disproportionately impacted by a decrease or loss of service
Health conditions (e.g., Urban air quality, extreme heat/cold, conditions for disease)	Accumulation of fecal wastes, etc., in low-lying areas (e.g., after flood) or build-up of ozone and temperatures during heat events	Potentially disproportionate impacts of disease on areas with high population density	Disproportionate impact on the poor; mitigation and adaptation costs constitute a disproportionately large share of disposable income	Disproportionate impact on the elderly and young, as well as some ethnic minorities

which is highly vulnerable to coastal flooding. For the analysis, the region was divided into the seven zones shown in Figure 7.1. The delineation of zones was guided largely by administrative borders and a reflection of differences in population density, economic make-up and expected changes over the next 50 years.

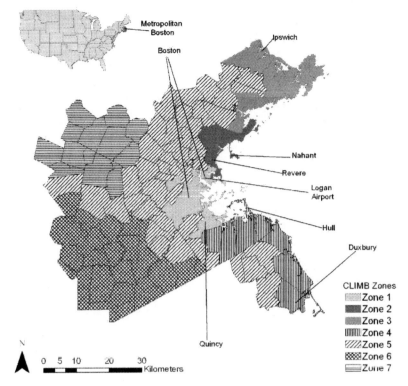

Note: Zone 1 = South Coastal Urban, Zone 2 = North Coastal Urban, Zone 3 = North Coastal Suburban, Zone 4 = South Coastal Suburban, Zone 5 = Developed Suburbs, Zone 6 = Developing Suburbs South, Zone 7 = Developing Suburbs North.

Figure 7.1   CLIMB zones

The analysis calculated the undiscounted cumulative coastal flooding costs to residential structures and contents over the period from 2000 to 2100. It assumes that no adaptation actions are taken (that is, damage is repaired after flooding) and that the eustatic sea level rise over the period is 0.45 m (approximately the mid range for current sea level rise (SLR) estimates from the IPCC Working Group I; IPCC 2007b) and the land subsidence is 0.15 m. The damage costs per hectare of residential property, versus population weighed household median 2000 incomes (from MAPC 2003) of the coastal communities in the five zones, are shown in Figure 7.2. Even though the sample is small, an inverse relationship can be seen between household incomes and damage per area.

The causes of this distributional impact could be multiple. Perhaps the

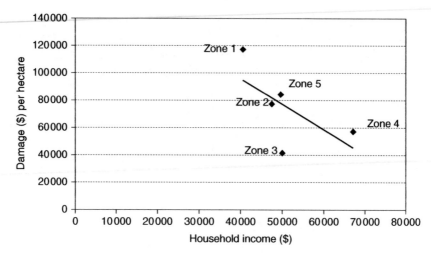

Figure 7.2   Unit area damage versus household income for CLIMB regions

less wealthy cannot afford the flood defenses of the more wealthy, and/or housing density is greater in less wealthy areas, making losses greater. A greater housing density in low-income areas would also mean more people are impacted.

Additional Studies

The research by Clark et al. (1998) presents an exception to the rule that few studies have explored the distributional impacts of climate change in urban areas. This research is on the vulnerabilities of coastal communities to extreme storms, with special focus on one community in Massachusetts. Clark et al. use a combination of factor analysis and Geographical Information Systems (GIS) to depict areas in Revere, Massachusetts, which historically have been the most vulnerable to hurricane-induced coastal flooding. They use their analysis to draw conclusions for local damage-reduction programs such as contingency plans for weather-robust transportation, as well as scenario analysis, to prepare better for climate-induced impacts.

Several researchers have also explored New York City's vulnerability to climate change and sea level rise. Their findings relate to the potential for impacts on coastal wetlands (inundation and migration), water, electricity and transportation infrastructure, and public health (Rosenzweig and Solecki 2001; Kinney et al. 2006; Knowlton et al. 2004). Rosenzweig and Solecki (2001) also examined the interconnections between elements of 'physical' infrastructure with 'social' infrastructure – institutions. For example, adaptations to the water supply infrastructure are dependent upon institutional capacity, while institutions such as health care are dependent upon a well-functioning water supply. In the case of New York City, major impacts from climate change could have national and international repercussions due to the city's economic prominence.

Differential impacts may stem not only from the direct effects of climate on the performance of infrastructure systems in urban areas but also, indirectly, from the extent to which adaptation and mitigation costs unevenly affect different parts of the population or economy (Adger 2001). For example, a detailed analysis of climate's impacts on water supply in Hamilton, New Zealand revealed that water demand (at the monthly aggregate level) will be largely driven by changes in population, and will not be significantly affected by changes in climate. However, as populations increase, the effect of climate variables on per capita water consumption will be magnified. Monthly aggregate changes may further mask potentially significant short-term shortages. In several scenarios, water supply shortages in 2030 occur with a 30–40 percent probability. This suggests the need for long-term capacity expansion or aggressive demand-side management, rather than implementation of short-term management of water demand (Ruth et al. 2007). Costs associated with capacity expansion constitute larger shares of disposable income among low-income groups. Further, rationing supply disproportionately affects larger and poorer households, as well as those with the very young or elderly.

A US report by the Congressional Black Caucus Foundation and Redefining Progress (2004) highlights the disparity between those who benefit from, and those who bear the burden of, climate change relative to national climate change policies. It makes the argument that the African American community is less responsible for, yet bears the greater social and economic burden of, climate change. Specifically, the report found that to the extent African Americans are associated with poor urban communities, climate change will exacerbate existing inequalities with respect to health effects (from exposure to air pollution and heatwaves in the north, outbreaks of infectious diseases in the south) and unemployment (from volatile oil prices and economic shifts). Similarly, poorly structured energy policies could disproportionately harm the African American community if energy prices rise in a non-progressive structure. Notably, on the whole African Americans spend a 25 percent greater share of their personal income on energy or energy-related goods (for example, gasoline, energy for heating and cooling their homes).

The sources of vulnerabilities are diverse and often interrelated. General urbanization trends change social and economic characteristics across the urban landscape. Investments in infrastructure and institutions – often because of their lumpiness and irreversibility – may ameliorate some problems but then magnify others. For example, expansion of an urban transport route may help move people and goods more efficiently in and out of the area. It may also, however, have detrimental impacts on the characteristics of adjacent neighborhoods, fragmenting social structures and perhaps even reducing the accessibility of some areas severed by the new route. Changes in the material and energy flows through a region, stimulated by urbanization and investments, tie urban dynamics to broader social, economic and environmental changes. In many instances, those ties help avert, prepare for or buffer adverse impacts of global (environmental) change by providing resources and knowledge essential for mitigation and adaptation. In many cases, urbanization, development of infrastructures and institutions, and the evolution of the urban 'metabolism' – for example, the flow of materials and energy through an urban system – also contribute to increased vulnerabilities. Each source of vulnerability is discussed in the following section.

SOURCES OF VULNERABILITIES IN URBAN AREAS

Urbanization Trends

Urbanization, though characterized by significant regional differences, is following an overwhelming upward trend. The world has seen a fifteen-fold increase in urban populations since the beginning of the twentieth century. Both total population, and urban population, are increasing at all levels of development – though at a decreasing rate (see Tables 7.2 and 7.3). Consistently, wealthier and more developed nations are characterized by greater levels of urbanization, though the majority of urban growth is occurring in less developed countries (UNDP 2003, 2006; World Bank 2005). Indeed, the rate of urbanization in the least-developed places is as much as seven times that in the most-developed nations (UNDP 2003).

Approximately half of the world's population now lives in urban areas, with more than 50 percent of those in cities of less than 500 000 people (McGranahan and Marcotullio 2006). Though some of the world's largest cities have experienced slowed growth rates in recent decades, the average size of the world's 100 largest cities has increased from 200 000 in 1800 to 5 million in 1990 (Cohen 2004). This trend in urban expansion is anticipated to continue as transportation and communication networks, two of a

Table 7.2   Trends in global population growth

	Total population (millions)			Annual population growth rate (%)	
	1975	2004	2015	1975–2004	2004–2015
High human development	1012.5	1275.0	1350.0	0.8	0.5
Medium human development	2743.2	4433.1	4995.8	1.7	1.0
Low human development	255.0	571.7	737.1	2.8	2.3
World	4073.7	6389.2	7219.4	1.6	1.1

Source: Adapted from UNDP (2006).

Table 7.3   Trends in global urban population growth

	Urban population (as % of total)				
	1975	2001	*% change*	2015	*% change*
High human development	71.7	78.3	*9.2*	81.5	*4.01*
Medium human development	28.1	41.6	*48.0*	49.4	*18.8*
Low human development	19.1	31.6	*65.5*	39.7	*25.6*
World	37.9	47.7	*25.9*	53.7	*12.6*

Source: Adapted from UNDP (2003).

city's most extensive infrastructure systems, expand outside of traditional inner city boundaries.

As populations age across the board, the age composition within nations and within cities is also changing. That demographic change has far-reaching implications for migration to and from cities. These implications also address demand for urban infrastructure, urban material and energy use, environmental quality, mobility and quality of urban life. The most pronounced changes can be seen in middle and high human development nations where between 2004 and 2015 United Nations (UN) projections are for an almost 12 percent decrease in the percentage of population under the age of 15; and an 18.5 percent increase in the percentage of population over the age of 65, respectively (Table 7.4). Decreases in youth

Table 7.4   Trends in global age demographics

	Population under age 15 (as % of total)			Population aged 65 and above (as % of total)		
	2004	2015	*% change*	2004	2015	*% change*
High human development	19.6	17.8	*−9.2*	13.5	16	*18.5*
Medium human development	28.8	25.4	*−11.8*	6.1	7.2	*18.0*
Low human development	44.8	42.6	*−4.9*	2.9	3.1	*6.9*
World	28.5	25.9	*−9.1*	7.3	8.4	*15.1*

Source: Adapted from UNDP (2006).

populations of 9.2 and 4.9 percent are anticipated in high and low human development nations, respectively. Increases of 18.5 and 6.9 percent in the elderly population are anticipated in these nations (UNDP 2003).

In addition to purely demographic changes there is a suite of environmental conditions influencing, and being affected by, urbanization. Most cities are located in, and are growing toward, coastal zones. This is in part due to the importance of access to natural resources and transportation networks in an increasingly globalized world. Population densities in coastal areas are approximately 45 percent greater than global average densities (McGranahan and Marcotullio 2006). As the size and make-up of cities change, new urban economic and social inequalities come to the forefront and new pressures on the local environment are created. For example, increased demand for land often leads to settlement in ecologically vulnerable areas or an increase of imperviousness (that is, paved and built-up surfaces) in the urban landscape. As a result, the ability of wetlands and forested areas to protect coastal zones, floodplains and rivers is reduced and the likelihood of flooding is increased. This has an associated impact on housing structures, transportation networks, water supply and water quality.

Increases in local densities of people, infrastructure and economic activity pose challenges for adaptation to both the seasonal changes and extreme events associated with climate change. Challenges from seasonal changes lie in the need to deliver, for example, ever larger amounts of water, energy and other infrastructure services to urban areas to meet increased demands during dry and hot periods. As temperatures rise, cooling needs increase. Urban heat island effects may further exacerbate those needs, creating a positive feedback process that results in larger energy demands, pronounced heat islands and higher emissions of greenhouse gases within the urban core (Stone 2006). Expansion of impervious surfaces may require more extensive and effective flood control during wet periods. Since flood control measures are typically designed to deal with 100- and 500-year floods, yet the definition of what constitutes those floods itself changes because of climate change (Kirshen et al. 2005; IPCC 2007b), investment in flood control infrastructure may actually lag behind needs. This may be the case even if it 'nominally' is able to handle the particular flooding events. As a result, a false sense of security may be created and ever larger populations and economic value will be placed at risk. If and when catastrophes hit, evacuation efforts will be challenged by the sheer numbers of individuals local governments have to deal with, and the rebuilding that damaged communities will require. This was vividly demonstrated by the demise of New Orleans during and in the aftermath of Hurricane Katrina (Petterson et al. 2006; Sherbinin et al. 2006; Christie and Hanlon 2001).

Urban Infrastructures and Institutions

Cities are able to grow and prosper when they have an adequate supply of infrastructure systems and services – such as water, sanitation, power, communication and transportation. In some regions, particularly in Africa and Asia, very basic deficiencies characterize urban systems of all sizes. According to the World Bank, in 2000 about 20 percent of the population in developing countries did not have access to safe drinking water, 50 percent did not have access to adequate sanitation, and upwards of 90 percent lived without wastewater treatment infrastructure (World Bank 2005). However, the challenges of inadequate or declining infrastructure are not confined to the developing world. In some developed nations, public spending on infrastructure has decreased over the last few decades. While some losses have been made up by increased private investment – for example, the provision of electricity and water distribution may suffer from decentralizing these services – concerns abound over the ability of profit-seeking firms to provide adequate public services equitably (Newton et al. 2001). In Australia, investment in the electricity, water, sewer, telecommunications and transportation sectors has become increasingly privatized (Newton et al. 2001). Private transportation providers (focusing on zones within Australia's major cities or on specific modes of transportation) have been diverting attention from an effective metropolitan system to private profit generation (Newton et al. 2001). In the US, during the time period between 2005 and 2010, infrastructure systems regularly received 'poor' or 'failing' grades and required more than $1.6 trillion in recommended infrastructure improvements (ASCE 2005).

It is the role of institutions – such as governments and planning agencies, markets and non-governmental organizations – to anticipate and assess the adequacy of existing infrastructure and the desirability of new infrastructure, to facilitate decision-making, and to oversee the implementation, operation, maintenance and decommissioning of infrastructure systems. A diversity of institutions is crucial, particularly in cities, given the spatial closeness of the individuals served by different organizations and infrastructure. Challenges in fulfilling this mission are often related to inabilities to secure adequate funds, inequitable access, the lumpiness and irreversibility of infrastructure investments, and the roles of risk, uncertainty and surprise in investment decision-making. Each challenge is discussed here, briefly, before we turn to the ramifications of urbanization for material and energy use, environmental quality and quality of life.

Infrastructure Investment

Typically, large-scale infrastructure investments are undertaken by the government to provide public goods. Examples include the building of dams, wastewater collection and treatment systems, energy supply systems, ports and roads. However, investments by private enterprises should not be overlooked. For example, private investments in office and residential buildings, and in communication and data storage systems, have paved the way for current advances in information exchange and Internet commerce. Public investments, unlike their private counterparts, are typically funded with long-term bonds or loans and with the goal of supporting the public good. Private infrastructure investments, by contrast, are generally focused on producing short-term pay-offs to the investing parties.

Increasingly, public–private partnerships are used to leverage access to capital with clear profitability goals, while at the same time creating synergistic effects among infrastructure investments, regional competitiveness and larger-scale socio-economic development. The reduction in investment risk is spread across different parties. This allows for longer planning horizons and more social and environmental concerns than would normally be chosen by private enterprises. Examples of public–private partnerships and similar arrangements are increasingly found in transportation development, wastewater treatment, water supply, and electricity generation and communication networks, where private enterprises receive revenues from user fees for their contributions.

In some cases, private investments replace public investments. The extent to which that replacement also reduces redundancy is a key factor in determining the overall ramifications for vulnerability. If, in the interest of profit making, provisions for backup systems in water treatment are reduced, or alternate transport routes are neglected, then short-term economic efficiency gains in infrastructure may eventually translate into increased vulnerability. New infrastructure may be perceived as reducing existing shortfalls, while in reality raising the possibilities for new disparities across space, time, and social and economic groups.

Trying to leverage private and public infrastructure investments can create special challenges in urban areas of developed countries. Places with deteriorating systems are not necessarily those of high growth in population or economic activity. These are not the places of greatest appeal to private investors. As a result, it is often the economically disadvantaged who are left with aging infrastructure, and the risks of infrastructure failure, that come with deterioration. This is especially true in times of increased climate-induced stress.

Equitable Access to Infrastructure Systems and Services

Criteria for equality and fairness must include the needs of current and future businesses and households at different locations in the economic landscape. Their needs for infrastructure services influence the choice of location and type of infrastructure system. Conversely, once in place, infrastructure affects the economic performance of businesses and household incomes, as well as the demand for services, susceptibility to climate impacts, and ability to adapt to climate change. Access to infrastructure determines access to resources and so affects quality of life.

As a consequence, equality and fairness in space are closely related to equality and fairness through time and across different parts of the socio-economic system (small and large producers, households from different income groups, and so on). This is true across the globe and perhaps even more so within developing countries (Kates 2000).

The international community recognizes differential mobility, access to education, provisions for clean water and sanitary sewer service, life expectancy, and exposure to disease in urban and rural areas, and that greater poverty is associated with rural areas (World Bank 2005). For example, enlarged transportation networks require dealing with water drainage from impervious surfaces, construction waste and managing larger traffic volumes. The presence, or enlargement, of one type of infrastructure system yields investments in another. Increased economic activity in cities and suburbs attracts companies and consumers to urban areas. Several consequences may be felt. Enlarging the urban–rural divide (that is, increasing income disparity and inequality) may reduce the sustainability of rural life and so undermine cultural and socio-economic integrity in some regions. Conversely, high concentrations of people and economic activities may result in diseconomies of agglomeration, such as congestion, social friction and an unsustainable urban system. Attention must be given to seeking optimum urban densities based on social and cultural characteristics, markets, natural resources and climate conditions.

The rate of change in urban densities can make it virtually impossible for planners and investors to take a long view on infrastructure investment. Current efforts to provide infrastructure may be too slow to keep up with growth in population and economic activity and, therefore, may not be able to address adequately either future needs or long-term environmental concerns. Such shortcomings are exacerbated by the fact that the very activity of creating a new infrastructure – both 'hard' structures (such as bridges and sewer systems) and the 'soft' structures of institutions – disrupts the performance of already existing systems. For example, expanding or building a new transportation route affects the accessibility to, and operation of, existing routes. This disruption is likely to occur both during construction and afterwards as users acclimatize to the new system. Creating new bureaucracies inevitably raises, at least in the interim, information and transaction costs. In both instances, the costs are not necessarily borne by those benefiting from the presence of new or more reliable infrastructure systems and services.

There is also the possibility for infrastructure change to leapfrog, as the example of wireless telecommunication technology shows. Notably, urban areas characterized by vandalism of, and underinvestment in, public communication systems may become more resilient as mobile phones proliferate. This is likely to occur to the extent that collective use of any available bandwidth does not overwhelm the system as a whole. Information about impending impacts may be accessed more easily, evacuation routes may be identified more efficiently, loved ones may be located more quickly, and help may be more readily directed where it is needed most.

Dealing with Indivisibilities, Complementarities and Irreversibilities in Investment

Infrastructure systems – such as water supply, flood control, and communication and transportation networks – are typically large and often function as a whole. A break in a water main, dyke or bridge can render the respective system incapable of providing a service. Investment in redundancy is critical for being prepared for disruptions, such as during construction or in an emergency. For example, having well-developed private transportation, bus and rail systems in place can help cut down on traffic jams when one of the three is disrupted. However, investing in redundancies is costly. Similarly, ensuring adequate and reliable performance by one kind of infrastructure system often requires coordination with other systems. The smooth operation of highways, for example, requires development of drainage and flood management systems. Redundancy is not only costly but may be affordable only for those localities and groups who stand to lose the most (economic assets) in the event of a system failure.

There are opportunity costs to sinking large investments in complementary infrastructure systems and such investments can cause both irreversible environmental degradation and degradation from putting the primary system in place. Developing complementary infrastructure systems can lead to technology lock-in (Arthur 1990) and the associated phenomenon of carbon lock-in (Unruh 2000). With few exceptions, urban transport systems around the world are largely fossil-fuel based – even with the increased popularity of vegetable-based fuels (ethanol and biodiesel). The ease and reliability of movement guaranteed by these systems spawned suburbanization in much of the Western hemisphere. In addition, it fostered an increase in private car ownership and the corresponding diminishing use of local buses and rail systems for other than long-distance commutes. With the enlarged role of transportation systems, institutions developed to manage these systems and to meet the needs of their users. As a result, they have further locked-in the existing infrastructure. Past institutional development has added to the inertia that makes adaptive management of infrastructure systems difficult in light of today's changing environmental conditions and technologies (Unruh 2002). This has calcified urban structures that rely on intense use of fossil fuels and whose combustion significantly contributes to the very impacts that development is supposed to ameliorate. To the extent that existing inequalities and differential vulnerabilities are the products of historic infrastructure development, locking-in particular development patterns will not likely offer major breakthroughs in reducing that vulnerability. For example, investment in old tried-and-tested fossil fuel systems may help lower the short-term costs of electricity generation, yet increase vulnerabilities among the poor, very young and elderly. Vulnerabilities may result from large price fluctuations, disruption of power from centralized generation, and regional air pollution.

Risk, Uncertainty and Surprise in Planning and Management of Infrastructure Systems

Since infrastructure systems typically have long lifespans, their presence reflects knowledge and perceptions that decision-makers have about the

physical, biological and economic environment, as well as their expectations for the future. To the extent that differential impacts of infrastructure development and differential vulnerabilities are not an integral part of
the decision-making process, those developments can exacerbate existing
inequalities and vulnerabilities.

Capacity and design criteria for infrastructure systems typically are
based on historic observations and extrapolations into the future. Planners
ask themselves: What will be the size and income of the population over
the next 20 years? What will be the rate of car ownership and travel
demand? What are likely changes in land use, industrial and residential
locations? How rapidly will relative employment and output shift among
sectors of the economy? Answers to such questions are often sought with
the help of economic and planning models – most of which base their projections on an analysis of historic data. Safety margins are introduced into
the projections to deal with risk and uncertainty. Yet, since planners and
decision-makers deal with socio-economic systems that co-evolve in close
relationship with other socio-economic systems and their environment,
there is ample room for surprises to occur and for projections to fail. For
example, few current and planned investments in sea and airports, tunnels
and roadways reflect the impacts that climate change may have on sea
level rise or increased adverse weather conditions. Thus, there is a need
for better drainage and flood management, or entirely different modes of
interaction across space. Current investments in transport infrastructure
may also be misplaced if telecommuting and Internet commerce gain in
economic importance. Those investments are too high when new communication technology leads to a reduction in transport demand; too
low, or geographically misplaced, when new communication technology
boosts economic activity and triggers increased (long-distance) transport
of goods, services and people (Golob and Regan 2001).

The size of capital requirements, long lifetimes, socio-economic development and environmental impacts of infrastructure all require institutions
to take the long-view approach. At times of rapid change in population
size, economic activity or technology, methods of forecasting future
infrastructure demands based on past trends are generally inadequate.
By the same token, a large-scale, long-term driver such as climate change
requires current design criteria to be revisited. Further, it necessitates that
infrastructures be (re-)built to withstand dramatic climate changes such
as higher winds, heavier snow and ice loads, higher surface temperatures,
increased drought and precipitation, or elevated sea levels. To the extent
that infrastructure investments help to overcome existing social and economic inequalities in urban areas, they can also help reduce the differential
impacts of climate change. As infrastructures adjust, the volumes and

patterns of material and energy used in urban areas (and their surroundings) change. In the next section we address urban metabolism and highlight changes in these flows.

Changes in Urban Metabolism

Urban metabolism is the total flow of materials, energy and information within an urban system in order to generate goods and services (physical output) and increase human well-being (non-material or social output) (Newcombe et al. 1978; Huang and Hsu 2003). Urban metabolism studies measure inputs, outputs and material recycling within a city or metropolitan area, often paying particular attention to associated energy flows (Huang and Hsu 2003). In general, though combined with decreased per capita energy consumption, urbanization increases total energy demand as the needs of physical and social infrastructure within cities grows (Huang and Chen 2005). Much of this increased energy demand has been met, and indeed facilitated, by the use of fossil fuels (Unruh 2000). By some accounts, urban metabolism has been understood more explicitly in terms of sustainability. Mitchell (1998) defines urban metabolism as the 'social as well as biophysical [means] by which cities acquire or lose the capacity for sustainability in the face of diverse and competing problems'. Here sustainability refers to the maintenance of resources and quality of life in the face of hazards and risk.

Two aspects of urban metabolism are particularly relevant in the context of differential climate impacts and vulnerabilities. First, there is the accumulation of 'metabolic wastes' in the environment. These could be liquids released onto soils or into water bodies, solids accruing in landfills or on brownfield sites (vacant, contaminated urban land), or gases emitted into the air. For example, with increased flash floods, storm and wastewater commingle, overwhelming local water treatment facilities and posing hazards to ecosystems and human health. With increased heatwaves, local air pollution is typically exacerbated, magnifying urban heat island effects and triggering respiratory problems among the very young, the elderly and the sick.

The second issue surrounding urban metabolism relates to its larger impacts on the regional and global environment. As hotbeds of economic activity and household consumption, urban areas largely drive the combustion of fossil fuels and corresponding CO_2 emissions. This makes them a source of their own problems. Building on the innovative capacity often found in urban areas, and leveraging the financial, cultural and technological resources at their disposal, may help reverse the trend towards unsustainable resource use and increased vulnerability. The diversity of urban areas along socio-economic dimensions needs to be embraced in that process.

Environmental Quality and Quality of Life

Urbanization means increasing rates of direct and indirect consumption of energy, materials and ecosystem services, as well as the significant displacement of natural ecosystems (McGranahan and Marcotullio 2006). Urban environmental problems, founded upon the appropriation and degradation of natural ecosystems, as well as stresses upon social institutions and urban infrastructure, vary regionally over time as cities develop economically. A number of researchers (for example, McGranahan et al. 2001) have supplied graphic representations of this phenomenon.

Figure 7.3 shows that local environmental concerns, such as indoor air quality and sanitation, are more pronounced in rural and low-income urban areas. These problems are largely driven by development paths characterized by rapid demographic change that do not significantly account for key biological and ecological processes. Examples include the dynamics of infectious diseases and the provision of ecosystem services. Regional problems, such as declining outdoor air quality, emerge as cities develop and incomes increase. Indirect drivers include the type of

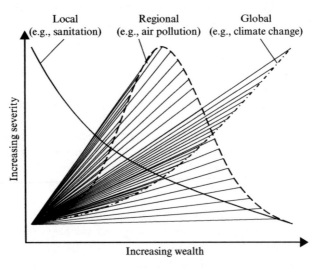

Source: Adapted from McGranahan and Marcotullio (2006).

Figure 7.3   Urban environmental problems along spatial and economic gradients

industrialization and the increased use of private automobiles, characteristic of larger cities which fail to consider the effects on regional ecosystems. More global problems, such as climate change, increase with increasing development and wealth. Excessive material wealth, exaggerated ecological footprints, generation of greenhouse gas emissions and solid waste, and a development path ignorant of (or unconcerned with) global effects of consumption, are driving these changes. The time scale over which these concerns are experienced also changes. Local concerns pose a more immediate threat to human health and well-being since global problems occur slowly and their damage is harder to see, understand and react to. Some of the most serious conditions are due to rapid urbanization causing more local and immediate environmental health issues (for example, inadequate sanitation and access to clean drinking water) to be experienced at the same time as more modern, global concerns (for example, climate change) effectively reduce a city's capacity to respond.

MANAGEMENT OPTIONS

While in many urban areas of the industrial world climate change is not likely to be the key driver behind socio-economic differences, it may highlight and exacerbate existing disparities. Consequently, strategies that generally reduce socio-economic differences may also reduce the differential impacts of climate change. Conversely, strategies to reduce vulnerabilities of individual social groups or economic sectors may generally reduce socio-economic disparities.

Two groups of management options address the differential impacts of climate change in urban areas. One set includes strategies that reduce the costs of impacts overall, recognizing that those costs are typically disproportionately borne by the socially and economically disadvantaged. Implementing broad-based adaptation strategies may not only reduce overall vulnerabilities but will do so disproportionately among the specific segments of society that are the most vulnerable. Examples of such strategies include the promotion of retreat from flood-prone coastal zones. This strategy will leave smaller numbers of people at risk, and will also keep insurance rates and public expenditure for evacuation and recovery down. Disposable incomes of the poor, and government budgets for social programs, may be less affected than in the absence of broad-based adaptation to climate change.

A second set of options includes strategies geared towards decreasing the vulnerability of individual social groups or economic sectors. Examples include improved monitoring and early warning systems to inform high-risk groups of impending severe weather and adverse outdoor temperatures or air quality. Similarly, subsidies to small businesses for water or fuel purchases may help reduce the impacts of drought and extreme temperatures on operating conditions and profitability.

Both sets of adaptation strategies – broad and group-specific – are further distinguished by those that address current or anticipated trends in climate change, and those that are event-specific. Examples of the former include responses to experienced or possible future increases in summer temperatures, or responses to changes in precipitation patterns. Specific illustrations are adaptation strategies that promote better insulation for houses, planting shade trees to reduce temperature-related morbidity and mortality, and the exploration of alternative water supply systems in preparation for drought. Event-specific adaptations include opening shelters during extreme storms (US Congress 2006), cold spells or heatwaves, providing generators and instructions for safe indoor use when electricity is lost due to a severe storm (DeGaetano 2000), and the distribution of bottled water during heat and drought periods.

The extent to which adaptation follows trend- or event-specific strategies, and is either broad-based or focused on group-specific vulnerabilities, depends largely on the communities' perception of risk, available resources to cope with change and potential disasters, the negotiation power of key interest groups, and the overall structure and functioning of the institutions charged with adaptation or amelioration of the consequences. Chapter 10 of this work, by Lange et al., addresses several of these issues in an international context.

Table 7.5 lists examples of adaptation strategies that explicitly target individual groups or economic sectors. More generic discussions of adaptation options are found in the Fourth Assessment Report of the IPCC Working Group II (IPCC 2007a).

SUMMARY AND CONCLUSIONS

Increases in urban populations, aging infrastructures, and global climate and environmental change have begun to highlight the need for, and urgency of, increasing urban resilience. There is an increase in the number of case studies for individual locations and on individual challenges – such as meeting water or energy demands. These studies frequently quantify impacts and, in several cases, monetize the cost of adaptation strategies. Additional studies reveal the complexity of managing the interrelations among population, infrastructure and institutions in order to reduce vulnerabilities and cost to society. Few studies, however, have addressed the

Table 7.5   Group and sector-specific adaptation strategies

Adaptation / Reduced vulnerability of . . .	Trend-specific	Event-specific
Public health	• Implementation of monitoring and early warning systems • Improved health education of high-risk groups • Increased capacity in local hospitals to deal with health conditions likely to result from temperature extremes (e.g., heat stroke) or warming (e.g., mosquito-borne diseases)	• Opening of cold or heat shelters • Opening of hydrants and provision of water for cooling and drinking • School and workplace closings
Water supply	• Subsidy for low-flow toilets, low-flow showers and other demand-side management options for low income households • Encourage and remove barriers to the use of grey-water recycling systems and rainwater capture	• Distribution of bottled water • Enforced restrictions on non-essential water use, such as for watering lawns or washing cars, during periods of drought
Water quality	• Subsidy for water purification technology in low income households • Use of desalination in the event of significant salt water intrusion in aquifers • Posting warning signs at poor water quality sites	• Distribution of bottled water, water filters, and disinfectants • Shutting down swimming beaches
Flooding	• Zoning to avoid concentration of poor in flood-prone areas • Building of sea walls to protect coastal property	• Sand-bagging and other short-term flood control methods • Evacuation

Table 7.5   (continued)

Adaptation / Reduced vulnerability of...	Trend-specific	Event-specific
	• Removal of emergency aid and phase-out of insurance coverage for property in major flood zones • Expansion of the federal buy-out program for high-risk properties in floodplains and coastal zones	
Energy demand and supply	• Free energy audits for small businesses • Subsidies for insulation of homes and energy efficient appliances and lighting • Fuel distribution to low-income households • Use of new building materials and designs to reduce energy consumption • Economic incentives for decentralized power generation	• Rolling brown-outs with preferential treatment of particular urban areas or kinds of businesses • Provision of generators in the event of significant electricity loss
Transportation	• Building of sea walls to protect transportation infrastructure • Changes in urban structure and personal travel behavior to reduce transport demand	• Road, rail and airport closings
Communication	• Distribution of mobile phones for emergency use • Standardization of emergency communication frequencies (e.g., for local and/or regional police, fire and rescue personnel)	• Emergency radio and television broadcasts • Emergency announcements on local government and news websites

need for policy and investment decision-making in order to increase the resilience of individual groups within urban populations of the regional economy. In this chapter we have addressed the differential impacts of interrelated population, infrastructure and institutional changes within an urban context and presented suggestions for adaptation strategies.

Given the lack of research in the field of climate impacts and adaptation in urban settings, it should not be surprising that our suggestions for reducing group-specific vulnerabilities are rather general, often speculative, and lack quantification. To advance research further in this area would require a heightened sensitivity to the impacts of climate change on the interrelated dynamics of population, infrastructure and environmental changes in the urban environment. Within that setting – but also for impact and adaptation research in general – it is necessary to pay attention to total cost and benefits as well as to those who bear the costs and enjoy the benefits. Such attention would significantly enrich scientific knowledge and debate on investment and policy making. Issues of social justice may have more bite in that dialog than current discussions about intergenerational welfare distribution in the light of climate change. In response, entirely new groups of actors may embrace the quest for economically and socially optimal ways of addressing the climate change challenge. It remains to be seen whether this confluence of social, economic and environmental concerns on adaptation to climate change ultimately promotes more sustainable societies.

REFERENCES

Adger, N. (2001), 'Scales of governance and environmental justice for adaptation and mitigation of climate change', *Journal of International Development*, **13**: 921–31.

Adger, W.N., N.W. Arnell and E.L. Tompkins (2005), 'Successful adaptation to climate change across scales', *Global Environmental Change*, **15**(2): 77–86.

ADRC, Japan, CRED-EMDAT, Université Catholique de Louvain, Brussels, Belgium and UNDP (2004), *Natural Disasters Data Book 2004*, http://web.adrc. or.jp/publications/databook/databook_2004_eng, accessed 28 April 2007.

Arthur, W.B. (1990), 'Positive feedback in the economy', *Scientific American*, **262**: 92–9.

ASCE (2005), *Report Card for America's Infrastructure*, American Society of Civil Engineers, http://www.asce.org/reportcard/2005/index.cfm, accessed 20 April 2007.

Black, D. and V. Henderson (1999), 'The theory of urban growth', *Journal of Political Economy*, **107**(2): 252–84.

Brenner, N. (2000), 'The urban question: reflections on Henri Lefebvre, urban theory and the politics of scale', *International Journal of Urban and Regional Research*, **24**(2): 361.

Christie, F. and J. Hanlon (2001), *Mozambique and the Great Flood of 2000*, Oxford: James Currey for the International African Institute.

Clark, G.E., S.C. Moser, S.J. Ratick, K. Dow, W.B. Meyer, S. Emani, W. Jin, J.X. Kasperson, R.E. Kasperson and H.E. Schwartz (1998), 'Assessing the vulnerability of coastal communities to extreme storms: the case of Revere, MA, USA', *Mitigation and Adaptation Strategies for Global Change*, 3: 59–82.

Clark, W.C., J. Jaeger, R. Corell, R. Kasperson, J.J. McCarthy, D. Cash, S.J. Cohen, P. Desanker, N.M. Dickson, P. Epstein, D.H. Guston, J.M. Hall, C. Jaeger, A. Janetos, N. Leary, M.A. Levy, A. Luers, M. MacCracken, J. Melillo, R. Moss, J.M. Nigg, M.L. Parry, E.A. Parson, J.C. Ribot, H.J. Schellnhuber, D.P. Schrag, G.A. Seielstad, E. Shea, C. Vogel and T.J. Wilbanks (2000), *Assessing Vulnerability to Global Environmental Risks*. Report of the Workshop on Vulnerability to Global Environmental Change: Challenges for Research, Assessment and Decision Making, 22–25 May, Airlie House, Warrenton, Virginia. Research and Assessment Systems for Sustainability Program Discussion Paper 2000-12. Cambridge, MA: Environment and Natural Resources Program, Belfer Center for Science and International Affairs (BCSIA), Kennedy School of Government, Harvard University.

Cohen, B. (2004), 'Urban growth in developing countries: a review of current trends and a caution regarding existing forecasts', *World Development*, 32(1): 23–51.

Congressional Black Caucus Foundation and Redefining Progress (2004), 'African Americans and climate change: an unequal burden', 21 July.

Cross, J.A. (2001), 'Megacities and small towns: different perspectives on hazard vulnerability', *Environmental Hazards*, 3: 63–80.

Dear, M.J. and J.D. Dishman (2002), *From Chicago to LA: Making Sense of Urban Theory*, Thousand Oaks, CA: Sage Publications.

DeGaetano, A.T. (2000), 'Climatic perspective and impacts of the 1998 northern New York and New England ice storm', *Bulletin of the American Meteorological Society*, 81(2): 237–54.

Freer, J. (2006), 'Insurance woes take toll on building sales', *South Florida Business Journal*, http://southflorida.bizjournals.com/southflorida/stories/2006/09/25/focus1.html?page=1, accessed 28 April 2007.

Fujita, M., P. Krugman and A.J. Venables (1999), *The Spatial Economy: Cities, Regions, and International Trade*, Cambridge, MA: MIT Press.

Golob, T.F. and A.C. Regan (2001), 'Impacts of information technology on personal travel and commercial vehicle operations: research challenges and opportunities', *Transportation Research, Part C – Emerging Technologies*, 9: 87–121.

Huang, S.-L. and C.-W. Chen (2005), 'Theory of urban energetics and mechanisms of urban development', *Ecological Modeling*, 189: 49–71.

Huang, S.-L. and W.-L. Hsu (2003), 'Materials flow analysis and emergy evaluation of Taipei's urban construction', *Landscape and Urban Planning*, 63: 61–74.

IPCC (2001), 'Human settlements, energy, and industry', in J.J. McCarthy, O.F. Canziani, N.A. Leary, D.J. Dokken and K.S. White (eds), *Climate Change 2001. Impacts, Adaptation and Vulnerability. Contribution of Working Group II to the Third Assessment Report of the Intergovernmental Panel on Climate Change*, Cambridge: Cambridge University Press, Chapter 7, pp. 381–416.

IPCC (2007a), 'Summary for policymakers', in M.L. Parry, O.F. Canziani, J.P. Palutikof, P.J. van der Linden and C.E. Hanson (eds), *Climate Change 2007: Impacts, Adaptation and Vulnerability. Contribution of Working Group II to the*

Fourth Assessment Report of the Intergovernmental Panel on Climate Change, Cambridge: Cambridge University Press, pp. 7–22.

IPCC (2007b), 'Summary for policymakers', in S. Solomon, D. Qin, M. Manning, Z. Chen, M. Marquis, K.B. Averyt, M. Tignor and H.L. Miller (eds), *Climate Change 2007: The Physical Science Basis. Contribution of Working Group I to the Fourth Assessment Report of the Intergovernmental Panel on Climate Change*, Cambridge and New York: Cambridge University Press, pp. 1–18.

ISDR/EIRD (2004), *Living With Risk. A Global Review of Disaster Reduction Initiatives*, Geneva: Inter-Agency Secretariat of the International Strategy for Disaster Reduction.

Kates, R.W. (2000), 'Cautionary tales: adaptation and the global poor', *Climatic Change*, **45**: 5–17.

Kinney, P.L., J.E. Rosenthal, C. Rosenzweig, C. Hogrefe, W. Solecki, K. Knowlton, C. Small, B. Lynn, K. Civerolo, J.Y. Ku, R. Goldberg and C. Oliveri (2006), 'Assessing the potential public health impacts of changing climate and land use: the New York Climate & Health Project', in M. Ruth, K. Donaghy and P. Kirshen (eds), *Climate Change and Variability: Consequences and Responses*, Cheltenham, UK and Northampton, MA, USA: Edward Elgar.

Kirshen, P., M. Ruth and W. Anderson (2005), 'Climate change in Metropolitan Boston', *New England Journal of Public Policy*, **20**(2): 89–103.

Kirshen, P., M. Ruth and W. Anderson (2008), 'Interdependencies of urban climate change impacts and adaptation strategies: a case study of metropolitan Boston USA', *Climatic Change*, **86**: 105–22.

Knowlton, K., E. Rosenthal, C. Hogrefe, B. Lynn, S. Gaffin, R. Goldberg, C. Rosenzweig, K. Civerolo, J.-Y. Ku and P.L. Kinney (2004), 'Assessing ozone-related health impacts under a changing climate', *Environmental Health Perspectives*, **112**: 1557–63.

Metropolitan Area Planning Council (MAPC) (2003), Boston Metropolitan Area Planning Council, http://www.mapc.org, accessed 13 May 2007.

McGranahan, G., P. Jacobi, J. Songsore, C. Surjadi and M. Kjellén (2001), *The Citizens at Risk: From Urban Sanitation to Sustainable Cities*, London: Earthscan.

McGranahan, G. and P. Marcotullio (2006), 'Urban Systems', in Millennium Ecosystem Assessment, *Ecosystems and Human Well-being: Current State and Trends*, Washington, DC: Island Press, pp. 795–825.

Mendelsohn, R., W. Morrison, M.E. Schlesinger and N.G. Andronova (2000), 'Country-specific market impacts of climate change', *Climatic Change*, **45**: 553–69.

Mitchell, J.K. (1998), 'Urban metabolism and disaster vulnerability in an era (Chapter X)', in H.-J. Schellnhuber and V. Wenzel (eds), *Earth System Analysis: Integrating Science for Sustainability*, Berlin: Springer.

Newcombe, K., J. Kalma and A. Aston (1978), 'The metabolism of a city: the case of Hong Kong', *Ambio*, **7**: 3–15.

Newton. P.W., S. Baum, K. Bhatia, S.K. Brown, S. Cameron, B. Foran, T. Grant, S.L. Mak, P. Memmott, V.G. Mitchell, K. Neate, N.C. Smith, R. Stimson, A. Pears, S. Tucker and D. Yencken (2001), *Australia State of the Environment 2001: Human Settlements*, Canberra: CSIRO Publishing on behalf of the Department of the Environment and Heritage.

O'Brien, K.L. and R.M. Leichenko (2003), 'Winners and losers in the context of global change', *Annals of the Association of American Geographers*, **93**: 89–103.

Petterson, J.S., L.D. Stanley, E. Glazier and J. Philipp (2006), 'A preliminary assessment of social and economic impacts associated with Hurricane Katrina', *American Anthropologist*, **108**(4): 643–70.

Pielke Jr, R.A., C. Landsea, M. Mayfield, J. Laver and R. Pasch (2005), 'Hurricanes and global warming', *Bulletin of the American Meteorological Society*, **86**: 1571–5.

Robson, B.T. (1969), *Urban Analysis: A Study of City Structure*, Cambridge: Cambridge University Press.

Rosenzweig, C. and W.D. Solecki (2001), *Climate Change and a Global City: The Metropolitan East Coast Regional Assessment*, New York: Columbia Earth Institute.

Rotmans, J. (2006), 'A complex systems approach for sustainable cities', in M. Ruth (ed.), *Smart Growth and Climate Change: Regional Development, Infrastructure and Adaptation*, Cheltenham, UK and Northampton, MA, USA: Edward Elgar.

Ruth, M., C. Bernier, N. Jollands (2007), 'Adaptation to urban water supply infrastructure to impacts from climate and socioeconomic changes: the case of Hamilton, New Zealand', *Water Resources Management*, **21**(6): 1031–45.

Ruth, M. and P. Kirshen (2001), 'Integrated impacts of climate change upon infrastructure systems and services in the Boston metropolitan area', *World Resources Review*, **13**(1): 106–22.

Sherbinin, A., A. Schiller and A. Pulsipher (2006), 'The vulnerability of global cities to climate hazards', *Environment and Urbanization*, **12**(2): 93–102.

Stone, B. (2006), 'Physical planning and urban heat island formation: how cities change regional climates', in M. Ruth (ed.), *Smart Growth and Climate Change: Regional Development, Infrastructure and Adaptation*, Cheltenham, UK and Northampton, MA, USA: Edward Elgar.

Turner, B.L., P.A. Matson, J.J. McCarthy, R.W. Corell, L. Christensen, N. Eckley, G.K. Hovelsrud-Broda, J.X. Kasperson, R.E. Kasperson, A. Luers, M.L. Martello, S. Mathiesen, R. Naylor, C. Polsky, A. Pulsipher, A. Schiller, H. Selin and N. Tyler (2003), 'Illustrating the coupled human environment system for vulnerability analysis: three case studies', *Proceedings of the National Academy of Sciences*, **100**(14): 8086–91.

UNDP (2003), 'Human development indicators 2003', Human Development Reports, http://hdr.undp.org/reports/global/2003/indicator/indic_38_1_2.html, accessed 28 April 2007.

UNDP (2006), *Human Development Report 2006. Beyond Scarcity: Power, Poverty and the Global Water Crisis*, http://hdr.undp.org/hdr2006/statistics, accessed 28 April 2007.

Unruh, G. (2000), 'Understanding carbon lock-in', *Energy Policy*, **28**: 817–30.

Unruh, G. (2002), 'Escaping carbon lock-in', *Energy Policy*, **30**(4): 317–25.

US Congress (2006), 'A failure of initiative: final report of the Select Bipartisan Committee to Investigate the Preparation for and Response to Hurricane Katrina', US House of Representatives, 109th Congress, 2nd Session. Washington DC.

World Bank (2005), *World Development Report 2006: Equity and Development*, New York: World Bank and Oxford University Press.

World Tourism Organization (2003), 'Climate change and tourism', in *Proceedings of the 1st International Conference on Climate Change and Tourism*, 9–11 April, Djerba, Tunisia and Madrid, Spain.

8. Climate information, equity and vulnerability reduction

Pablo Suarez, Jesse C. Ribot and Anthony G. Patt

INTRODUCTION

The last few decades have brought about a heightened awareness of the effects of climate change. We now know that climate change can increase the risk of natural disasters. Recent advances in science and technology now provide us with more reliable forecasting tools (Wang et al. 2004). Because these new tools hold great promise for reducing vulnerability, massive financial, technological and human resources are being invested in their development. Possible predictions from these tools range from short-term tropical cyclone tracks to shifts in rainfall patterns due to climate change. Humanity faces two new challenges: not just preparing for the foreseeable climate, but also modifying decision-making processes to incorporate information now available for vulnerability reduction (Brunner 1999).

Researchers and practitioners often disagree on how to define vulnerability (Ionescu et al. 2004) and how climate information can affect it. Vulnerability is broadly defined as the ability to be harmed. There are numerous concepts on vulnerability – depending on *what* people or systems are vulnerable *to* (Patt et al. 2005a). There are two major approaches to addressing this issue: vulnerability to hazard (for example, droughts) and vulnerability to outcomes (for example, famines). This distinction has profound implications regarding the appropriate policy, and resulting strategy, to reduce vulnerability.

Climate information can be used to reduce the negative effects of expected changes (Dilley 2000). However, mere availability is not a sufficient condition to ensure reduction in the vulnerability of all sectors of the population and the economy – particularly in cases where ignorance of future conditions is not the main factor impeding the fulfillment of basic needs. Adequate consideration of the most vulnerable sectors of the population is necessary. Without it, the widespread generation of climatic forecasts may result in a socially differentiated distribution of benefits. This distribution would increase the gap between those who are relatively safe and those who are most vulnerable and, therefore, need to be given the highest priority for their care (Sperling 2003).

In this chapter we explore the relationship between climate information and vulnerability in the context of competing worldviews. This analysis identifies the most pressing factors limiting the ability to put available information into use. In addition, it suggests innovative ways in which new predictions can help address the causal chain of disasters and related equity issues.

VULNERABILITY AND THE ROLE OF CLIMATE FORECASTS: THREE APPROACHES

Hansen (2002) presents a simple illustration depicting the determinants of the potential for human populations to benefit from climate predictions (Figure 8.1).

In this work, 'human vulnerability' refers to the elements of the human system that are susceptible to harm as a result of climate phenomena. 'Climate prediction' refers to climate phenomena that are predictable (that is, their causal processes are understood to the extent that available information at time t allows us to anticipate their occurrence in place s at time $(t + \tau)$). 'Decision capacity' refers to decisions the human system is capable of actually making to improve its future state (that is, the deliberate interventions that can be chosen by the system and are compatible with the goals, resources and constraints of decision-makers). Forecasts can be useful where these three determinants coexist in space and time – in other words, where the circles in Figure 8.1 overlap.

Building on Hansen's diagram, this section identifies categories with which to approach dealing with the threats of the climate phenomena depending on which of the three realms is the focus of the proposed action. We label these three approaches as 'perfect information', 'vulnerability to hazard', and 'vulnerability to outcome'. The perfect information approach emphasizes the decision-maker's need to improve knowledge of future conditions, and assumes that once that information is available the system will optimally adapt. The vulnerability to hazards approach recognizes existing limitations in response capacity, focuses on the multiple effects of a single cause (the predictable hazard), and allows for a conceptual means of prioritizing ways to address that causal vector. Finally, the vulnerability to outcome perspective identifies the multiple causes of each undesired outcome. This allows those interested in reducing vulnerability to that

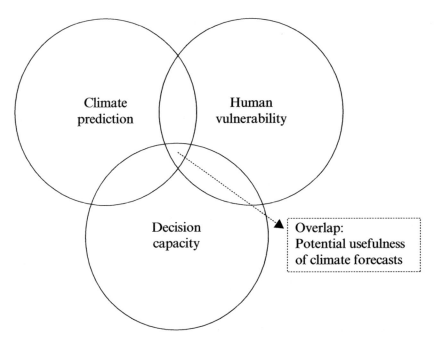

Note: This figure should not be interpreted strictly as a Venn diagram: the three sets exist in different realms (that is, they have different kinds of elements) and therefore from the perspective of set theory they do not intersect.

*Figure 8.1   Hansen's (2002) diagram relating predictions, decisions and
                     vulnerability*

outcome to target their investments in order to reduce the most salient set of socio-political causes.

Perfect Information and the Expansion of Climate Prediction

One approach for addressing the risks posed by climate change focuses on expanding climate prediction capabilities. For example, it looks to increasing investments in the monitoring and modeling of atmospheric and oceanic processes, and impact assessments, in order to improve our understanding of the potential consequences of changes in future climate conditions. In Figure 8.1, this implies expanding climate prediction and, thereby, increasing the area of overlap. Once a new prediction is made, the assumption is that this information will flow towards the relevant actors, who should properly weigh risks and uncertainties, and make rational decisions so that the system adapts to expected conditions. This approach resonates strongly with the quest for information, predictability and rationality embraced both by the scientific community and by proponents of perfect-market economic models (Jaeger et al. 2001).

The expansion of knowledge about future conditions is an essential element of the perfect-market economic paradigm. This paradigm is based on Adam Smith's postulation that the common good is reached most efficiently when each person seeks to maximize utility in a perfectly competitive market. The ability to foresee the near future has been a central topic in the history of economic theory (Coddington 1982). In the 1930s, Hayek (1935) maintained that the assumptions implied in the concept of market equilibrium 'are essentially that everybody foresees the future correctly' (pp. 139–40).

In theory, the Pareto-efficiency of market economies is obtained under a peculiar set of assumed circumstances defined initially by the Arrow–Debreu model of general equilibrium (Debreu 1959). A fundamental assumption is that of perfect information. The concept of perfect foresight captures the assumption that individuals with perfect access to information can modify their behavior in order to adapt to expected market conditions and maximize utility. Information is a key tool for production in a market economy, both in terms of connecting demand with supply, and in terms of increasing the productivity of labor, land and capital. Market forces require information. In Hayek's (1945) 'The use of knowledge in society', he refers to equilibrium prices in a decentralized market system as aggregators and conveyors of disperse information.

From the perspective of the perfect information model, markets are analogous to the luminiferous ether of physics: a medium which can be effective for transmitting all the types of physical action known to us. Just as 'substanceless' light waves were assumed to travel through the perfect substance of luminiferous ether, so the conceptualization of traditional economics sees the perfect market as the medium through which information is optimally transmitted to enable macroeconomic change (Hayward and Broady 1994).

Like other forms of information, weather and climate forecasts have economic impact insofar as they affect the decisions of individuals engaged in economic activities (Stewart 1997). The emphasis in improving climatic forecasts is a positive step forward as it allows land, labor and capital to adjust optimally to expected conditions. Whatever vulnerability is left in the system, it would be 'the right amount of vulnerability' as dictated by market forces. The assumption that the mere availability of information about the future will lead to the adoption of necessary action is still at the core of many initiatives involving the production of climate forecasts (Stern and Easterling 1999).

More than two decades ago, Lamb (1981) stated that achieving the ultimate goal of climate prediction (that is, the reduction of the negative consequences of climate variability) has two prerequisites. First, the activities and regions most affected by climate variability require identification. Second, the affected regional economies must have the flexibility to adjust to, and capitalize on, the availability of skillful forecasts. He argued that it is only after these two prerequisites are met that we can develop truly useful climate prediction systems. These requirements imply that the most vulnerable regions, sectors and individuals (for example, those unable to adjust and capitalize on the availability of forecasts) will be marginalized from the benefits of climatic information. Accordingly, this chapter chiefly argues that if the development of climate forecasts remains embedded in (and directed by) the perfect-market paradigm, those with the most pronounced need are unlikely to reap the benefits of improved climate predictability.

Imperfect Information Flow and the 'Vulnerability to Hazard' Model

Stiglitz (1986) points out that the assumption of perfect information, if questionable in more developed economies, is clearly irrelevant in less developed countries. Stiglitz's 'imperfect information model' views people as rational individuals operating in environments where information is imperfect, scarce and costly.

Johnson and Holt (1997) note that the existing system for sensing, recording and reporting weather conditions and producing forecasts has been developed primarily in response to the demands of specific market needs, such as airline navigation and agribusiness. The result is that the system for producing, storing and disseminating weather and climate information has strong linkages to the demands of major clients. There are growing discussions about the possibility of treating some meteorological services as private goods (Freebairn and Zillman 2002). Johnson and Holt suggest that discussions will continue to focus on the appropriate division between private and public responsibility.

Buckland (1991) distinguishes between the following three meanings: (1) 'information-as-process'; (2) 'information-as-knowledge'; and (3) 'information-as-thing'. While it is natural to view items that embody information as commodities, information itself is increasingly commodified (Baron 2001; Malone and Elichirigoity 2003). There is a tension between perspectives of information as a commodity with compelling 'public good' characteristics, and information as inherently a value-added product (Koenig 1995). This tension grows with increasing tensions in information technology. Several commentators have highlighted the social implications of a differentiated production of, and access to, the commodity of information (Baron 2001; Doctor 1991; Lievrouw and Farb 2003). For example, like any other commodity, the value of information is often greater from the perspective of an individual who owns it when it is not widely disseminated. For example, if only a small group of individuals know that a drought is expected, they can profit from that information. Such commodification of forecasts, however, can be very damaging.

A natural consequence of the 'information as commodity' paradigm is that the ability to acquire valuable information is determined by the consumer's assets. When climatic information is relegated as a private good it can be subject to the exclusion principle. Under this principle, those unable or unwilling to pay are excluded from the product's benefits. For example, even the cost of batteries for listening to radio programs communicating seasonal forecasts, or agricultural extension advice, may be prohibitive for some subsistence farmers who are excluded from markets that affect climate information policies.

The recognition of market imperfections in dealing with the threats of climate variability highlights an alternative means of viewing the relationship between predictions, decisions and vulnerability. Dilley and Boudreau (2001) argue that the 'vulnerability to hazard' framework – embraced by the disaster risk community since 1979 (United Nations Disaster Relief Coordinator 1979) – provides a useful theoretical structure for an easy, transparent translation of concepts into practice. In essence, the disaster risk literature delineates the following key terminology: 'hazard' (event that causes harm), 'vulnerability' (susceptibility of a certain unit to a specific event) and 'risk' (likelihood of an undesirable outcome, based on the potential occurrence of harmful events and of the susceptibility to them among those likely to be exposed). In this context, 'vulnerability is contingent on the specification of hazards or shocks' (Dilley and Boudreau 2001). By identifying the specific causal risk factors and relative degree of risk, this approach informs relative to the types of interventions, locations, timing, target population and level of effort necessary to avoid the undesired outcome. This formulation assumes exogenous causal factors. In other words, 'one key conceptual element required is a clear separation between selected causal *events* and outcomes' (p. 235, emphasis added).

For this approach, the essence of vulnerability reduction is to rearrange intrinsic characteristics of exposure units (ranging from households to regional economies) with respect to exogenous climatic factors that put them at risk. In this context, climatic information is essential for reducing vulnerability. For example, if a seasonal precipitation forecast indicates that a drought is likely to strike a certain area, this information can facilitate the process of getting food aid in time, or helping farmers to anticipate the changes and choose a type of seed that might reduce the magnitude of the anticipated food shortage.

The 'vulnerability to hazard' model argues that the key policy intervention is to expand decision capacity through preparedness and response. In this context, targeted delivery of forecasts is essential. Given the existence of information about expected extreme events, this model suggests that it is necessary to increase the ability to take action in response to the predicted climatic conditions. In the case of climate change and agriculture, examples may range from promoting and enabling the planting of appropriate seed varieties, to setting food aid distribution systems in motion. A key challenge emerging from this framework is that new climatic predictions imply the need to adapt to the potential availability of new forecasts. Thus, people and institutions need to learn about changes in climate predictability, as well as how to respond to newly available information.

A good example is provided by the Regional Climate Outlook Forum. This annual event brings together climate scientists – those who develop regional climate forecasts – and representatives from the user community. These community representatives can include disaster managers, health officials, water managers, agricultural extension agents and the media. Initiatives of this type need to be strengthened, expanded and articulated in order to ensure that the management of forecast information becomes embedded in the institutional decision-making processes of relevant actors. In addition, efforts should be made at promoting dialogue across a variety of boundaries such as those separating administrative jurisdictions, academic disciplines, economic sectors, institutional frameworks and geographic scales.

Expanding the Understanding of Causality: The 'Vulnerability to Outcome' Model

Ribot (1995) views the issue of vulnerability from a different perspective (see also Downing 1991). He begins by stating that it is misleading to designate undesired outcomes as 'impacts' of external hazards such as climate variability or change. Further, he explains that there is an initial need to explain why households came to be vulnerable in the first place. Being more concerned with social and political-economic relations and processes, Ribot embraces a 'vulnerability to outcome' approach. This approach builds on Sen's (1981) work on entitlements. Entitlements are the bundle of goods and services that a particular unit can obtain through production, exchange or extra-legal legitimate conventions. Extreme events become disasters only when entitlement systems fail. From each instance of entitlement failure, chains of causality can be traced through a historical analysis of the 'production of vulnerability' (processes involving socially differentiated access to resources and opportunities).

From this perspective, the root causes of vulnerability are related to the dynamics of social systems such as extraction, accumulation and marginalization. The fact that vulnerability is produced by ongoing processes must be considered in responses. Ultimately, the 'vulnerability to outcome' approach proposes to identify the social, political and economic processes that produce vulnerability through the allocation of state funds and through the structuring of socially differentiated access to alternative opportunities. Once identified, these processes need to be confronted, going 'beyond redistribution to identify and nurture countervailing processes' (Ribot 1995, p. 121). In this approach, climate information is welcome, but not indispensable, for vulnerability reduction. An increase in entitlements would result in climate extremes having relatively less influence on the food security of the population. Such is currently the case with localized droughts in regions of Europe and the Americas. The key to vulnerability reduction is to address resilience, increasing the options to satisfy basic needs.

In the case of climate predictions, this approach embraces the 'bundles of powers' framework. This framework is defined by Ribot and Peluso (2003) as follows: identifying the constellations of means, relations and processes that enable various actors to derive benefits from access to information. Additionally, the 'vulnerability to outcome' paradigm seeks to concentrate efforts on addressing the root causes of vulnerability. Options may include collective democratic action to reduce the price of farming inputs suitable for expected conditions. Additional options include risk-sharing through market- or community-based mechanisms, diversifying the local economy, investing in capacity building, strengthening the role of subsistence farmers' associations in the definition of regional agricultural policies, and incorporating the concerns of marginal sectors in the development of the research agenda of the natural and social sciences involving climate. In short, the idea is to identify and transform the processes that perpetuate the production of vulnerability, increasing the bundle of entitlements so that the ability to meet basic needs is not so dramatically affected by climatic extremes.

There is a need to harmonize the fields of disaster risk reduction and regional development (World Bank 2000). Sen (1996) concludes that the goal of development should be to replace the dominance of circumstances and chance over individuals by the dominance of individuals over chance and circumstances. The same could be said of climate change adaptation, particularly with regards to those disproportionately at risk.

RETHINKING THE ROLE OF CLIMATE PREDICTIONS

The large amount of resources currently being used to improve our ability to make accurate climate forecasts is not well harmonized with efforts to increase our preparedness to act on that information, or strategies to reduce our susceptibility to climate variability. This is especially true among the most vulnerable sectors of the global rural population. The current emphasis on forecast development offers us the opportunity to simultaneously embrace the recommendations of the perfect information, vulnerability to hazard, and vulnerability to outcome approaches through the process of forecast communication. Even though they reflect very different views of political economy, the policies implied by these approaches are neither inconsistent nor mutually exclusive (Table 8.1).

The dissemination of predictions at local and regional levels could be embedded in a larger process aimed at: (1) seeking to facilitate the flow of available forecasts, and identifying the critical aspects of climate phenomena that people would want to have predicted with better accuracy at the local level; (2) identifying and addressing the bottlenecks in the potential use of forecasts; and (3) exploring opportunities to address the root causes of vulnerability. This integration can lead to synergies between these three policy approaches and also innovative strategies for increasing human security and well-being. For this to occur, the use of climate forecasts needs to be incorporated not only into hazard mitigation efforts, but also into the design of regional development initiatives. By so doing, people may be assured of having the means to take advantage of climate forecasts.

There is an opportunity to integrate the three approaches, bringing together all levels of analysis in a search for short- and long-term risk reduction. The objective should be to foresee climate-related threats and reduce their direct negative effects, as well as to reduce the numerous other causes that make the direct climatic events disasters. As Dilley and Boudreau suggest, the hazards approach works best for bolstering the security of those most vulnerable to a well-defined climatic threat. The question of why those households came to be vulnerable in the first place requires a 'second level of analysis', looking into 'historical, social, political and economic developments that determine who has sufficient access to the means for ensuring their own well-being and who does not' (Dilley and Boudreau 2001).

Information about future climate conditions is most useful in two ways. First, it can serve to help people prepare to cope with the hazard. Second, it can serve as a trigger for beginning to reverse existing processes of

Table 8.1 Policy recommendations emerging from each approach

Approach	Policy recommendation	Focus
Perfect information	Produce better forecasts in order to fulfill the requirement of 'perfect foresight'. *Example:* Invest in science and technology for monitoring and modeling climate system. Improve skill of forecasts, expand their spatial and temporal coverage. Assumption: actors and markets will adjust to expected conditions.	Expand *Climate prediction*
Vulnerability to hazard	Increase the ability to take action in response to climate forecasts. *Example:* Invest in early warning systems. Improve communication and understanding of predictions. Enhance preparedness, response and recovery mechanisms.	Expand *Decision capacity*
Vulnerability to outcome	Address root causes of vulnerability. Increase ability to meet basic needs by reversing processes of marginalization. *Example:* Reduce price of agricultural inputs through collective democratic action. Diversify local economies. Strengthen role of vulnerable communities in	Reduce *Human vulnerability*

Table 8.1 (continued)

Approach	Policy recommendation	Focus
	definition of public policies. Assure fair market access and access to land and other resources.	

marginalization which contribute to converting an event into an undesired outcome. Climate predictions – when combined with analysis of likely outcomes – are particularly well suited for attracting the attention of vulnerable people who tend to be both sensitive to, and have reason to be interested in, weather and climate patterns. Participatory workshops for forecast communication convened in collaboration with local leaders can provide an opportunity for the community to come together, learn the basics of climate science as they relate to forecasting, identify and prioritize their most critical sensitivities to climate variability, and explore ways to respond to the forecast. There is evidence that this participatory approach can lead to significantly better decisions (Patt et al. 2005b). Ultimately this approach could be expanded in its scope, aiming to build resilience through action at the individual or collective level, as well as with help from government or aid organizations. Once the discussion gets started, it is possible to introduce questions about the processes that perpetuate conditions of vulnerability. This, in turn, should lead to an exploration of ways in which the community, with the help of policymakers at all levels, can fortify its assets and increase its ability to meet basic needs.

The synergies created by integrating the three approaches could provide many positive feedbacks. For example, if potential users of forecasts identify ways to put that information to good use, they may become advocates for increased investment in the development of climatic knowledge and add strength to efforts aimed at securing resources for monitoring and research. Farmers who learn about a useful prediction may also want to increase their access to other forms of information, from new agricultural practices to expected market conditions for their products, therefore improving the overall flow of information. Similarly, regional development policies that increase the bundle of entitlements of poor peasants in rural Africa would also enhance the subsistence farmers' capacity to take action to reduce risk or improve yields based on the contents of a seasonal precipitation forecast.

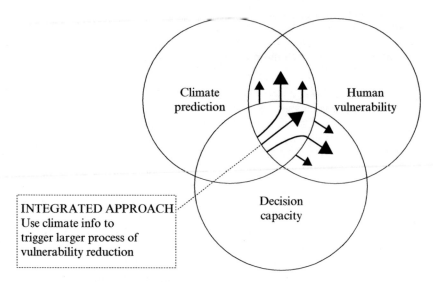

*Figure 8.2   Innovative approaches can combine the three policy
               recommendations listed in Table 8.1, aiming to reduce
               vulnerability while promoting the improvement of climate
               predictions and augmenting decision capacity*

Figure 8.2 portrays the recommended approach: a concerted, simultaneous reduction of human vulnerability and expansion of climate predictions
and decision capacity in response to those predictions, through participatory processes and government engagement aimed at increasing the usabil-
ity of climate forecasts and at reducing the risk of undesired outcomes.

CONCLUSIONS

The value of climate information depends not only on how it is used but
also on the method by which it is introduced into a particular environment. This can also contribute to vulnerability reduction by helping to
reshape the internal dynamics of the socio-economic system. The potential
role of forecasts with respect to differential vulnerabilities across regions,
productive sectors and socio-economic characteristics deserves further
investigation.

This chapter argues that the best use of climate forecasts is not just to
anticipate the future, but also to integrate them in processes aimed at identifying and resolving bottlenecks in the flow of information. In addition,
such information can be used to explore the possibility of creating and

nurturing processes that can countervail the production of vulnerability. Forecast dissemination could be implemented in creative participatory ways, thinking of information-as-process rather than information-as-commodity. In the case of climate change, efforts to communicate new knowledge will also need to address global, national and local economic, social and political obstacles to putting that information to use among the most vulnerable.

Increased understanding of atmospheric processes will, and should, continue to grow. Undoubtedly, climatic forecasts can be of high value for agricultural production and other economic activities; their potential applications for improving livelihoods are undeniable. However, market forces alone are not effective for channeling climatic information to where it can best help reduce vulnerability to famine and other disasters. If forecasts are to be used for reducing the probability of negative outcomes among the poor and most vulnerable, it is imperative to give adequate consideration to how this particular type of information is produced and disseminated. Likewise, it is important to address the constraints faced by households that deserve the highest priority with respect to this information. Without an effort to integrate forecast development with the policy options derived from the 'vulnerability to hazard' and 'vulnerability to outcome' approaches, the causal factors that perpetuate the reproduction of vulnerability will continue to create conditions of avoidable risk for marginal populations.

REFERENCES

Baron, P. (2001), 'Databases and the commodification of information', *Journal of the Copyright Society of the USA*, **49**(1): 131–63.

Brunner, R.D. (1999), 'Predictions and policy decisions', *Technological Forecasting and Social Change*, **62**(1–2): 73–8.

Buckland, M.K. (1991), 'Information as Thing', *Journal of the American Society for Information Science*, **42**(5): 351–60.

Coddington, A. (1982), 'Deficient foresight: a troublesome theme in Keynesian economics', *American Economic Review*, **72**(3): 480–87.

Debreu, G. (1959), *Theory of Value: An Axiomatic Analysis of Economic Equilibrium*, New York: Wiley.

Dilley, M. (2000), 'Reducing vulnerability to climate variability in Southern Africa: the growing role of climate information', *Climatic Change*, **45**(1): 63–73.

Dilley, M. and T.E. Boudreau (2001), 'Coming to terms with vulnerability: a critique of the food security definition', *Food Policy*, **26**(3): 229–47.

Doctor, R.D. (1991), 'Information technologies and social equity: confronting the revolution', *Journal of the American Society for Information Science*, **42**(3): 216–28.

Downing, T.E. (1991), 'Assessing socioeconomic vulnerability to famine: Frameworks, concepts and applications', Final report to the US Agency for International Development, Famine Early Warning Systems Project.

Freebairn, J.W. and J.W. Zillman (2002), 'Funding meteorological services', *Meteorological Applications*, **9**(1): 45–54.

Hansen, J. (2002), 'Realizing the potential benefits of climate prediction to agriculture: issues, approaches, challenges', *Agricultural Systems*, **74**: 309–30.

Hayek, F.A. (1935), 'Preiserwartungen, monetäre Störungen und Fehlinvestitionen', *Nationaløkonomisk Tidsskrift*, **73**(3). Translated in English as 'Price expectations, monetary disturbances and malinvestments', in F.A. Hayek (1939), *Profit, Interest and Investment and Other Essays on the Theory of Industrial Fluctuations*, London: Routledge & Kegan Paul, pp. 135–56.

Hayek, F.A. (1945), 'The use of knowledge in society', *American Economic Review*, **35**(4): 519–30.

Hayward, T. and J.E. Broady (1994), 'Macroeconomic change: information and knowledge', *Journal of Information Science*, **20**(6): 377–88.

Ionescu, C., R.J.T. Klein, K.S. Kavi Kumar and J. Hinkel (2004), 'Towards a formal framework of vulnerability to climate change', unpublished manuscript, PIK, Potsdam, Germany.

Jaeger, C.C., O. Renn, E.A. Rosa and T. Webler (2001), *Risk, Uncertainty, and Rational Action*, London: Earthscan.

Johnson, S.R. and M.T. Holt (1997), 'The value of weather information', in A.H. Murphy (ed.), *Economic Value of Weather and Climate Forecasts*, Cambridge: Cambridge University Press.

Koenig, M.E.D. (1995), 'Information policy – the mounting tension (value additive versus uniquely distributable public good)', *Journal of Information Science*, **21**(3): 229–31.

Lamb, P.J. (1981), 'Do we know what we should be trying to forecast – climatically?', *Bulletin of the American Meteorological Society*, **62**: 1000–1001.

Lievrouw, L.A. and S.E. Farb (2003), 'Information and equity', *Annual Review of Information Science and Technology*, **37**: 499–540.

Malone, C.K.L. and F. Elichirigoity (2003), 'Information as commodity and economic sector: its emergence in the discourse of industrial classification', *Journal of the American Society for Information Science and Technology*, **54**(6): 512–20.

Patt, A.G., R.J.T. Klein and A. de la Vega-Leinert (2005a), 'Taking the uncertainty in climate change vulnerability assessment seriously', *Comptes Rendus Geosciences*, **337**: 411–24.

Patt, A.G., P. Suarez and C. Gwata (2005b), 'Effects of seasonal climate forecasts and participatory workshops among subsistence farmers in Zimbabwe', *Proceedings of the National Academy of Sciences*, **102**(35): 12623–8.

Ribot, J.C. (1995), 'The causal structure of vulnerability: its application to climate impact analysis', *GeoJournal*, **35**(2): 119–22.

Ribot, J.C. and N.L. Peluso (2003), 'A theory of access: putting property and tenure in place', *Rural Sociology*, **68**(2): 153–81.

Sen, A. (1981), *Poverty and Famines: An Essay on Entitlement and Deprivation*, Oxford: Oxford University Press.

Sen, A. (1996), 'Development: which way now?', in C.K. Wilber (ed.), *The Political Economy of Development and Underdevelopment*, New York: McGraw-Hill.

Sperling, F. (ed.) (2003), 'Poverty and climate change: reducing the vulnerability of the poor through adaptation', Washington, DC: AfDB, ADB, DFID, EC DG Development, BMZ, DGIS, DECD, UNDP, UNEP and the World Bank.

Stern, P.C. and W.E. Easterling (eds) (1999), *Making Climate Forecasts Matter*, Washington, DC: National Academy Press.

Stewart, T.R. (1997), 'Forecast value: descriptive decision studies', in A.H. Murphy (ed.), *Economic Value of Weather and Climate Forecasts*, Cambridge: Cambridge University Press.

Stiglitz, J.E. (1986), 'The new development economics', *World Development*, **14**(2): 257–65.

United Nations Disaster Relief Coordinator (1979), *Natural Disasters and Vulnerability Analysis: Report of Expert Group Meeting (9–12 July 1979)*, Geneva: UNDRO.

Wang, Y.Q., L.R. Leung, J.L. McGregor, D.K. Lee, W.C. Wang, Y.H. Ding and F. Kimura (2004), 'Regional climate modeling: progress, challenges, and prospects', *Journal of the Meteorological Society of Japan*, **82**(6): 1599–1628.

World Bank (2000), *World Development Report 2000/2001: Attacking Poverty*, New York: Oxford University Press.

9. The security challenges of climate change: who is at risk and why?

Timothy Gulden

INTRODUCTION

This chapter focuses on identifying the potential security problems posed by climate change. Where the security challenges of the twentieth century were largely defined in terms of large-scale interstate conflicts (for example, World War II and the Cold War), the challenges of the twenty-first century have been typified by civil conflicts (for example, the genocide in Rwanda), and asymmetric conflicts (for example, the 'Global War on Terror'). The drivers and dynamics of such civil conflicts cannot be explained by extensions of theories developed in an interstate context (Steinbruner and Forrester 2004). Because climate change is a fundamentally disruptive force, it is important to think carefully about the implications of these disruptions for different forms of armed conflict and for human security in general.

Like the direct impacts of climate change, many of the associated conflict-related risks are likely to fall most heavily upon the poor. This fact is acknowledged in studies of resource scarcity as a driver of conflict. Still, there are other important, but less direct, connections between climate change and human conflict that add another aspect to the distributional analysis. Civil conflicts in the less developed parts of the world can pose real threats to wealthy nations. Technological responses, if not handled adequately, may threaten the wealthiest citizens of the most powerful countries.

The security challenges of climate change can be broken down into two overarching categories: (1) those which stem from the environmental disruptions of climate change itself (including uncoordinated human reactions to these events); and (2) those which stem from our coordinated attempts to avoid more catastrophic change by shifting the structure of our economies and energy production systems. The first class of problems needs to be assessed in order to understand the costs of inaction. The second class needs to be assessed in order to weigh the relative worth of various courses of action.

What follows is not an attempt to deal exhaustively with the contents of these classes, but instead to populate them along with their subcategories. An important argument contained in this chapter is that, while nuclear fission is likely to play a major role in decarbonizing the world energy supply system, security concerns make a simple scaling-up of current nuclear technologies and institutions unworkable. The production of nuclear power on the scale required to make a real contribution to climate stabilization will require a deeper reworking than has generally been appreciated of both the related technology and global institutions aimed at preventing the proliferation of nuclear weapons.

ENVIRONMENTAL SCARCITY AS A DRIVER OF CONFLICT

Climate change poses direct threats to human security through its disruptive impacts on our ability to meet the basic needs of food, water and shelter. Rising sea levels and more powerful storms threaten to displace large numbers of people, particularly in low-lying areas. At the same time radical shifts in climate pose real threats to agricultural production and to the supply of clean drinking water.

Developing countries are more vulnerable than industrialized countries to the impacts of climate change for several reasons (Moss et al. 2001). First, their economies are generally less diversified, leaving them fewer options for adaptation. Second, they generally depend on primary agricultural products and are located in warm regions which stand to lose the most in agricultural terms from climate change. Third, people in these countries tend to live more traditional lifestyles, which are more closely tied to their particular environment, than people in industrialized countries. When that environment shifts, traditional lifestyles adapt much more slowly than do industrial economies. These and other factors place the populations of developing countries in a position to be highly vulnerable to the impacts of even modest changes in climate (McCarthy et al 2001). The same can generally be said for the poorest people within all nations.

Many studies have analyzed the role of environmental scarcity as a conflict driver (Gleditsch and Theisen 2006; Khagram and Ali 2006). Notably, Homer-Dixon identified three distinct classes of scarcity and various mechanisms by which their interactions can lead to violence (Homer-Dixon 1991, 2001). He classifies environmental scarcities as demand-induced (that is, stemming from increasing population and/or increasing per capita consumption), supply-induced (that is, stemming from environmental degradation which leads to a reduced supply of such resources as clean water or arable land) and structural (that is, stemming from the uneven distribution of access to resources which leaves the majority with inadequate supply). These scarcities can interact and reinforce one another through resource capture. Resource capture occurs when a scarce resource becomes valuable and is taken over by powerful minority groups within a society. Resource capture can be caused by ecological marginalization, wherein impoverished people are driven to make use of increasingly marginal resources (for example, arable land) which are then damaged by overuse so as to lead to increased scarcity and poverty. These patterns of scarcity can lead to destabilizing social effects such as lower agricultural production, economic stagnation or decline, massive migrations out of areas of scarcity, and a weakening of governing institutions (Homer-Dixon 2001).

INDIRECT EFFECTS OF CLIMATE CHANGE ON DRIVERS OF CONFLICT

There is an intuitive relationship between climate change, resource scarcity and conflict. Thus, it is noteworthy that none of the major cross-national quantitative studies of factors that make some countries more conflict-prone than others have identified resource scarcity or other environmental factors directly affected by climate change as an important driver of conflict. The fact that environmental scarcity has not played a major role in the mainstream of quantitative conflict literature does not indicate that its role is unimportant. Its absence is likely due to the fact that its effects are indirect and often too complex to be picked up in a regression model.

Using a case-control-based logistic regression model to predict the onset of political instability (defined in such a way that political instability correlates closely with civil violence), the Political Instability Task Force (Goldstone et al. 2005) identified several consistent drivers of conflict between the middle of the twentieth century and the early years of the twenty-first century. The most notable is the combination of a factional political system with one that is only partially democratic. A factional political system is here defined as one where the major political parties represent ethnic, religious or regional groups, rather than differing policy approaches. Other consistently significant variables include having several neighboring countries also in conflict, having a government that actively condones ethnic discrimination, and having a high rate of infant mortality.

Infant mortality is not a likely driver in its own right. Instead, it is a proxy for the combination of economic development and inequality of distribution of that development. Other research has independently demonstrated that conflict is often associated with poor economic performance (Collier and Sambanis 2002). The fact that Goldstone et al. found infant mortality to be a better indicator than other measures of economic performance offers evidence that inequality, as broadly defined, is also an important contributor to political instability and violence.

There is good reason to assume a connection between poverty and scarcity on the one hand, and civil conflict and violence on the other. These two phenomena are linked regardless of whether the conditions in question consist of absolute poverty (that is, incomes below levels required for subsistence) or relative poverty (that is, the perception of inequality irrespective of income). The existence of widespread hunger and desperation, or resentment and frustration, among populations appears likely to increase competition for scarce resources. In addition, it tends to exacerbate existing social, ethnic, racial and religious tensions and encourages political and social movements to use such tensions to mobilize supporters to violence. Demonstrating these relationships, and establishing a causal link, is a challenging task for scholars.

Other quantitative work conducted by researchers at the World Bank shows a strong link between conflict and dependence on primary commodity exports (Collier 2000; Collier and Hoeffler 2001). This line of thought is known as the 'greed' theory of conflict and is distinguished from more traditional 'grievance' theories. Civil conflict, in this conception, is not driven so much by political disagreement or resistance to oppression, but rather by the desire for profits that can be used to fund further rebellion. Diversified economies are generally resistant to this kind of activity because of the mutual interdependence of their various sectors. Primary commodity exports (for example, diamonds, oil and timber), are more suited for control by an elite group, which can then operate more or less independently of the rest of the nation's economy and use the revenues from these exports to fund efforts to gain control over additional resource streams.

Though the field has not reached consensus on the relative importance of these drivers, it appears likely that greed and grievance both play major roles in the development of conflict. Sambanis (2001, 2003), using a case study approach, found that understanding the relative importance of these drivers requires appropriate categorization of conflicts according to their origin in ethnicity or economics.

Work on the relationship between economic performance and subjective well-being also has implications here (Graham and Pettinato 2002). Graham and Pettinato found that people's satisfaction with their economic

lot and with their government depends more on their performance relative
to their perceived comparison group than it does on their absolute level of
income. While rapid economic growth can go some way toward offsetting
the dissatisfaction engendered by radical inequality, people in high-growth
economies are particularly frustrated when this growth slows. In a highly
connected world where the comparison group for the average person in
the developing world includes members of the industrialized world, and
where economic growth needs to be tempered by the need to maintain a
livable atmosphere, these feelings of frustration must be anticipated and
taken seriously.

The threads of democratization, ethnic factionalization, economic inequality, elite dominance of resources and shocks to subjective well-being
are not fully integrated within the formal conflict literature. Chua provides
a relevant way of combining these issues (Chua 2003). She documents a
series of cases in which economic liberalization collided with democratization to create an environment conducive to violence. She observes that
unrestrained capitalism has, in many cases, concentrated economic power
in the hands of an ethnic minority. Examples include ethnic Chinese in
Southeast Asia, people of European decent in Latin America, and Indians
in East Africa. These groups tend to become targets of resentment on the
part of the broader population. In this environment, Chua observes that
the introduction of democratic rule empowers this broader population,
leading to potentially deadly conflict between economic and political
power centers. She notes that examples of this dynamic include the emergence of Milosovic in Serbia, Mugabe in Zimbabwe and the Hutu leader-
ship in Rwanda. Further, she analyzes the terrorist threat against the US
in these terms, casting it in the role of the economically dominant ethnic
minority, and modern communications technology as the democratizing
force that is empowering the resentful masses.

In short, while the relationship between climate change and the drivers
of civil violence is indirect and hard to quantify, it appears to be both
powerful and important. Changes in climate may create an abundance of
specific resources in some areas (for example, rainfall in northern India).
However, climate disruptions will generally lead to increased supply-
induced scarcity. This can reinforce scarcity and inequality in a way that
may eventually lead to violence.

MITIGATION AND CIVIL CONFLICT

The security challenges posed by climate change itself are among a list
of hazards to be avoided by undertaking efforts to reduce greenhouse

emissions. These are either impacts of climate change itself (for example, flooding of low-lying areas, crop failures, and so on), or they are impacts of adaptation to climate change (for example, shifting social structures as a nation grapples with decreased fresh water supply). It must be remembered, however, that many strategies for greenhouse gas reduction have their own security implications. Although the security impacts of climate change mitigation are generally harder to forecast than the effects of climate change, they are just as important.

Another important difference between threats related to adaptation and those created by mitigation policies is that the effects of climate change are essentially given (if not entirely understood), while the effects of mitigation strategies depend on the strategies chosen. The policy-maker who chooses a mitigation strategy chooses its corresponding security implications. This makes an understanding of the implications of mitigation strategies even more important because we are in a position to choose not only the degree of impact we are willing to tolerate, but also the types of problems that we are likely to face.

If not implemented with care, the measures employed to address the global climate change problem could have significant negative, and often regressive, impacts on incomes, thereby contributing to social tensions within nations that may lead to violence. For example, efforts to decrease the use of fossil fuels, or increase the use of higher-cost renewable sources, could raise electricity prices and slow the expansion of the electricity supply. Actions to address climate change could produce broader societal changes as well. Graham (Graham and Pettinato 2002) points out the dangers of stunting development in societies that have been growing, while Chua (2003) identifies the potential for violence that might emerge if a change in fuel consumption patterns or prices were to alter economic relations between an ethnic minority and the rest of society.

In countries where low-carbon energy resources are found in areas that are poor or populated by distinct ethnic or social groups, national efforts to develop these resources could galvanize opposition to such development or lead to charges of inequitable distribution of benefits. This could in turn worsen conflicts between central governments and local ones or indigenous peoples. The Indonesian province of Aceh on the island of Sumatra is an example of this kind of conflict (Ross 2002). The exploitation of this region's rich oil and natural gas deposits has figured prominently in the conflict between the government and the local separatist movement.

Research by Collier and Hoeffler (2001) has disturbing implications for a future where much of the industrialized world's energy needs are met with fuels derived from biomass. Early experience with growing corn in the US, and sugar cane in Brazil, for the manufacture of ethanol have raised concerns about energy crops driving up food prices. A major expansion of energy crops would require the use of large swaths of land. This land is likely to be located in tropical nations where growing seasons are long, water is plentiful and land prices low. In such a scenario, grower countries would be made even more dependent on primary agricultural exports, along with the concentrated streams of income and conflicts that they tend to produce.

The production of export commodities leads to the concentration of wealth among those who command the resources and have the ability to bring them into the international market. For example, if the world shifted from petroleum to ethanol for transport fuel, we might expect to see further destabilization of the current generation of petro-states with economies that are dependent on high demand for petroleum. In addition, we could find the emergence of a new class of 'biomass-states' in tropical regions. The production of commercial biomass (for example, sugar cane or – assuming advances in the manufacture of cellulosic ethanol – crops like switchgrass) involve high-volume, low-value crops which lend themselves better to mechanized production, as opposed to labor-intensive crops like coffee, cocoa or bananas. The fact that the conversion of biomass to ethanol might be most efficiently done in the originating nation does not help here since the process is highly capital-intensive. Accordingly, it is hard to see how either smallholders, or other small businesses, might fit into an economy based on ethanol production.

While such a shift might be an aggregate economic boon for tropical nations, it is likely to lead to an increased concentration of wealth in these nations. At the same time, such a shift could create the kind of hijackable resource stream shown by Collier and Hoeffler (2001) to be destabilizing. This increase of concentrated wealth, without a corresponding increase in internal economic activity, can lead to rapid urbanization and a host of related maladies. This type of phenomenon, as demonstrated in the Middle East, was dubbed by Bonine (1997) as 'petroleum urbanization'. In 1979, reflecting on the effect of the oil boom on his nation, Sheik Yamani, Oil Minster of Saudi Arabia said: 'All in all, I wish we had discovered water.' If not handled with care, large-scale exploitation of biomass has the potential to move the often unstable nations of tropical regions along a similar path.

Studies show that mitigation policies, such as carbon taxes and other measures that increase the cost of energy are also likely to impose greater burdens on poorer households (Brendemoen and Vennemo 1994; Cornwell and Creedy 1996; Aasness et al. 1996; Harrison and Kriström 1999; Barker and Kohler 1998). This is largely the case because energy expenditure consumes a larger share of the income of poorer families.

Appropriate revisions to national tax structures could go a long way toward mitigating the regressive nature of carbon taxes. The difficulty in making such revisions, however, should not be underestimated. Fully offsetting the increased basic commodity prices that poor people would face might require strong redistributive measures, such as negative income taxes. Such measures are bound to face strong opposition from more powerful groups. It seems likely that the theoretical possibility of distributionally neutral carbon taxes would be difficult to realize in poor nations.

Even more difficult would be the task of offsetting the distributional impacts of policies that raise energy prices on the global market. Strong arguments can be made that wealthy nations should compensate less wealthy ones for sacrifices made in the name of climate stabilization. However, compensation on the scale required might prove more politically difficult than national redistributive measures.

It is generally recognized that to be both widely accepted and effective, mitigation measures must also be fair. Most of the excess CO_2 emissions in the atmosphere came from industrialized countries that used the energy from its production to build wealthy, flexible economies. Less developed countries are understandably hesitant to commit to restrictions on their CO_2 emissions until they have reached a similar level of development.

Raising global living standards to a more equitable level would likely require a threefold increase in global energy production over the next 50 years. Under business-as-usual conditions, such an increase would necessarily entail a huge increase in global CO_2 emission levels – even under an optimistic assumption of relatively rapid future declines in carbon intensity. It is generally agreed that the climate will not support the kind of emissions associated with the full industrialization of the 80 percent of the world's population currently living in non-OECD (Organisation for Economic Co-operation and Development) countries. Without a corresponding commitment to reduce the use of fossil fuels dramatically, a global poverty amelioration effort would greatly exacerbate the climate change problem. The resulting climate-related impacts would then likely feed back on the entire effort, providing incentives for renewed conflict and eventually diminishing or eliminating the impact of the original anti-poverty program. However, global policies that deny the right to equal development are bound to breed resentment and discord.

To address this concern, policies must be designed to provide opportunities for sustainable development on the part of poorer nations without breaking the global carbon budget. The 1998 United Nations Development Programme (UNDP) *Human Development Report* stated: 'Poor countries need to accelerate their consumption growth – but they need not follow the path taken by the rich and high-growth economies over the past half century' (UNDP 1998). However, the responsibility for making such alternative growth paths feasible and attractive may lie as much with industrialized as it does with developing nations. Such equity concerns are being integrated into analyses of the climate change problem (for example, Munasinghe 2000; Jamieson 2000; Schelling 1997; Byrne et al. 1998; Parikh and Parikh 1998; Tolba 1998; Agarwal et al. 2000). The likely impact of these concerns on the formation of effective control regimes has also received considerable study. There exists extensive economic and political science literature that has been reviewed by the Intergovernmental Panel on Climate Change (Metz et al. 2001: 620–30).

THE CHALLENGES OF INCREASED RELIANCE ON NUCLEAR FISSION

Pacala and Socolow (2004) analyzed the mitigation problem in terms of 'stabilization wedges'. These are changes from business as usual that are intended to deflect the global greenhouse gas production curve from its current growth pattern and stabilize it at current levels for the next 50 years. They found that a combination of proven technologies is capable of achieving stabilization in emissions. Among these technologies, they propose a doubling of current world nuclear power generation (from 700 GW to 1400 GW) over 50 years. This constitutes one stabilization wedge – accounting for one-seventh of the required deflection from the business-as-usual scenario.

In a study with similar aims, Fetter (2000) identifies nine major sources of carbon-free energy. Of these, he determines that four (hydroelectric, geothermal, ocean and nuclear fusion) are unlikely to provide significant sources for additional power by the year 2050. He then identifies five technologies (nuclear fission, biomass, solar, wind and decarbonized fossil fuel) which might make significant contributions. He finds that no single technology can serve all of the carbon-free energy needs of the planet. However, it is entirely plausible that a combination of strategies will enable the world to stabilize climate while producing the 300 to 900 EJ/y of carbon-free energy needed by 2050. This amount is necessary to maintain a high level of material well-being in the OECD countries while substantially improving the material well-being of those in less developed parts of the world. He makes the case that it is difficult to envision a successful combination of policies that does not involve a major increase in the use of nuclear power.

Nuclear power is the most mature of the carbon-free technologies, and is the only one currently deployed on a significant scale. While each of the other technologies shows promise, they are unlikely to produce enough power to stabilize greenhouse gas emissions by 2050 without an increase in nuclear power. Even if an optimistic assumption of sustainable source biomass energy production is made (for example, on the order of 100 EJ/y), another 200 to 800 EJ/y would be needed from the remaining carbon-free sources.

Nuclear power also has operational advantages over other carbon-free energy sources. Nuclear power plants can be situated almost anywhere – unlike solar, wind and fossil fuel plants with CO_2 disposal. These plants can only be sited in countries and in areas with the appropriate resources. There is also an important qualitative difference between the operation of nuclear plants and renewables. Notably, the former can provide reliable 'baseload' power during most hours throughout the year on a scale sufficient to replace fossil-fired electricity. The latter can provide only intermittent power and could not supply more than 10 to 20 percent of electricity without large-scale energy storage or intercontinental electricity transmission. Neither option is affordable using current technologies (Fetter 2000).

While the exact amount of additional capacity depends on the outcomes of a host of other policy decisions, most stabilization scenarios involve a substantial increase in the use of nuclear fission. Pacala and Socolow's suggestion of a doubling of current capacity is at the low end of current estimates. Feivesion uses an eightfold increase in global nuclear capacity (to 3000 GW) by 2075 as an analytical benchmark (Feiveson 2004). Fetter and Gulden suggest that as many as 2500 GW of new nuclear capacity may be needed by 2050 (Fetter and Gulden 2005).

The number of countries reliant on nuclear power will increase as well, especially fast-growing countries that currently depend upon fossil fuels to meet much of their energy needs. Whereas countries with current nuclear power programs either already have nuclear weapons, or are industrialized democracies with a strong commitment to non-proliferation, the countries whose future energy needs are growing most rapidly are a more diverse group. Nuclear fission is only effective at reducing carbon emissions if it is brought on line as a substitute for carbon-intensive methods. One reason that Pacala's and Socolow's estimate is lower than others is that they are assuming that all of the new nuclear capacity is offsetting potential generation from coal (which has nearly double the carbon intensity of natural gas).

Population growth, growth in per capita consumption and current patterns of energy generation technology all combine to create a situation where a two- to eightfold expansion of the nuclear industry is likely to slant heavily toward the developing world. Currently, China and India are dependent on coal and have massive coal resources (IEA 2002). They are expected to increase greatly their use of nuclear fission, and their current coal reliance makes this expansion efficient in terms of reducing global carbon emissions. Nuclear fission may also become attractive for other countries with rapidly growing populations that use little or no nuclear power, including Indonesia and Pakistan. Such a large, rapid and diverse global expansion will heighten concerns about accidents, materials management and secure waste disposal. There will need to be more open international discussions concerning the best practices for handling these problems. In addition, there should be a concerted effort to develop and exchange safer nuclear technologies that can keep the risk of accidents as low as they are today; even with the expected eightfold increase in nuclear power production.

A major increase in nuclear power use will also exacerbate concerns about the proliferation of nuclear weapons. If nuclear power grows substantially, demand for low-enriched uranium will increase and the reprocessing of spent fuel may become necessary or economically attractive. Since bomb-grade plutonium is a major by-product of current reprocessing technology, additional technical and institutional barriers will be needed to prevent, deter or detect theft and diversion. This could include novel reactor concepts such as lifetime cores; new reprocessing techniques that do not involve the separation of pure plutonium; and fuel cycles that minimize the production of high-quality plutonium (for example, the thorium fuel cycle) (Galperin et al. 1997; Kasten 1998; Feiveson 2004).

INTERNATIONAL CONTROL OF NUCLEAR ENERGY

Currently, nuclear safety concerns are handled at the national level, while nuclear proliferation concerns are addressed by the Nuclear Non-Proliferation Treaty (NPT). The NPT was designed in 1970 to prevent the spread of nuclear weapons beyond the five states that already had them when the treaty was negotiated (the USA, Russia, the UK, France and China). This is achieved through a bargain in which the non-nuclear weapon states pledge not to acquire nuclear weapons and to accept International Atomic Energy Agency (IAEA) safeguards on their civilian nuclear programs. The nuclear weapon states promise not to help non-nuclear weapon states proliferate, to share nuclear technology with appropriate safeguards, and to reverse the nuclear arms race. The treaty has been largely successful. Three key states with known nuclear weapons programs (India, Pakistan and Israel) are not signatories to the treaty and so are not required to have full-scope IAEA safeguards on their civilian nuclear programs. North Korea was accused of violations and withdrew from the treaty in 2003. In 2006 it conducted a nuclear test. Iran has been embroiled in a controversy with the international community over its desire to have uranium enrichment capabilities and its nuclear weapons ambitions.

Currently, the NPT gives non-nuclear weapons states in good standing the right to enrich uranium for civilian reactors and to reprocess spent fuel for reuse under IAEA supervision. Both activities could be misused since the same processes can be used to make weapons-grade uranium or plutonium. NPT member states have devised an IAEA Additional Protocol to improve oversight at declared facilities and to help the IAEA detect clandestine nuclear activity. Compliance with the Additional Protocol is currently voluntary, and there is serious doubt as to whether full adoption of the Additional Protocol could prevent all diversion of weapons material from all nuclear facilities under national control. This is particularly likely to occur if there is a great deal of growth in civilian nuclear power and related fuel processing in non-nuclear weapons states.

Various proposals to strengthen the non-proliferation regime have been put forward (Bush 2004; Wolfsthal 2004), but these proposals suffer from political and/or technical problems. For example, the Bush administration proposed that all NPT members agree to follow the IAEA's Additional Protocol in addition to their current safeguards, and that no new countries be allowed to have their own advanced fuel-cycle capabilities. Because participation in any new obligations related to the NPT is voluntary, the burdens and benefits of additional measures must be equitably shared. Non-nuclear weapons states tend to view any extensions that further restrict their access to nuclear technology, without corresponding new commitments on nuclear disarmament, as unfair and against their national interests – thus making their broad adoption impossible.

The Director General of the IAEA has proposed an alternative approach that would reduce proliferation risks while expanding access to peaceful nuclear technology and creating a more equitable system. The proposal builds on the NPT and IAEA safeguards system while adding several new elements. Notably, it would restrict all processing of weapon-usable materials to facilities under multinational control. In addition, it proposes that all nuclear energy systems should be proliferation-resistant by design, including the accelerated conversion of all highly enriched uranium (HEU) reactors to low-enriched uranium (LEU) reactors. Further, the proposal advocates consideration of multilateral arrangements for the management and disposal of spent fuel and radioactive waste. It stresses the need for all countries to end the production of fissile material for nuclear weapons and to make further progress on nuclear arms reductions. Incentives for proliferation would be reduced through an inclusive effort to address all countries' security concerns by developing a new collective security system that does not depend on nuclear weapons or deterrence. Once in force, this new framework would be a 'peremptory norm' of international law without a right of withdrawal (El Baradei 2003; IAEA 2005).

The fundamentally international approach to fuel supply proposed by the IAEA Director General would be a real step forward in preventing the diversion or misuse of fissionable material. It would provide strong international assurance to non-nuclear weapons states that they could have reliable access to nuclear fuel and, therefore, would not need to develop a domestic fuel processing or reprocessing capability. This would place the most dangerous part (from a weapons standpoint) of the nuclear cycle under direct international control. The approach would do little to protect against accidents and the diversion of non-bomb grade nuclear material which could be used in a 'dirty bomb'.

A novel approach to integrated international control of the entire fuel cycle involves the centralization of all sensitive nuclear facilities in a few heavily guarded 'energy parks' which would be under international control. Long-life reactor cores could be sealed and exported to faraway users who would plug them into their electrical generation system, operate them for 15–20 years, and then return the sealed core with the spent fuel to a central international repository (Feiveson 2004). There would be a number of difficult technical, institutional and political problems involved in any approach that is so different from current practice. Given the magnitude of the global warming problem, a serious effort should be made not only to assess incremental expansion of existing arrangements but also to think creatively about new reactor designs and novel institutional arrangements that would be proliferation-resistant.

Any major change in the international regulation of atomic energy will require a protocol to the NPT or the adoption of an additional treaty. Since such agreements must be voluntarily adopted, the distributional implications must be considered carefully. Less powerful states will not be inclined to sign on to a treaty that leaves them worse off after signing than they were before. Further, they may not comply fully if they sign under duress (as is evidenced by the withdrawal from the treaty of North Korea). The current nuclear states should recognize that it is in their interest to promote the adoption of such a framework by making it progressive. Unlike most of the impacts of climate change, the increased threat of nuclear weapons proliferation falls at least as heavily on the urban residents of wealthy nations as it does on the rural poor of less developed ones.

CONCLUSIONS

This discussion indicates the fine balance that must be maintained if the world is to address successfully the twin problems of armed conflict and global climate change. Both represent important challenges to future global security that must be confronted. Simultaneously, however, an intensive effort to address either problem in isolation can make the other worse. There is a strong case to be made for global recognition of the interdependence of these issues, and for tackling them together, with complementary measures and approaches.

Environmental scarcities resulting from climate change can drive conflicts as societies strive to adapt. These scarcities are often hardest on the poor and those living traditional lifestyles because they tend to concentrate wealth further and lead to destabilizing resource capture by conflicting elites. Existing studies provide some leverage for thinking about these relationships, but more needs to be done to synthesize the various strands of research on civil conflict and its relationship to environmental scarcity and climate change.

Climate change mitigation strategies also raise security concerns. An abrupt shift away from oil would be extremely destabilizing for petroleum-producing nations, many of which are already marginally stable. A major shift toward biomass as a source of energy could give tropical nations some of the same problems that petroleum-producing states currently suffer. These stem from reliance on a single export commodity, concentrated wealth and hijackable income streams.

While most of the security-related impacts of climate change adaptation and mitigation will fall hardest on the poor in developing nations, the likely need for increased reliance on nuclear fission is a major exception. The most direct threat stemming from a greatly expanded and more widely distributed nuclear industry would be the potential for the illicit development or diversion of bomb-grade fissionable materials by additional states or non-state actors. Nuclear weapons threaten cities – even in wealthy nations. It is therefore in the interest of wealthy nations to take strong steps to place the nuclear fuel cycle under credible international control. It may even be in the interest of developed nations to place the whole of the nuclear power generation system under such control by underwriting international efforts to supply sealed nuclear cores on terms that are sufficiently attractive that non-nuclear nations would be willing to give up the right to independent nuclear programs. This would likely require real concessions on the part of wealthy nations, and security threats associated with free-market development of sufficient nuclear power capacity may justify such an investment.

Understanding the distributional impacts of the security implications of both climate change, and efforts to control climate change, is far from simple. Thus there remains a great deal of work to be done in this area. This chapter has outlined some of the major issues and makes the case that this area is an important one. Our analysis indicates that failure by wealthy nations to consider these security implications is not only unjust but also unwise.

REFERENCES

Aasness, J., T. Bye and H.T. Mysen (1996), 'Welfare effects of emission taxes in Norway', *Energy Economics*, **18**(4): 335–46.

Agarwal, A., S. Narain and A. Sharma (2000), *Green Politics*, New Delhi: Center for Science and Environment.

Barker, T., and J. Kohler (1998), 'Equity and ecotax reform in the EU: achieving a 10% reduction in CO_2 emissions using excise duties', *Fiscal Studies*, **19**(4): 375–402.

Bonine, M.E. (1997), 'Population, poverty and politics in the urban Middle East: an overview', in M.E. Bonine (ed.), *Population, Poverty, and Politics in Middle East Cities*, Gainesville, FL: University Press of Florida.

Brendemoen, A. and H. Vennemo (1994), 'A climate treaty and the Norwegian economy: a CGE assessment', *Energy Journal*, **15**(1): 77–93.

Bush, G.W. (2004), 'Remarks on weapons of mass destruction: Proliferation', National Defense University, Washington, DC, http://www.whitehouse.gov/news/releases/2004/02/20040211-4.html.

Byrne, J., W. Young-Doo, H. Lee and J. Kim (1998), 'An equity and sustainability-based policy response to global climate change', *Energy Policy*, **26**(4): 335–43.

Chua, Amy (2003), *World on Fire: How Exporting Free Market Democracy Breeds Ethnic Hatred and Global Instability*, New York: Doubleday.

Collier, Paul (2000), 'Economic Causes of Civil Conflict and their Implications for Policy', World Bank, 15 June 2000.

Collier, Paul, V.L. Elliot, H. Hegre, A. Hoeffler, M. Reynal-Querol and N. Sambanis (2003), *Breaking the Conflict Trap: Civil War and Development Policy*, Washington, DC: World Bank.

Collier, Paul and Anke Hoeffler (2001), 'Greed and grievance in civil war', World Bank, 21 October.

Collier, Paul and Nicholas Sambanis (2002), 'Understanding civil war: a new agenda', *Journal of Conflict Resolution*, **46**(1): 3.

Cornwell, A. and J. Creedy (1996), 'Carbon taxation, prices and inequality in Australia', *Fiscal Studies*, **17**(3): 21–38.

El Baradei, Mohamed (2003), 'Towards a safer world', http://www.iaea.org/NewsCenter/Statements/2003/ebTE20031016.shtml.

Feiveson, H.A. (2004), 'Nuclear proliferation and diversion', *Encyclopedia of Energy*, Volume 4. San Diego: Elsevier, pp. 433–47.

Fetter, Steve (2000), 'Energy 2050', *Bulletin of the Atomic Scientists*, **56**(4): 28–38.

Fetter, Steve and Tim Gulden (2005), 'Decarbonizing the global energy system:

implications for energy technology and security', CISSM Working Paper, April, http://cissm.umd.edu/papers/display.php?id=5.

Galperin, A., P. Reichert and A. Radkowsky (1997), 'Thorium fuel for light water reactors: reducing the proliferation potential of nuclear power fuel cycle', *Science and Global Security*, **6**(3): 265–90.

Gleditsch, N.P. and O.M. Theisen (2006), 'Resources, the environment, and conflict', Centre for the Study of Civil War, PRIO, Norwegian University of Science and Technology, Trondheim, Norway, http://www.prio.no/files/file48356_gleditsch_theisen_160906.doc.

Goldstone, Jack A., Robert H. Bates, Ted Robert Gurr, Michael Lustik, Monty Marshall, Jay Ulfelder and Mark Woodward (2005), 'A global forecasting model of political instability', presented at American Political Science Association, Washington, DC, 1–4 September, http://globalpolicy.gmu.edu/pitf/PITFglobal.pdf.

Graham, Carol and Stefano Pettinato (2002), *Happiness and Hardship: Opportunity and Insecurity in New Market Economies*, Washington, DC: Brookings Insitution Press.

Harrison, G.W. and B. Kriström (1999), 'General equilibrium effects of increasing carbon taxes in Sweden', in R. Brännlund and I.-M. Gren (eds), *Green Taxes: Economic Theory and Empirical Evidence from Scandinavia*, Cheltenham, UK and Northampton, MA, USA: Edward Elgar.

Homer-Dixon, Thomas F. (1991), 'On the threshold: environmental changes as causes of acute conflict', *International Security*, **16**(2): 76–116.

Homer-Dixon, Thomas F. (2001), *Environment, Scarcity and Violence*, Princeton, NJ: Princeton University Press.

International Atomic Energy Agency (IAEA) (2005), 'Multilateral approaches to the nuclear fuel cycle: Expert Group report submitted to the Director General of the International Atomic Energy Agency', INFCIRC/640, 22 February, http://www.iaea.org/Publications/Documents/Infcircs/2005/infcirc640.pdf.

International Energy Agency (IEA) (2002), *Coal in the Energy Supply of India*, IEA, http://www.iea.org/Textbase/publications/free_new_Desc.asp?PUBS_ID=1101.

Jamieson, D. (2000), 'Climate change and global environmental justice', in P. Edwards and C. Miller (eds), *Changing the Atmosphere: Expert Knowledge and Global Environmental Governance*, Cambridge, MA: MIT Press.

Kasten, P.R. (1998), 'Review of the Radkowsky thorium reactor concept', *Science and Global Security*, **7**(3): 237–69.

Khagram, S. and S. Ali (2006), 'Annual review of environment and resources', *Environment and Security*, **31**: 395–411.

McCarthy, J., O. Canziani, N. Leary, D. Dokken and K. White (eds), (2001), *Climate Change 2001: Impacts, Adaption, and Vulerability*, Contribution of Working Group II to the Third Assessment Report of the Intergovernmental Panel on Climate Change, Cambridge: Cambridge University Press.

Metz, B., O. Davidson, R. Swart and J. Pan (eds), (2001), *Climate Change 2001: Mitigation*, Contribution of Working Group III to the Third Assessment Report of the Intergovernmental Panel on Climate Change, Cambridge: Cambridge University Press.

Moss, Richard H., E.L. Malone and A.L. Brenkert (2001), *Vulnerability to Climate Change: A Quantitative Approach*, Pacific Northwest National Laboratory, http://www.globalchange.umd.edu/publications/PNNL-13765.pdf.

Munasinghe, M. (2000), 'Development, equity and sustainability in the context of climate change', in M. Munasingha and R. Swart (eds), *Proceedings of the IPCC Expert Meeting on Development, Equity and Sustainability*, Colombo, 27–29 April 1999, Geneva: IPCC and World Meteorological Organization.

Pacala, S. and R. Socolow (2004), 'Stabilization wedges: solving the climate problem for the next 50 years with current technologies', *Science*, **305**(5686): 968–72.

Parikh, J. and K. Parikh (1998), 'Free ride through delay: risk and accountability for climate change', *Journal of Environment and Development Economics*, **3**(3): 347–409.

Ross, Michael L. (2002), 'Resources and rebellion in Aceh, Indonesia', paper prepared for the Yale–World Bank project on the economics of political violence, University of California Los Angeles, Department of Political Science, 7 November, http://www.polisci.ucla.edu/faculty/ross/ResourcesRebellion.pdf.

Sambanis, Nicholas (2001), 'Do ethnic and nonethnic wars have the same causes?', *Journal of Conflict Resolution*, **45**(3): 259–81.

Sambanis, Nicholas (2003), 'Expanding economic models of civil war using case studies', Yale University, unpublished paper, http://www.nyu.edu/gsas/dept/politics/seminars/ns1110.pdf.

Schelling, T.C. (1997), 'The cost of combating global warming', *Foreign Affairs*, **76**(6): 8–14.

Steinbruner, John and Jason Forrester (2004), 'Perspectives on civil violence: a review of current thinking, in W. Lahneman (ed.), *Military Intervention: Cases in Context for the 21st Century*, Lanham, MD: Rowman & Littlefield Publishers, pp. 1–27.

Tolba, M.K. (1998), *Global Environmental Diplomacy: Negotiating Environmental Agreements for the World, 1973–1992*, Cambridge, MA: MIT Press.

UNDP (United Nations Development Programme) (1998), *Human Development Report 1998*, New York: Oxford University Press.

Wolfsthal, J.B. (2004), 'Assessing proposals on the international nuclear fuel cycle', Weapons of Mass Destruction Commission paper no. 11, June, http://www.wmdcommission.org/files/No11.pdf.

10. Distributional effects and change of risk management regimes: explaining different types of adaptation in Germany and Indonesia

Hellmuth Lange, Heiko Garrelts, Winfried Osthorst and Farid Selmi

INTRODUCTION

For a long time, the primary concern of both environmentalists and political decision-makers was to mitigate human activities that negatively impact climate systems. However, climate research shows that even when such mitigation efforts succeed, for a long time the specific inertia of the climate system will still confront societies with negative follow-on consequences of past human impacts on the system. Adaptation, which has been identified as an issue of increasing importance in the Third, and Fourth, Assessment Reports of the Intergovernmental Panel on Climate Change (IPCC), has thus become an additional core challenge.

Adaptation to potential future damage that, due to prognostic uncertainty, can only be extrapolated in terms of probabilistic equations means coping with risk. Risk typically derives from processes of both man-made climate change and 'normal' natural extreme events. The general aim is to reduce the vulnerability of society and of particularly exposed social groups with regard to expectable impacts from nature. This understanding links adaptation to socio-economic and institutional factors, as well as political and cultural processes, that determine how people respond to external hazards (Adger et al. 2004: 6; Lindseth 2005: 64).

Adaptation thus includes changes in institutional arrangements, public policies, public and private spending, and investments in infrastructure and other durable goods. All of these changes have considerable distributional effects. Besides a redistribution of risks and resources between different social groups, resources between institutions may also be redistributed (Paavola and Adger 2004: 175). Relevant differentiations are between long-term incremental adaptation, and short-term modifications, in order to prevent exceeding critical thresholds and flipping to alternative states of equilibrium (resilience) (Barnett 2001: 980). Further distinctions with relevance to adaptation in general, and political decision-making in particular, are between autonomous and planned reactions, and between reactive or anticipatory adaptation, respectively (IPCC 2001: 884).

The growing demand for adaptation has triggered a vivid academic discussion on types, forms and core characteristics of adaptation. The 'anatomy of adaptation' can be framed by the following three questions as posed by Smit et al. (2000): (1) Adaptation to what? (2) Who or what adapts? (3) How does adaptation occur? The core question here is how adaptation becomes an issue of political decision-making and, therefore, leads to conceptual changes. At the heart of our analysis are factors decisive for the design, scope and choice of policy instruments, as well as the timing and pace of their introduction.

Following Nancy Roberts (1998), policy change can happen in two dimensions: pace and scope. Kingdon's policy window approach (Kingdon 1984) provides a suitable framework for analyzing such differences in more detail. He interprets policy change as an interaction between external events (such as natural hazards), activities of political or societal actors, and particularities of the political system that result in situational opportunities for change. In this perspective different types of adaptation can be analytically connected to different constellations of social concern, institutional settings, political activities and actor constellations. Kingdon highlights non-rationality as an obvious feature of political action. However, political action is not beyond all rationality. It can be analyzed by focusing upon the underlying rationales of discursive struggles between actors and actor coalitions. Discourses are of particular relevance for either legitimizing or delegitimizing existing political and conceptual arrangements (Hajer 1995), which is an important prerequisite of almost any political change.

We demonstrate this idea by referring to three empirical cases of conceptual adaptation to risk. In doing so, we restrict our analysis to observable changes in the perceptions of problems and related political concepts. Our main focus is on changes at the discourse level; it is not on the respective implementation processes with their distinct problems and contradictions. The first two cases are closely related to forecasted effects of climate change; the third case is a response to the threats of 'normal' natural disasters:

- The first case deals with limited change within the German regime of coastal protection at the storm-prone German North Sea coast, an area assumed to be affected by ongoing sea level rise (Case A).
- The second case investigates the rapid introduction of new forms of risk management in Germany after a severe river flooding event in 2002 (Case B).
- The third case bears on the post-2004 introduction of a fundamentally different disaster risk management concept in Indonesia in response to a series of devastating natural disasters (Case C).

Differences between Germany and Indonesia are obvious in both geophysical respect and related risk patterns as well as in socio-economic and political respect. However, these differences are clearly not congruent with the pace and scope of the conceptual change that occurred in the realm of risk management. Instead, all cases reveal a striking significance of risk analysis, capacity building and institutional learning in multilevel contexts; in short, the introduction of adaptation-related governance schemes.

Our cases elucidate the conditions in which the employment of adaptive concepts is likely. It is not the mere intensity of natural events in terms of (for example) meteorological and geological features that explains significant differences in the pace and scope of conceptual change. Even in the two cases in which far-reaching concepts were introduced (Cases B and C), other factors exerted relevant influence on the orientations and situational perceptions of public actors. In doing so, they contributed significantly to the resulting concepts of disaster management and risk management. In particular, overarching shifts in power relations and governance structures proved relevant. In the Indonesian case (Case C) the ongoing decentralization process of the entire political system proved to be important. In the case of the German flood management regime (Case B), the political orientation and specific political concerns of the former government of Social Democrats and the Green party[1] impacted heavily. As for the case of the German coastal protection regime (Case A), we will argue that it is not only the absence of severe disasters since 1962 that accounts for the slow and only gradual adaptation, despite increasing pressure to prepare for changing vulnerability. Rather, the existing institutions had remarkable difficulties in attuning to the core implications of the more recent scientific debate on climate chance.

Our argument will be deployed in five sections. In the second section we develop a conceptual framework that provides criteria for the investigation of our case studies with regard to the relevance of external events, the stability of the overall political environment, decisive political actors' constellations, and the proliferation of risk management concepts. The third section presents an account of the three case studies. The fourth section discusses the core characteristics of these cases in light of the analytical framework from a comparative perspective. Finally, the fifth section draws some conclusions that highlight the interdependence between political processes, situational factors and external events. Further, it addresses constellations that foster the emergence of risk management concepts requiring profound change.

CONCEPTUAL FRAMEWORK

As a fundamental prerequisite for an assessment of adaptation, we apply the typology of Nancy Roberts (1998) which identifies four ideal types of change by distinguishing them according to pace and scope (Table 10.1). Changes can be slow (adjustment[2]) or fast (transformation); their scope can embrace the entire system, separate subsystems or even elements. Roberts (1998) defines the resulting types, which may overlap in reality, as follows. Element adjustment refers to minimal modifications in one part of the system to ensure that the elements are converging with other parts. A system adjustment is a change in the system itself rather than a modification in one of its parts that occurs over a long period of time. Element transformation can be understood as a dramatic break in a system's element in a short period of time. The system itself, however, does not undergo a radical reconfiguration. System transformation, finally, represents a shift from one system to another in a very short period of time (Roberts 1998: 110).

Despite all differences, all types of change, as identified above, are reactions to the perceived necessity to take action in spite of uncertainty. Whether the resulting form of adaptation really leads to adequate political response is another story (Yohe and Tol 2002). This is true even in cases where there exists a potentially high adaptive capacity based on indicators such as economic resources, technology, skills and infrastructure (Naess

Table 10.1   Four ideal types of change

		Scope of change	
		Part	Whole
Pace of change	Slow	Element adjustment	System adjustment
	Fast	Element transformation	System transformation

Source: Based on Roberts (1998, p. 109).

et al. 2005: 125). In any case, response can take very different routes. This raises the question why adaptation occurs – and why and when it does not (Lindseth 2005: 65). The research on adaptation identifies some factors that are relevant in this context:

- First, institutions have a considerable effect. They decide which localities or social groups are particularly vulnerable to conse-quences of climate change or more general risks. Further, they are decisive in providing mechanisms for management of specific aspects of the society that are risk sensitive. Thus, they affect the capacity to adapt (Adger 2000; Naess et al. 2005: 126).
- Second, policy-driven recommendations for adaptive measures have a normative character. Obviously, the perceptions of climate change, as well as the necessity and the extent of adaptation, differ substantially between (natural) scientists, politicians and among various stakeholders. Their starting points to assess the effects and priorities for reactions are shaped not only by diverging interests but also by varying beliefs and social preferences (Burton et al. 2002; Lindseth 2005).

These findings highlight that adaptation interferes with the internal dynamics of political and societal processes to achieve a specific outcome. Therefore, an 'objective' demand for adaptation needs to be linked to political constellations and to the political and societal structures as frame conditions. Hence, it is evident that adaptation is not solely a technical matter of implementation but a case of complex policy change, too.

This is accompanied by a redistribution of resources between social groups or societal sectors, but also between levels of government, different branches of administrations and relevant policies. Further, it encompasses shifts in approaches and shared beliefs embedded in institutions, as well as in interaction between actors that legitimate the distribution of resources and competencies among institutions. These aspects highlight the contested nature of change and, in our context, the need for theoretical perspectives that help understand the interdependence between problems, perceptions, institutions and actors, as different dimensions of such processes.

An approach that addresses the relation between these aspects, and thus may be particularly valuable to explain the emergence of risk management regimes, is the 'policy window' approach of John Kingdon (1984). Similar to the approach of Roberts, it is rooted in organizational and political theory which analyzes change as a multi-faceted and therefore not always unequivocal process. Both approaches reject the idea of given problems and preferences (which rational choice approaches assume; compare

Olson 1965), and of well-defined, target-oriented and coordinated processes (which the problem cycle approach takes for granted; compare Easton 1965).

At the heart of Kingdon's approach lies the differentiation between three process streams: namely a problem stream, a policy stream and a politics stream. Kingdon holds that each stream is largely independent of the others. Further, each develops according to its own dynamics and rules. Elements of the problem stream may be events like crises and disasters. Problems are recognized independently of available solutions. The policy stream refers to instruments, conceptions, ideas, proposals, speeches, and so on that are generated by a community of specialists like bureaucrats, politicians, interest groups or academicians. The politics stream contains changes in the political environment such as election results or a new administration. Far-reaching policy changes occur when the three streams (problems, policies and politics) coincide with a choice opportunity. These 'policy windows' – sometimes predictable, sometimes not – are opened by events, in either the problem or the political stream, such as catastrophes or shifts in socio-economic and political contexts. Linkage of the streams often depends on skilful policy entrepreneurs (for example, scientists, politicians or citizens) willing to invest resources to develop concepts and to engage in bargaining. In many cases these actors collaborate in so-called advocacy coalitions (Sabatier 1988) or epistemic communities (Haas 1992). Thus, the appearance of the right entrepreneur at the right time is crucial for the scope and pace of change.

In policy windows, the three streams are 'coupled into a package' (Kingdon 1984: 21), and 'advocates push their solution' (p. 173). The question remains: what are these packages and solutions about? While the policy window approach rightfully points to the irrationality of political processes by underlining the aspect of anarchic interactions between different spheres of social reality, we need to go into more detail regarding the 'result' of such processes. At this point, discourses become relevant, not least in elucidating underlying rationalities of political decision-making.

According to Hajer (1995: 44), discourses can be seen as a specific ensemble of concepts and categories giving meaning to physical and social realities. The aim of actors in discourse coalitions is to maintain or to gain discourse dominance by delegitimizing the discourses of their scientific and/or political opponents (Hajer 1995: 62). Issues are framed in a strategic manner (Szarka 2004: 318) in order to provide answers to four questions: What is the problem? What information is relevant? What has to be done to cope with the problem? Who can do it best? This framing can occur in public controversies or in professional circles. The outcomes of discursive struggles assign roles as well as competencies and resources for

Table 10.2   Two constellations for policy windows resulting in limited and profound change

	Conceptual change – the policy stream	Reality test – the problem stream	Political environment – the politics stream
Case of element adjustment	Weak	None	Stable
Case of system transformation	Strong	Yes	Profound change

their fulfillment to institutions, agencies, actors and even levels of government. As a consequence, they have a significant distributional effect

Investigation of these dimensions of change, when applied to different cases of the emergence and evolution of risk management regimes, provide us with insights into mechanisms that drive the development of distinct forms of management. In comparing the elements that characterize cases of strong change and the outcomes of such processes, we can identify conditions by which adaptation actually occurs. Our expectation is that forms of strong change will be fostered by constellations in which elements of all streams coincide. Cases of limited change will be characterized by weak values for the different elements (see Table 10.2). In these contexts, discursive struggles between actor coalitions are core elements in change processes and are thus parts of the frames for policy windows.

In our three cases we analyze whether external events occurred (problem stream); whether and to what extent changes in the political environment contributed to the growth of new risk management concepts (politics stream); and whether promoters of new concepts were able to offer alternative problem perceptions (policy stream) that challenge established institutions in discursive struggles. Further, we will highlight which distributional effects can be identified in the different cases: first, with regard to different potential consequences for groups of the population; and second, concerning the allocation of resources, competencies or power between competing institutions. For both forms of (re)distribution, the (de)legitimizing role of discursive struggles is highlighted.

Methodologically, all three case studies build on interviews with administrative officers and selected stakeholders. The interviews provided both expert knowledge on the cases under investigation, and insights into different conceptual approaches, problem perceptions and normative backgrounds of the various actors. Further, documents were analyzed in a manner which provided additional background information on, and an extended understanding of, the actors' perceptions of the problem. The studies combine elements of both an actor-oriented policy analysis, and a discourse analysis (Hajer 1995).

THREE CASES: SLOW AND RAPID ADAPTATIONAL CHANGE

Flood Protection on the German North Sea Coast: Between Safety and Risk[3]

Coastal protection in Germany is being planned and executed on the state level. The pivotal actor is the public administration in charge. Its core assignments are threefold:

1. Technical maintenance of the dykes and other protective buildings (like sluices and water barriers).
2. Dimensioning: assessing and fixing the necessary height, firmness and related constructive features of the protective constructions.
3. Monitoring and integrating external expertise on technical, meteorological and climate issues.

The most relevant point here is the procedure by which the necessary height and strength of the protective constructions are assessed. The procedure currently in force is strictly empirical. The highest tide gauge ever reported has served, and is still serving, as a reference point. All other technical data are derived from this gauge. The only element without a clear empirical basis is a safety margin to be added to this measurement.[4] Flood occurrence is thus conceived as swinging within the boundaries of the highest and lowest tides ever reported. As far as changes in the swings as a consequence of climate change are concerned, they are – more implicitly than explicitly – assumed to evolve in a continuous and essentially linear way. Therefore, the potential consequences of climate change are considered as calculable in principle, and the procedure that builds on this assumption is seen as one that can provide (and guarantee) equal safety at all sections of the coastline. Actually, this way of assessing the necessary dimensions of flood protection facilities has worked well.

Hence, the formula 'Equal safety at all sections of the coastline' has become the general guideline of how to manage coastal protection successfully.[5] However, it is this 'safety discourse' which stands in partial contrast to the current findings of climate research (IPCC 2001, 2007a, 2007b). As the climate system may react in an unprecedented way, safety will become an aim that can hardly be calculated any longer on measurements of past extreme events. Instead, and due to the absence of knowledge based on practical experience, (different) risks must be considered probabilistically and decided politically. Risk-related decisions can be seen as following a precautionary principle. In that sense, a 'risk discourse' emerges that questions conventional assumptions regarding date of occurrence, frequency, extent and regional specifics of future extreme events. Such a discourse challenges any claim of the ability to guarantee equal safety and manageability of future extreme events. The subsequent questions are whether, and how, administrative officers are ready to shift from the firmly established safety discourse to a risk discourse; and what decisions must be made to reassess and adjust the system of coastal protection today and in the future.

Unsurprisingly, our interviews[6] give evidence that the administrative officers in charge feel very uneasy in view of such widespread uncertainty. On the one hand, uncertainty about what will, and what can, happen does not mesh with the specific responsibility and professional ethos of the administrative officers. They are responsible for assuring that the protective constructions will be strong enough under any conditions. It is a matter of professional self-esteem to be able to ensure that this goal will be achieved. As the safety discourse builds on assessing the required features of the protective constructions in a retrospective and strictly empirical way, it tends systematically to repel uncertainty as core feature of model-based climate research and its probabilistic assumptions. On the other hand, the scientific debate on climate change with its emphasis on uncertainty as an ever more constitutive element cannot not be ignored.

Monitoring and assessing the scientific debate, as one of the three core assignments of the administration in charge (assignment 3, see above), initially was just an add-on. Its main purpose was to ensure that new information was continuously assessed in technical terms and, if necessary, utilized in improving the technical quality of the constructions. Now, being faced with the challenge to consider conceptual readjustments, considering the emergence of risk instead of consistently insisting on providing for safety, the assignment of observing and monitoring the scientific debate has gained importance. In fact, meanwhile, more emphasis has been placed on:

• assessing the findings of the scientific debate on climate change more systematically; and
• filtering out findings of potential importance for coastal protection on the German North Sea coast.

In practice, this tends to boil down to dividing the findings of climate research into two: findings that are judged to be relevant and findings that are denied to be of relevance. Although there is basically nothing wrong with this, the important question is: what is the criterion for ascribing or denying relevance?

Our interviews exhibit one general criterion: the degree of certainty with which data and scenarios are associated. Looking at the subunits of the administrations which are in charge of the more technical and practical dimensions of coastal protection (assignment 1), another tendency can be recognized: to consider only those findings that have been approved by their own 'in-house' specialists who are in charge of monitoring and assessing the ongoing scientific debate (assignment 3).[7] The expected practical use of this process is to reduce uncertainty in administrative planning and thus to avoid costly precautionary investments.

Thus, the administrative officers entrusted with coastal protection in both the subunits in charge of monitoring and assessing new scientific knowledge, as well as in the subunits in charge of more practical and technical responsibility, tend to only readjust the conceptual framework of coastal protection by accepting uncertainty and risk when the findings of the general scientific debate are accepted to be sufficiently certain. In this way, a rather paradoxical transformation of knowledge takes place. It strives for precaution without accepting the element of uncertainty which lies at the core of the precautionary principle. It aims at retaining the deterministic and empirically based safety discourse, and the related routines of assessing and safeguarding coastal protection, without openly rejecting the probabilistic approach of the risk discourse so dominant within the framework of today's climate research community.

In the investigated coastal area, this procedure for political decision-making continues as the accepted norm for matters related to coastal protection. Reasons for this adherence include the fact that this does not require additional investment. Further, the respective coastal zone, so far, has not been hit by a heavy or disastrous meteorological extreme event in a long time.

Flood Protection in German River Basins: Incorporating Risk and Uncertainty

In August 2002 heavy rains led to unprecedented floods in Central Europe and caused severe damage and the loss of 100 human lives in Austria, the Czech Republic and southeast Germany. Compared to floods in the past (along the River Rhine in the 1990s, for example), the damage was much greater. Around 100 000 people had to be evacuated. The total economic losses due to natural disasters in that year were estimated at about €15–16 billion, much of this uninsured. The highest losses occurred in Germany, at €9 billion (Becker and Grünwald 2003). Although Europe had not been exempt from floods in the past, the severity of that disaster seemed to have shocked not only the victims, but governments, planners and insurers as well: 'It was as if wealth, infrastructure and order were being unfairly challenged by nature, in societies that considered themselves immune or robust, unlike the less developed countries' (Wisner et al. 2004: 201). Immediately after the flood, discussions relative to its causation began. Two primary arguments surfaced from these discussions. One was represented by the mass media. It referenced the impacts of global warming and climate change, as the frequency of both floods and extreme rainfall events has increased (Nachtnebel 2003: 6–8; Wisner et al. 2004: 201). The second was loosely connected to environmentalists and the Green movement (Wisner et al. 2004: 202). It focused on the loss of retention capacity in the river basin and sparked a widespread debate considering direct human intervention as an additional and worsening cause. Urbanization, accumulating economic value in flood-prone areas, as well as river engineering like the canalization of rivers, was regarded as particularly relevant (Mechler and Weichselgartner 2003).

After 2002, discussions on floods and on how to cope with an increased flood risk in the future intensified in several affected European countries, dealing with the question of how to cope with flood risk in future. Popular conceptions of floods gained influence, emphasizing the 'needs of nature' and the inappropriate behavior of man in relation to such needs (Wisner et al. 2004: 202).

In Germany, this debate took place shortly before the general elections. This resulted in what was widely perceived as a very close race. Against this background, the intense and immediate assistance provided during the floods and immediately after 'boosted the government's poor standing in the polls during the run-up to the elections' (Mechler and Weichselgartner 2003: 2). The government followed up its firm handling of this crisis by proposing recommendations aimed at avoiding a repeat of the devastation. These recommendations included calling a halt to all construction projects designed to improve rivers for shipping traffic until the government had completed its review of the environmental consequences. The government also proposed an end to building on flood plains and the removal of some flood defenses like dykes to allow rivers to swell naturally, thus reducing pressure downstream.

In 2005 these measures were enacted as the Flood Control Act (BMU 2005). This enactment, however, was the result of a contentious policy debate in which the government appeared on one side, with the German

Länder (federal states) on the other (Jekel 2005). This Act envisages amendments in the Water Resources Act, the Town and County Planning Code, the Federal Regional Planning Act, the Federal Waterways Act, and the law governing the German Weather Service. Under the new law the *Länder* are required to develop plans which coordinate flood protection along the rivers for the next four years. In developing these plans, the interests of upstream and downstream users of a water body must be coordinated. The underlying rationale is that every upstream flood defense construction could increase risks downstream. In addition, the *Länder* are required to designate flood-prone zones, assuming a flood that has the likelihood of occurring once in 100 years (BMU 2005). Flood plains and flood-prone zones must be marked in spatial and development plans in order to point to the danger of flooding at an early stage. The concerned public must also be involved in the decision-making process. The aim is to raise awareness among both the general public and planning authorities. It was the first time that a federal law had prohibited planning new buildings in flood plain areas. Another 'innovation' of this Act is its focus on ensuring that potential damage will be as minor as possible. For example, in flood zones, computing centers and oil-fired heating systems are no longer allowed to be installed in the basement of a building (BMU 2003).

The key message consists of a paradigm shift from a 'safety mentality', with its promise of protection, to a 'risk culture' and strategies to cope with floods. The latter message fits into the precautionary principle. This means that the separation between those involved with flood risk reduction and those involved with coping with the floods has to be overcome. Flood risk reduction and flood response are 'cross-sectional tasks and require a great deal of communication, cooperation and management. All participants from different specialist and spatial areas must be better integrated with each other' (DKKV 2004: 6; Friesecke 2004: 14–15). In addition, as more weight is given to participatory procedures, a risk culture can be regarded as a process (compare Stirling 2003).

These measures are not novel. They are very similar to guidelines recommended by the Working Group on Water of the German *Länder* (LAWA) which depict a forward-looking model of flood protection. In June 1994 the German *Länder* Ministers for the Environment instructed the LAWA to develop the guidelines which were drawn up in November 1995 (ZENEB 2002). Unlike the governmental program of 2002, its stipulations never became mandatory regulations due to political resistance by different stakeholders (local and regional development actors). It needed exceptional political circumstances to disprove and delegitimize the so far dominant safety discourse.

A New Disaster Risk Discourse in Indonesia

The Republic of Indonesia is the largest archipelagic nation in the world and geographically straddles three tectonic plates (the Eurasian, Indo-Australian and Pacific plates). This location makes Indonesia particularly prone to natural disasters, whose impacts are frequently exacerbated by human activities. Over the decade 1994–2004, approximately 6.8 million people in Indonesia fell victim to one of these disasters (MPBI 2006). Although most disasters are natural occurrences, their roots often lie in human activities. This is particularly true for rapid and poorly adapted economic growth which may lead to substantial changes in environmental conditions and higher levels of vulnerability in ecosystem and social respect. These impacts are partially aggravated by social, cultural, religious and political conditions.

The focus of this case study lies on the political aspects because – since the fall of President Soeharto in 1998 – Indonesia's population, institutions and sectors have undergone a remarkable transformation. Government reform has triggered a tremendous push towards democratization and decentralization by introducing a series of laws shifting both political power (Law 32, 2004) and financial control (Law 33, 2004) from the central government to regional and local governments. The policy of local autonomy – and consequently the devolution of tasks, authorities, resources and responsibilities – aims to empower local governments and provide better access and basic services to the people. Besides enhanced access to coastal natural resources, communities have to be involved in the development of regional regulations in order to increase public participation at all levels of political decision-making. This includes a substantial redistribution of the revenues gained from regional natural resources. Nowadays, the central government receives 20 percent of the revenues (prior to decentralization 80 percent) and the regional government receives 80 percent; 26 percent of this amount goes to the province and 64 percent to the district.

The result of this decentralization process is nothing less than a revolution in governance (Patlis et al. 2001). These fundamental changes in governance were, however, not accompanied by adjustments in sectors such as the system of disaster management with regard to the responsibilities, rights and obligations of the different actors involved (central and local governments, non-governmental organizations and citizens). In other words, local governments were formally empowered by the new regulation while in the relevant sub-system they have not been enabled to achieve the new tasks. Here, the regulations, decrees and executive orders were overlapping and partially contradictory. As a result, the capacity to respond to disasters was weakened. Despite these obvious difficulties, the creation of a comprehensive new disaster risk management law, as a possible solution, was not on the government's agenda. This did not change even after the tragic and devastating consequences of the 2004 (26 December) disaster, the Indian Ocean earthquake and the following so-called Asian Tsunami. This disaster dramatically highlighted the vulnerability of Indonesian society and the weakness of the existing disaster risk management system.

Against this background, international and domestic non-governmental organizations (NGOs) started to introduce new disaster risk management approaches independently. One approach led to the creation of the 'Community Based Disaster Risk Management' (CBDRM). The CBDRM is devised to increase resilience, overcome the lack of awareness among the Indonesian population, and focus on ways to encourage active participation from the community. This approach is in line with the UN International Strategy for Disaster Reduction (ISDR).

A second concept led to the creation of a new Disaster Risk Management Law. The underlying discourse encourages a shift in the current view of disaster management. Under this new view, disaster management should not be: (1) an emergency response, but risk management; (2) an obligation of the government to protect, but instead protection should be understood as a basic right of the public; or (3) a government responsibility but, instead, a public matter.

CARE International, a relief and development organization, was the first international agency to respond to the need for a new law. In February 2005 it provided funds for a project implemented through the NGO the Indonesian Society of Disaster Management (MPBI). The aim of the MPBI was to enhance the national capacity in disaster risk reduction by translating conceptual principles into practical measures at the regional level (CARE 2005). In early March 2005 the MPBI facilitated the formation of a working group entitled Disaster Management Legislative Reform. This group involved a wide range of civil society and government actors.[8] It was only due to the diverse activities and lobbying efforts of this working group that the House of Representatives placed the Disaster Risk Management Bill onto its list of priorities. Eventually, the version developed by the working group was used as a reference in formulating the actual draft bill (CARE 2005).

The draft law aimed to structure the National Coordination Board for Natural Disaster Management according to the new decentralization laws. In order to accomplish this task, the draft proposed establishment of the Board at the provincial, district and subdistrict levels. In addition, it proposed an increased independence of the Board regarding funding.

This independence stood in contrast to its then reliance on funding from different ministries that share the responsibility of disaster risk management. Furthermore, the proposal strengthened the districts as centers for implementation of disaster management and disaster preparedness. Up to the finalization of this chapter in 2009, the board acted only after a disaster occurred. Thus, it was not required to develop or conduct pre-disaster measurements.

With this process already started by CARE International (MPBI 2005), and taken over by the House of Representatives, the central government could not withstand the momentum towards a more comprehensive proposal. To do otherwise would have meant losing its international prestige, especially on the ASEAN[9] stage. Here, the Indonesian government had actively advocated disaster preparedness in the past. The momentum thus resulted from the combination of two processes which changed the perspective on risks substantially: a social (democratization) process and a natural (increase of disasters and their effects) process. It shifted the approach from an emergency response to a risk management approach with significant contributions to decentralization (devolution and participation). All these sociopolitical changes occurred in a very short time – approximately five years (1998 to 2001). In the case of the new disaster risk management system that was enacted in June 2007, the fundamental changes took place only within the three years 2005–07.

EXPLAINING POLICY CHANGE IN RISK MANAGEMENT REGIMES

A comparison of the three cases reveals both striking similarities, and differences, that shed light on particular factors that foster adaptation. As a preparatory step, we briefly characterize the three processes with reference to the basic lines of differentiation identified in our conceptual framework. In its most abstract form, we highlighted that adaptation can be distinguished according to its scope and range. Applying the resulting typology of Roberts (1998), the first example of the German coastal protection (Case A) can be interpreted as a case of element adjustment where change occurs slowly and is restricted to one component: the introduction of cautious mechanisms reviewing the results of climate research; whereas the institutional design remains untouched. The second example of the German riparian flood protection regime (Case B) appears as an element transformation where the fast adaptation occurred within the existing institutional framework. The third example of the Indonesian disaster management regime (Case C) can be understood as a system

Table 10.3   Occurrences of change in the investigated cases

		Scope of change	
		Part	Whole
Pace of change	Slow	Element adjustment Case A	System adjustment
	Fast	Element transformation Case B	System transformation Case C

transformation characterized by a fast change embracing the entire institutional framework of disaster management (Table 10.3).

In order to understand the factors that explain the characteristics of the cases with regard to scope and range as the two core dimensions of change, three variables prove to be highly relevant: (1) institutional settings and actors who take the initiative to impose change with distributional implications; (2) situational factors like the occurrence or non-occurrence of external events that function as reality tests for problem perceptions; and (3) changes in the political environment.

Within the case of the German coastal protection regime (Case A), a well-equipped public administration uses its institutional capacities and resources to span the 'boundary' between science and policy in a way that predominantly accepts those findings of climate research which match with the 'safety discourse'. This discourse is based on experience derived from retrospection and historically proven and tested routines ensuring dyke safety. It is also based on a more or less linear understanding of climate behavior. Elements of the 'risk discourse' which underline the potential non-linearity of further climate change and related effects, like sea level rise, are challenged or ignored unless they can be categorized as proven results. Thus, risk is neither publicly addressed nor is uncertainty publicly considered. This allows both maintaining the given distribution of responsibilities and the resources that the institutions of coastal protection dispose of; as well as retaining the principle of equal safety along the coastline that assumes equal risk distribution among social groups. According to our assumption, the underlying tendency to continue treating adaptation to climate change as a non-issue can prevail as long as there are no relevant changes in the political environment or – in the worst-case scenario – as long as real extreme events do not lead to a substantial delegitimization of the concept in force.

In contrast, in the case of the riverine floods in Germany (Case B), the German federal government addressed the precautionary principle and publicly stated that risky constellations could be avoided forever and that flood protection measures guarantee only limited safety. Here, the pivotal role of the government may explain why it was possible quickly to institutionalize the risk discourse and require the responsible administration to adopt it conceptually. With regard to distribution, this perspective implies a restricted use of flood-prone areas, thus affecting the property rights of stakeholders (such as farmers), investors and citizens. Realty located in flood-prone areas might lose value. Thus, erecting new attractive riverine buildings will be more difficult in the future. Moreover, regulatory competencies for these zones are to be redistributed to higher political levels. This restricts the development strategies of municipalities, in particular, which are competing with non-riparian localities for economic growth and inhabitants. The required coordination of interests between downstream and upstream municipalities may reduce the power of the latter. New modes of cooperation and communication between those involved in flood risk reduction, and those involved in coping with the floods, may be confronted with conflicting interests.

In the Indonesian example (Case C), concepts emerged to introduce more flexible disaster risk management mechanisms with an enhanced reactive capacity. This emergence was at a supranational level in international organizations and, independently, in non-governmental organizations working in the field of aid and development assistance. The application of these concepts is inevitably linked to a redistribution of competencies and resources between political levels, and a strengthening of the lower tiers of government and administration. Further, its application implies the introduction of new and complex technical devices and their embedding into local practices. While the crucial role of NGOs results from their conceptual abilities and their access to know-how, financial resources and technical capacities, their access to the political arena depended on the consent of the Indonesian national government. The departments within this government now had to accept a far-reaching shift of their prior roles within society.

Apart from institutional factors, situational ones are of crucial importance to explain these conceptual and discursive shifts. The example of coastal protection on the North Sea coast (Case A), while staying within the boundaries of a deterministic perspective, can be explained by the fact that its constitutive promise to ensure safety, up to now, has not had to pass a reality test that exceeded the safety level as provided by the existing structures and the present pace of its extension. Consequently, the legitimacy of the existing paradigm, together with its affiliated institutions, remained widely uncontested.

As for case B, in contrast, the severe riverine floods of 2002 can be interpreted as an external impact, thereby disproving the idea that one is able to calculate and to ensure safety under all realistic circumstances.

The 'collapse of confidence in engineered flood protection' (Wisner et al. 2004: 203) fostered a paradigm shift towards 'living with floods' being considered something that was normal and had to be accepted. This shift includes the opinion that rivers, their banks and flood plains provide valuable 'ecological services' (including the partial absorption of flood water).

In the Indonesian example (Case C), the devastating natural disasters of 2004 and 2005 finally revealed the inappropriateness of any existing institutional mechanisms, employed technologies or distribution of competencies. Aware of the extent of the threat, a legitimate concept had to include plausible proposals for adequate changes in all these dimensions. Since the disaster risk management concepts that emerged among experts and NGOs aim at the combination of innovative technologies (such as high-tech early warning systems) with decentralized and responsive local institutions, both the activities of NGOs as independent actors and the upgrading of local and regional response capacities received acceptance.

In the first example (Case A), the political environment for the responsible institutions remains stable and, in principle, unchallenged. In Case B, by contrast, the imminent federal elections of 2002 became a decisive factor. There is no doubt that the coincidence of the damage produced by the floods in August 2002 and the imminent elections challenged the political class. This aim to demonstrate commitment and conceptual competency fostered acceptance of a risk perception at the political level. In fact, the combination of spatial planning and the precautionary principle meshed well with the discourse of 'ecological modernization' pursued by the Social Democrat and Green government in charge during that period. This situational 'conceptual superiority' fostered a response that, at the same time, highlighted the limited ability of the *Länder* to frame the problem adequately. At this time, the *Länder* were predominantly controlled by the political opposition. As a consequence, the Five Points Program, that under different conditions certainly would have provoked political conflicts at the federal and *Länder* levels, was accepted without major opposition.

In the Indonesian example (Case C), the profound and far-reaching response implied by the new disaster management regime must be understood as a component of the overarching reform of both the constitutional structure and the administrative system of the country. Under Soeharto, the political system sought to achieve national unity and economic development by authoritarianism. The reform sought to maintain political stability under changed internal and external frame conditions. This became possible through increased decentralization. As with the concepts for disaster management, the success of this paradigm is ensuring enhanced flexibility. However, its effectiveness relies on the change of roles of political

Table 10.4   Configuration of adaptational change

	Pivotal actors	Reality test	Political environment
Case A: Element adjustment	Public administration	None	Stable
Case B: Element transformation	German Federal Red–Green government	Severe floods in 2002	Federal elections in Germany
Case C: System transformation	National/ international NGOs, international organizations, national parliament	Various disasters, especially the tsunami of 2004	Reform of the entire Indonesian political system

and societal actors at all levels. Thus, the correspondence between both governance approaches is by no means accidental but the result of the same understanding between the societal processes and the normative assessment of development. Thus, the decentralized disaster management regime inevitably depends on the dynamics of the political system as an institutional environment. It was only under these conditions that NGOs could enter into the arena and, thereby, expand the system's complexity. Table 10.4 summarizes the configuration discussed so far for our cases.

This comparison highlights the following. External events that function as 'reality tests' for dominant discourses up to that time, may play a major role as factors that enhance change. Additionally, contextual political and institutional processes (that may be rather weakly related to the issue at hand and may cause adaptation in the investigated field rather by coincidence) can be of pivotal importance. As proposed by the approach of policy windows, scope and pace of adaptation result from the interaction of these dimensions, or 'streams', as Kingdon calls them, which follow their own dynamics.

As theoretically assumed, system transformation – the most radical change among our cases – occurred when all three streams coincided. The weakest form – slow pace and a limited scope of adjustment (element adjustment) – occured associated with stable political frame conditions and the absence of external events.

Policy change is closely related to the distribution of risks and resources. First, risk management concepts touch upon the vulnerability of social groups or locations. As the two German cases illustrate, adaptation to increasing sea levels (Case A) or the risks of riparian floods (Case B) may include the acceptance of higher risks for some locations in order to improve the level of protection for others. In the Indonesian case (Case C), the zoning of coastal strips for security reasons has the same effect. Thus, not only do disasters show distributional effects but also policy changes that seek to reduce vulnerability through adaptation. This applies not only to social groups but also to institutions. For the latter, policy change implies the redistribution of tasks, staff and resources from institutions that are regarded as inappropriate to ensure adaptation, to institutions or even levels of government expected to improve risk management.

A further aspect is the reduction of chances for development of locations in favor of other localities, as Case B illustrates. The faster policy change occurs, and the more substantial its consequences are, the more it affects the stakes of the actors involved. Regarding both concerned institutions and potentially affected social groups, related costs and losses are substantial hindrances to accepting policy change. Such obstacles can only be overcome if promoters of a new risk management concept are supported by changes in politics and backed by reality tests that delegitimate opposing discourses and related concepts. In addition to some clearly identifiable interests, normative perceptions of affected social groups or of concerned professionals have a considerable impact on the conceptual responses being accepted or refuted. In discursive struggles, all of these aspects become amalgamated and assorted into a limited number of conceptual alternatives.

CONCLUSION

Societies are undoubtedly now concerned with climate change due to the recognized risks associated with it. Although the probabilities of occurrence and specifics of regional impacts of these risks are uncertain in principle, societies must adapt in order to reduce their vulnerability and strengthen their resilience.

This begs the question, what is adaptation? In this chapter, we have drawn on three aspects: on the reference points of adaptation (Adaptation to what?), on the substance, and on the levels of adaptation (Who or what should adapt?). The main focus is on understanding substantial differences in the scope and pace of adaptation processes (How does adaptation occur?) and the resulting distributional effects.

Even though climate change can affect almost every country, the patterns of adaptation to the related risks differ substantially. Adaptation may encompass changes in the whole regulatory framework, or just in particular elements. Further, these changes may take place rapidly or even slowly.

Different amplitudes, in terms of pace and scope, can be explained by the policy window approach. Occurring extreme events, as well as novel information in terms of warnings launched by the climate change scientific community, represent the problem stream. Conceptual frameworks of how to cope with, and adapt to, such problems represent the policy stream. Whether, and how, modification of elements – or even of whole concepts – takes place depends on the politics stream. Here redistribution of responsibilities, modifications of hierarchies, and demands for new competencies, new resources and the involvement of new actors are decided upon. The course of the politics stream implies, from a political science perspective, the redistribution of resources and thus of power. Here, 'winners' and 'losers' get set up.

The first two streams are of crucial importance. Not surprisingly, resistance against the redistribution of resources due to new risk management or general adaptation concepts can only be overcome under exceptional conditions. The interaction between policy stream, problem stream and politics stream, as proposed by the policy window approach, provides a framework to improve the understanding of these constellations. Competing discourses can be seen as a means of striving for, and finally achieving, changes in problem definitions (What is the problem and how to cope with it?) and power relations and actor constellations (Who is to resolve the problem best?). Thus, discourses have an explicit distributional quality since they assign roles and resources to actors and institutions. Beyond their effect on social groups, they legitimize or delegitimize institutional settings. In our cases, contrasting discourses (safety discourse, risk discourse) proved to be important. They were the medium in which these conceptual struggles for adaptation took place.

In spite of many remarkable differences between the cases we analyzed, the risk discourses we identified led to similar strategies of adaptation to risks that have the following features in common.

The main feature is that adaptation goes far beyond technical risk provisioning (for example, dykes). It also has to go beyond pure disaster management. Rather, adaptation at its best should make disaster management superfluous. Adaptation, firstly, requires a risk management approach which starts with prevention (precautionary principle), thus integrating the potential occurrence of risks into policies aiming at fostering preparedness mainly on the regional and local levels. This holds true particularly for spatial planning. Secondly, this cannot be done effectively unless the risks to be considered are communicated publicly, thereby enabling potentially affected groups to understand the rationality behind the measures in question, to let them have their say and, finally, to help them to react adequately. As distributional effects are a part of every policy, and as risk-related adaptation policies refer to future extreme events, the potential distributional effects of adaptation policies must be considered in advance. Such public communication inevitably leads to contestation, negotiation and bargaining in the public arena. Managing these processes in a way that allows for both efficiency and equity is a prerequisite of gaining the ample acceptance which, beyond being desirable in the normative respect, is also of crucial importance in the functional respect, to attain a cooperative citizenry. Hence, adapting to contemporary and future risks of climate change is ultimately also a challenge to develop further the efficiency of democracy.

ACKNOWLEDGEMENT

We would like to thank the referees and the editor for helpful comments. We also wish to thank all persons who provided information on the empirical cases.

NOTES

1. This government was in office between 1998 and 2005.
2. In the original treatise, Roberts (1998) uses the term 'adaptation' for slow change. We prefer to use the term 'adjustment' to avoid conceptual confusion with the use of the term in the literature on climate change that this chapter refers to.
3. The area under investigation comprises the coastline of northwestern Germany, including the River Weser up to the city of Bremen. Because of the low topology, and consisting largely of five-grained marine sediments, the coastal area is prone to erosion and flooding.
4. Actually the procedure is more complicated. For details see Lange et al. (2005: 31).
5. The equal-safety formula is included in the respective legal regulation and defines the official mission of the administrative units in charge of coastal protection in the region in question (Niedersächsisches Deichgesetz).
6. The empirical basis of our finding consists of 50 interviews conducted in 2003. The interviewees included officers in charge of different subtasks in the realm of coastal protection at all levels (local, district, federal state) and the involved political entities in geographical respect (Land Niedersachsen, Land Bremen). The interviewees were selected in a way that assures a full-fledged coverage of the political-administrative system of coastal protection in the area.
7. For details, see Lange et al. (2005).
8. Environmental-focused NGOs, women-focused NGOs, religious-based groups, the Indonesian Red Cross, United Nations agencies (UN-Office for the Coordination of Humanitarian Affairs (UNOCHA) and United Nations Development Programme (UNDP)), international organizations (European Commission Humanitarian Office (ECHO)) through CARE International Indonesia, OXFAM GB, International Federation of Red Cross and Red Crescent Societies (IFRC)).
9. ASEAN (Association of South East Asian Nations) commitments: Regional Emergency Alleviation Plan; ASEAN Concord-1 Declaration (1976) and Concord-2 Declaration

(November 2003) are promising to reduce the burdens of other members affected by disasters and to cooperate in the alleviation of problems and in disaster management. As a reaction to the tsunami of 2004, ASEAN agreed in January 2005 to improve the efficiency of disaster management and to provide mutual assistance in cases of major disasters.

REFERENCES

Adger, W.N. (2000), 'Institutional adaptation to environmental risk under the transition in Vietnam', in *Annals of the Association of American Geographers*, **90**: 738–58.

Adger, W.N., N. Brooks, G. Bentham, M. Agnew and S. Eriksen (2004), 'New indicators of vulnerability and adaptive capacity', Tyndall Centre Technical Report 7, Norwich.

Barnett, J. (2001), 'Adapting to climate change in Pacific Island countries: the problem of uncertainty', *World Development*, **29**(6): 977–93.

Becker, A. and U. Grünwald (2003), 'Flood risk in Central Europe', *Science*, **300**: 1099.

BMU (2003), 'Trittin presents draft Flood Control Act. Give our rivers more room – before they take it themselves', Press statement No. 143, 8 August.

BMU (2005), 'New Flood Control Act enters into force. Preventive flood protection is improved significantly', Press statement No. 111, 9 May.

Burton, I., S. Hug, B. Lim, O. Pilifosova and B. Schipper (2002), 'From impact assessment to adaptation priorities: the shaping of adaptation policy', *Climate Policy*, **2**: 145–59.

CARE (2005), 'The DRM-Draft Bill activities', Jakarta.

DKKV (2004), 'Flood risk reduction in Germany: lessons learned from the 2002 disaster in the Elbe region', Bonn: DKKV Publication 29e.

Easton, David (1965), *A Systems Analysis of Political Life*, New York: Wiley.

Friesecke, F. (2004), 'Precautionary and sustainable flood protection in Germany: strategies and instruments of spatial planning', paper presented at the 3rd FIG Regional Conference, Jakarta, Indonesia, 3–4 October.

Haas, P.A. (1992), 'Introduction: epistemic communities and international coordination', *International Organization*, **46**: 1–35.

Hajer, M.A. (1995), *The Politics of Environmental Discourse: Ecological Modernization and the Policy Process*, Oxford: Clarendon Press.

IPCC (2001), 'Summary for policymakers', in J.J. McCarthy, O.F. Canziani, N.A. Leary, D.D. Dokken and K.S. White (eds), *Climate Change 2001: Impacts, Adaptation and Vulnerability. Contribution of Working Group II to the Third Assessment Report of the Intergovernmental Panel on Climate Change*, Cambridge: Cambridge University Press, pp. 1–20, available at: http://www.ipcc.ch/ipcc reports/tar/wg1/pdf/WG1_TAR-FRONT.PDF, accessed 18 April 2009.

IPCC (2007a), 'Summary for policymakers', in S. Solomon, D. Qin, M. Manning, Z. Chen, M. Marquis, K.B. Averyt, M. Tignor and H.L. Miller (eds), *Climate Change 2007: The Physical Science Basis. Contribution of Working Group I to the Fourth Assessment Report of the Intergovernmental Panel on Climate Change*, Cambridge: Cambridge University Press, pp. 1–18, available at: http://www.ipcc. ch/pdf/assessment-report/ar4/wg1/ar4-wg1-spm.pdf, accessed 18 April 2009.

IPCC (2007b), 'Summary for policymakers', in M.L. Parry, O.F. Canziani, J.P. Palutikof, P.J. van der Linden and C.E. Hanson (eds), *Climate Change 2007: Impacts, Adaptation and Vulnerability. Contribution of Working Group II to the Fourth Assessment Report of the Intergovernmental Panel on Climate Change*, Cambridge: Cambridge University Press, pp. 7–22, available at: http://www.ipcc.ch/pdf/assessment-report/ar4/wg2/ar4-wg2-spm.pdf, accessed 18 April 2009.

Jekel, H. (2005), 'Das Gesetz zur Verbesserung des vorbeugenden Hochwasserschutzes', *Zeitschrift für Umweltrecht*, **16**(9): 393–400.

Kingdon, J.W. (1984), *Agendas, Alternatives, and Public Policies*, Boston, MA: Little, Brown & Co.

Lange, H., M. Haarmann, A. Wiesner-Steiner and E. Voosen (2005), 'Klimawandel und präventives Risiko- und Küstenschutzmanagement an der deutschen Nordseeküste (KRIM) – Teilprojekt IV: Politisch-administrative Steuerungsprozesse (PAS)', http://www.artec.uni-bremen.de/files/papers/paper_129.pdf, accessed 18 April 2009.

Lindseth, G. (2005), 'Local level adaptation to climate change: discursive strategies in the Norwegian context', *Journal of Environmental Policy and Planning*, **7**(1): 61–83.

Mechler, R. and J. Weichselgartner (2003), 'Disaster loss financing in Germany: the case of the Elbe River floods 2002', Interim Report IR-03-021, International Institute for Applied Systems Analysis (IIASA), Laxenburg, Austria.

MPBI (2005), 'Chronological progress of academic text and disaster management bill drafting', 5 June, Jakarta.

MPBI (2006), 'Establishing the most appropriate format of CBDRM for Nangroe Aceh Darussalam', Community Based Disaster Risk Management, GTZ Supported Project SLGSR, Banda Aceh.

Nachtnebel, H.P. (2003), 'New strategies for flood risk management after the catastrophic flood in 2002 in Europe', Disaster Prevention Research Institute (DPRI) of the Kyoto University and International Institute of Applied Systems Analysis (IIASA), Laxenburg, Austria: Third DPRI-IIASA International Symposium on Integrated Disaster Risk Management (IDRM-2003), 3–5 July, Kyoto International Conference Hall, Kyoto, Japan.

Naess, L.O., G. Bang, S. Eriksen and J. Vevatne (2005), 'Institutional adaptation to climate change: flood responses at the municipal level in Norway', *Global Environmental Change*, **15**: 25–138.

Olson, Mancur (1965), *The Logic of Collective Action*, Cambridge, MA: Harvard University Press.

Paavola, J. and N.W. Adger (2004), 'Knowledge or participation for sustainability? Science and justice in adaptation to climate change', in F. Biermann; S. Campe and K. Jacob (eds), *Proceedings of the 2002 Conference on the Human Dimensions of Global Environmental Change 'Knowledge for the Sustainability Transition. The Challenge for Social Sciences'*, Amsterdam, Berlin, Potsdam and Oldenburg: Global Governance Project.

Patlis, J., R. Dahuri, M. Knight and J. Tulungen (2001), 'Integrated coastal management in a decentralized Indonesia: how can it work', *Jurnal Pesisir & Lautan*, (*Indonesian Journal of Coastal and Marine Resources*), **4**(1): 25–39.

Roberts, Nancy (1998), 'Radical change by entrepreneurial design', *Acquisition Review Quarterly*, Spring: 107–27.

Sabatier, P. (1988), 'An advocacy coalition framework of policy change and the role of policy oriented learning therein', *Policy Sciences*, **21**: 129–68.

Smit, B., I. Burton, R.J.T. Klein and J. Wandel (2000), 'An anatomy of adaptation to climate change and variability', *Climatic Change*, **45**(1): 223–51.

Stirling, A. (2003), 'Risk, uncertainty and precaution: some instrumental implications from the social sciences', in F. Berkhout, M. Leach, I. Scoones (eds), *Negotiating Environmental Change*, Cheltenham, UK and Northampton, MA, USA: Edward Elgar, pp. 33–76.

Szarka, J. (2004), 'Wind power, discourse coalitions and climate change: breaking the stalemate?', *European Environment*, **14**: 317–30.

Wisner, B., P. Blaikie, T. Cannon and I. Davis (2004), *At Risk: Natural Hazards, People's Vulnerability and Disasters*, London and New York: Routledge.

Yohe, G. and R.S. Tol (2002), 'Indicators for social and economic coping capacity: moving toward a working definition of adaptive capacity', *Global Environmental Change Part A*, **12**(1): 25–40.

ZENEB (Zentrum für Naturrisiken und Entwicklung Bonn/Bayreuth) (2002), 'Zusatzbeitrag. Floods in Europe: lessons learned?', http://www.giub.uni-bonn.de/zeneb/hauptseiten/aktiv/inframe/inhalt/vr/download/bericht_wvr.pdf.

11. Conclusions

María E. Ibarrarán and Matthias Ruth

The anticipated ramifications of climate change, especially the increased frequency and severity of weather events, can have disastrous implications for communities, economies and environments. As such, research into vulnerability to disasters needs to be sensitive to differences within and among socio-economic and geographically distinct segments of the population.

The chapters in this volume have described the many facets of climate change, and focused on impacts and vulnerabilities, as well as mitigation and adaptive actions. Some of the chapters have presented empirical or modeling analyses that point towards policies to reduce the unequal impact of climate change, while other chapters have highlighted the need for more analysis to tackle an underexplored issue among scientific and policy researchers. This final chapter discusses the recommendations made and indicates areas of research for the future.

The first part of the book presented an overview of the impact of climate change and natural disasters on the poor, and ranked countries according to their vulnerability. Overall, since the poor are more vulnerable to natural disasters and climate change tends to increase the frequency and intensity of these disasters, investment in disaster prevention, awareness and mitigation will positively affect inequality and poverty reduction.

Vulnerability and resilience to climate change can be addressed by combining economic, social and environmental factors. In Chapter 2, Malone and Brenkert discussed a way to integrate these three sets of factors into a single indicator. It follows from their analysis that there are several factors that may reduce a region's sensitivity to disasters and improve its coping capacity. Results showed a country-level ranking and showed how appropriate investment can contribute toward lowering vulnerability across countries. The methodology shown may help individual countries carry out similar analyses at a state or finer level, depending on available data. This type of exercise has been done for India (Brenkert and Malone 2002), and Mexico (Ibarrarán et al. 2007).

In Chapter 3, Ibarrarán and Ruth discussed how the macroeconomic impact of these disasters falls largely upon the poor but, even among the poor, it affects some groups more than others. However, empirical evidence shows that through physical, economic and institutional development, a region may somewhat insulate itself from the negative effects of natural disasters. Additionally, there is a pressing need to plan and budget resources for catastrophes, making sure to address subgroup vulnerability. This chapter therefore stressed the need for tailor-made policies and institutions to reduce vulnerability.

While the first part of the book developed frameworks for analysis, the second part concentrated on the differential effects of climate change, such as on health, income distribution and security, as well as gender, urban conditions, communication and the development of institutions for risk management.

The research presented in the second part of the book covered examples from a wide range of countries in the developing and industrialized world. The impact of climate change on health and cities was studied in industrialized countries, whereas income distribution and gender issues were discussed mainly in a developing country context. Security and risk management issues were analyzed across the globe. All of these chapters offered important pieces of the overall picture on how climate change affects countries with different needs and institutional frameworks.

The impacts of climate change on health were explored in the context of Western industrialized countries in Chapter 4, by Kalkstein, Koppe, Orlandini, Sheridan and Smoyer-Tomic. They argued that even though both heat-related illnesses and asthma prevalence may increase if the climate warms, there are still many uncertainties. Demographic changes, the effectiveness of mitigation measures, urban structure changes and adaptation will all play roles in determining how humans respond to climate change. However, heat-related mortality is already the leading weather-related killer in the Western world and asthma prevalence is increasing among the young. Thus, regardless of the climate change impacts, it is important that we become more aware of the vagaries of weather upon the human body, and develop means to lessen the negative health outcomes. An issue for further research is whether these health effects may be different for developing countries, where the diseases related to climate change are mainly vector-borne, like malaria and dengue fever. This will affect millions, so some comparison between expected health effects in developing and industrialized nations will be of great interest.

In Chapter 5, Patt, Dazé and Suarez stated that gender differences must be considered not just in terms of differential vulnerability, but also differential adaptive capacity. Women suffer disproportionately the harms of climate-related natural disasters and slower-onset, chronic events such as food insecurity. Women also tend to make decisions differently than do men in several fundamental ways. Firstly, they take greater account of risk. Secondly, they have a more realistic appraisal of the range of possible consequences of acting or failing to act. Thirdly, women tend to seek out help and listen to advice more than men. Fourthly, women are more likely to change their behavior in response to success and failure. Therefore, the empowering of women to make family decisions in response to climate change may lead to more adaptive behavior and a reduced vulnerability to the effects of climate change. Cultural aspects also play a role and site-specific research may be of great value to assess how women may become less vulnerable.

Not only does climate change increase income inequality, but the adoption of mitigation and adaptation policies have a clearly redistributive impact as well. For the case of Mexico, Boyd and Ibarrarán, in Chapter 6, described the effect of different mitigation policies on income distribution because the highest usage of energy occurs in the lowest-income groups. Consequently, increased investment and exploration in the natural gas sector have a progressive effect on income distribution, although the deregulation of electricity prices and carbon taxes hits the lower-income groups more severely than higher-income groups. Additionally, Mexico's lower-income groups are disproportionately affected by the negative externalities associated with air pollution. Energy policies that reduce local pollutants are generally progressive with regards to income distribution. This type of analysis may be replicated for other countries to find the specific magnitudes of these, and other, mitigation policies, but most of these general conclusions are very likely to hold elsewhere.

Urban areas in industrialized countries are vulnerable to climate change, was the point made by Ruth, Kirshen and Coelho in Chapter 7. Urban vulnerabilities are to a large extent the result of the growing water and energy demands. The authors produced a set of suggestions to reduce group-specific vulnerabilities in the urban context. They also highlighted that to advance research in that area would require heightened sensitivity to the impacts of climate change on population and infrastructure in the urban environment. This analysis may help determine both the cost and cost distribution of adaptation. As the authors argued, issues of social justice may have more relevance to local decision-making than the current discussions about intergenerational distribution in the light of climate change.

Many of the effects and costs of climate change may be significantly reduced through the dissemination of information about vulnerabilities and possible adaptation. The value of climate change information depends on how it is used. The method by which information is introduced into a particular environment can contribute to vulnerability reduction by helping to reshape the internal dynamics of the socio-economic system.

Chapter 8, by Suarez, Ribot and Patt, argued that the best use of climate forecasts would be not just to anticipate the future, but also to integrate them in processes aimed at identifying and resolving bottlenecks in the flow of information.

Climate change impacts will also bring with them security challenges. Gulden, in Chapter 9, indicated the fine balance that must be maintained if the world is to address the twin problems of armed conflict and global climate change. Scarcities resulting from climate change can drive conflicts as societies strive to adapt. These scarcities are often hardest on the poor and those living traditional lifestyles; they tend to concentrate wealth further and lead to destabilizing resource capture by conflicting elites. Climate change mitigation strategies also raise another security concern. An abrupt shift away from oil and toward biomass energy would be extremely destabilizing for petroleum-producing nations. It could also make tropical nations turn to a single export commodity and the concentrated wealth that comes with it. One of the other energy options is nuclear fission, with the usual threats that nuclear power imposes. Thus, this chapter indicated that failure by wealthy nations to consider these security implications would be unjust and unwise.

Finally, in Chapter 10, Lange, Garrelts, Osthorst and Selmi argued that societies must adapt in order to reduce their vulnerability and strengthen their resilience. The authors touched on three aspects to understand the motivations behind increased adaptive capacity and actions. Their exposition demonstrated that adaptation goes far beyond technical measures and pure disaster management. Adaptation requires a risk management approach aimed at prevention, and hence integrating the occurrence of risk into relevant policies, particularly spatial planning. Moreover, in order to cope with and manage risks successfully, the fostering of preparedness proves crucial on the regional and local level. This cannot be done effectively unless risks and adaptation strategies to those risks are communicated publicly and their distributional effects considered in advance. Managing these processes adequately may help to create a cooperative citizenry. Hence, adapting to the risks of climate change is, ultimately, a challenge to develop democracy further.

Overall, the chapters in this book have suggested that information sharing and the development of knowledge are crucial prerequisites to climate change mitigation and adaptation, and the reduction of vulnerabilities of societies and economies. Policies should be put in place to empower traditionally disenfranchised groups, such as the poor and women, and thus reduce further negative effects on their health, social standing or prosperity. Many of the policies suggested here would have clear benefits beyond the groups they target.

With its focus on concepts and cases, the book lays the ground for a more structured and systematic analysis of how costs of climate change and its mitigation and adaptation processes are distributed across and within countries, and of measures that increase equity that might lower these costs and distribute them more evenly. Subsequent work will need to enrich the portfolio of methods and cases presented here, particularly by giving special attention to spatial scale. A refined 'spatial' resolution will be particularly relevant to those who make mitigation and adaptation decisions 'on the ground' in both developing and industrialized countries – the local stakeholders as well as investors and policy-makers dealing with place-specific distributional issues, mitigation efforts and adaptation strategies. We invite them, and the research community, to combine forces in what must be a collective endeavor to address the causes of climate change as well as the expected impacts that affect the social fabric, the economic base and the environment, that will ultimately shape humanity for the centuries to come.

Index